DJe Conincklijcke Maiesteyt / be...

de dat een yeghelijcken kennisse hebbe vande nieuwe Goud...
Penninghen / die gheordonneert zijn met consent vande ge...
van dese Nederlanden / onder den Naem Tytel Wapen e...
zyne Maiesteyt / heeft den generael Meesters vander Munten van zyne ... van her
waertsouer beuolen / te doen Drucken de Figueren vande voorseyde nieuwe Penninghen
metten ghewichte en prijs / alsoe hier naer volght.

EEnen Gouden Penninck, diemen noemen sal den
dobbelen Nederlantschen Gulden weghende eenE
Enghelschen en dertich Aes en drp quaert, diemen we
gheuE sal voor veertich stupuers, vandE nieuwE slaghe.

DEn Nederlantschen Guldk weghende eenender
tich ende een quaert en half Aes / salmen wegh
uen voor twintich stupuers banden nieuwen slaghe.

EEnen Zilueren Penninck / diemk noemen sal den
zesthien stupuers Penninck / weghende neghen
Enghelschen dertich Aes drp quaert / zalmen beghe
uen voor zesthien stupuers / vanden nieuwen slaghe.

EEnen anderen Zilueren Penninck / diemen noe
men zal eenen acht stupuers Penninck / weghende
vier Enghelsche / eenendertich Aes / een quaert en half
zalmen wtgheuen voor acht stupuers banden nieuwE
slaghe.

EEnen anderen Zilueren Penninck / diemen noe
men zal den vier stupuers Penninck / weghende
twee Enghelschen vijfthien Aes en half salmen wt
gheuen voor vier stupuers banden nieuwen slaghe.

EEnen anderen Zilueren Penninck / diemen noe
men zal den twee stupuers Penninck / weghende
eenen Enghelschen zeuen Aes en drp quaert / zalmen
begheuen voor twee stupuers vandE nieuwen slaghe.

DEn nieuwen Stupuer / weghende eenE Enghel
schen / twaelf Aes en half / diemen begheuen sal
voor eenen stupuer.

DEn haluen nieuwen Stupuer weghende tween
twintich Aes een quaert / diemen begheuen sal
voor eenen haluen stupuer.

THantwerpen / by Guilliame van Parijs / ghezwoten Drucker van sConinc Munte /
Met Priuilegie ende Verbode expres / tenlaste van allen anderen Druckers niet te prenten /
dat der Majesteyts Munte aengaet. 1577.

Typis Gualteri Manilij.

Coins in history

Coins in history

John Porteous

G. P. Putnam's Sons 200 Madison Avenue New York

Acknowledgements

The following illustrations are reproduced by courtesy of the authorities, directors, keepers and curators of the following museums, companies and institutions: Administration des Monnaies, Paris, figures 55, 246, 263, 273; Archivio di Stato, Venice, figure 93; Ashmolean Museum, Oxford, figures 28, 36, 41, 46, 68, 70, 129, 130(i), 200, 211, 235, 247, 254, 264; Bank of England, figure 266; Bibliothèque Nationale, Paris, figures 65, 69, 71, 110, 128, 138, 164, 166, 186, 204, 205, 209, 241, 245, 271; Bibliothèque Royale de Belgique, Brussels, figures 137, 147; British Museum, London, figures 3, 4, 6, 8, 9, 11, 12, 15, 16, 18, 19, 21, 22, 23, 24, 25, 26, 27, 29, 30, 32, 33, 34, 35, 37, 38, 39, 40, 42, 43, 44, 45, 48, 53, 64, 66, 72, 73, 74, 75, 99, 105, 106, 123(i), 127, 133, 134, 150, 161, 164, 167, 169(ii), 176, 177, 178, 185, 188, 189, 190, 198, 203, 207, 224, 225, 226, 227, 229, 232, 236, 239, 240, 242(i), 244, 249, 250, 252, 258, 259, 267, 276, 277, 278, 280, 281, 283, 284, 285; Coins and Medals, figures 251, 253, 270; D. J. Crowther Ltd, figure 268; Gemeentelijke Archiefdienst Dordrecht, figures 212, 223; Fitzwilliam Museum, Cambridge, figures 49, 160, 275; the late C. W. Peck, figure 279; Istituto Italiano di Numismatica (formerly collection of King Victor Emmanuel III), figures 89, 199; Koninklijk Penningkabinet, The Hague, figures 81, 83, 100, 104, 131, 144, 145, 146, 148(ii), 149, 153, 168, 169(i), 170, 182, 183, 184, 192, 196, 208, 213, 214, 215, 242(ii), 260, endpapers; Kunsthistorisches Museum, Vienna, figures 218, 219; Mestske Museum Kremnici, figures 221, 230; Metropolitan Museum of Art, New York, figure 151; Museo Bottacin, Padua,

figures 91, 92, 95, 117(i), 119(i)(ii), 121, 136, 140; Museo Correr, Venice, figure 117(ii); National Museum, Budapest, figures 87(ii), 119(iii), 180, 217; National Museum, Prague, figures 77, 111, 115, 139, 152, 154, 233, 234, 261; National Portrait Gallery, London, figures 248, 269; Österreichische Nationalbibliothek, Vienna, figures 156, 171; Royal Mint, London, figure 206; Santamaria, Rome, figures 1, 2, 5, 10, 14, 17, 20, 31, 94, 141, 157, 158, 162, 165, 197, 201, 202, 222, 274; J. Schulman NV, Amsterdam, figure 255; Schweizerisches Landesmuseum, figures 50, 90; SPADEM, figure 97; Staatliches Münzkabinett, Berlin, figures 51, 84, 85, 88, 113; Staatliche Münzsammlung, Munich, figures 52, 78, 79, 80, 84, 112, 114, 142, 173, 174, 175, 191, 220, 237, 238, 286; Stadtarchiv Schaffhausen, figure 82; Swedish National Collection, figure 256; The Times, figure 243; Westminster School, figure 228. Figures 54, 62, 97, 101, 122, 155, 176, 257 are from the collection of Philip Grierson Esq; figures 7, 47, 56, 57, 59, 60, 61, 63, 65, 67, 76, 96, 98, 102, 103, 107, 108, 116, 118, 119(iv), 120, 123, (ii), 124, 125, 132, 135, 143, 148 (i), 159, 163, 179, 181, 187, 193, 194, 195, 210, 262, 265, 272, are from the author's collection.

Figure 58 was photographed by Archives Photographiques, Paris; figure 137 by Paul Bijtebier; figures 3, 4, 6, 7, 8, 9, 11, 12, 18, 21, 22, 23, 24, 25, 26, 27, 29, 30, 32, 33, 34, 35, 37, 38, 39, 40, 42, 43, 44, 45, 47, 48, 53, 54, 56, 60, 61, 62, 63, 64, 66, 67, 96, 98, 102, 105, 106, 107, 108, 118, 119(iv), 122, 123, 124, 127, 132, 133, 134, 143, 155, 159, 161, 163, 164, 169 (ii), 176, 177, 179, 181, 187, 188, 189, 190, 203, 207, 210, 224, 225, 226, 227,

229, 232, 236, 239, 240, 242(i), 244, 249, 252, 256, 257, 258, 259, 265, 267, 272, 276, 277, 278, 280, 281, 283, 284, 285 by Brompton Studios; figure 130 (ii) by Editions Argra, Toulouse; figures 84, 85, 86, 88 by Hirmer Verlag, Munich; figures 87(i), 126, 172, Inz. Jan Horák; figures 103, 148(i) by Koninklijk Penningkabinet, The Hague; figures 89, 199 by Oscar Savio; figures 49, 57, 59, 76, 101, 116, 120, 125, 135, 160, 275, by Derrick Witty.

ENDPAPERS: (right) Placard of Philip II of Spain giving notice of coins struck in the Netherlands after the Pacification of Ghent, Antwerp, 1577 (left) Placard of Philip II giving notice of new small silver and copper coins, Brussels, 1571

PAGE 1: Saxony; silver thaler 1584, Elector August, Dresden mint-master Hans Biener (actual size)

FRONTISPIECE: Bavaria, silver thaler, 1626 (reverse) Elector Maximilian I, Munich (enlarged approx 4:1)

PAGE 5: Transylvania; silver thaler 1661 (obverse) John Kemény, Segesvár (enlarged 1.25:1)

Contents

Preface

Coin collectors tend to be interested in rare coins. This book is mostly about the common ones. The great interest of coinage is that it holds up a sort of mirror (sometimes only a dim one) to history, especially to economic and social history. The coins which do this are above all those which were traded and spent again and again, whose names were written in every banker's ledger or housewife's accounts book, Shylock's ducats, for example, or the Pied Piper's guilders. It is these, considered against the background of the rise and decline of coinage as a monetary instrument, which are the subject of this work.

The story is a continuous one going back to the time of Diocletian. It would be a bold historian who suggested that the decisive break between the ancient and modern worlds took place so early as 295. Most would agree that it occurred during the economic and cultural hibernation which Europe underwent in the sixth and seventh centuries. However, an understanding of those years can only be reached by referring back to Diocletian and Constantine, so it is best to start with them.

The theme is primarily European. In the modern world it is the European concept of money, as rooted originally in European coinage, which lies behind all the world's currencies. Except for the coinage of Islam, which played a decisive part in European developments in the early middle ages, the many and interesting coinages of the east have made little contribution to the picture. These therefore are not dealt with here. I should perhaps also admit that their proper consideration requires much more knowledge of oriental languages and history (to say nothing of oriental numismatics) than I am master of.

The historian of coinage faces this difficulty, that his material becomes more plentiful as it becomes less interesting. Less interesting especially in that from the seventeenth century onwards, it has made up a progressively smaller part of the total money supply. The monetary role of coinage is now nugatory, even in undeveloped economies. A book remains to be written about modern coinage, its design, its size, its manufacture, its raw materials and its use. The theme of this one, however, ends with the monetary upheavals caused by the bimetallic crises in the United States and Europe in the later years of the nineteenth century. However this is not wholly irrelevant to modern times. These chapters have been written during three years of recurrent monetary crisis in which governments have in turn been constrained to adopt the same expedients of devaluation and exchange control as their medieval predecessors. Coinage as such no longer plays a significant part in these events, but the events themselves do perhaps give more insight into the workings of past currency mutations than was given to students of an earlier generation. They have undoubtedly coloured the writing of this book, though whether the book itself throws any light on modern problems is another matter.

A book such as this is bound to lean heavily upon secondary sources. The select bibliography on page 250 lists those learned authors to whom I am principally indebted. To some of those whose names appear there I owe a stronger obligation. Much of the pleasure in writing the book has lain in the chance that it has given me of travelling to see coins and mints and to meet those who have charge of them. These have been generous with their help and advice. Dr. H. Enno van Gelder, director of the Koninklijk Penningkabinet at the Hague, whose department has provided many of my pictures, has done much to help me understand the intricacies of Dutch coinage. Monsieur Jacques Yvon of the Cabinet des Médailles in the Bibliothèque Nationale, also a provider of photographs, has saved me from one or two fundamental errors in my treatment of the coins of the crusaders. Mrs. Jarmila Hasková of the National Museum, Prague, drew my attention to the principal features of the coinage of medieval Bohemia. A journey to Kremnica (Kremnitz) would have been a complete waste of time but for my good fortune in meeting Inz. Jan Horák, formerly director of the mint there and now its historian, who generously gave me photographs from his own history of the mint.

I must also express my thanks to the following who have shown me what I wanted to see in their collections, who have given me advice and information and some of whom I have pestered for photographs: Signor Ottorino Murari of Verona, Dott. Giovanni Gorini, director of the Museo Bottacin, Padua, Dr. Kütthmann of the Staatliche Münzsammlung, Munich, Fräulein Radomersky of the Staatliche Münzsammlung, Berlin, Dr. B. Koch, director of the Münzkabinett of the Kunsthistorisches Museum, Vienna, Mademoiselle J. Lallemand, director of the Cabinet des Médailles, the Bibliothèque Royale, Brussels. Madame Y. Goldenberg of the Administration des Monnaies, Paris, and Dr. L. Huszár, keeper of the coin collection at Budapest, Miss Heather Salter, editor of *Coins and Medals*, and the keepers of the Stadtarchiv, Schaffhausen, and the Rheinische Landesmuseum, Trier have all been kind enough to give me photographs. I have a long standing debt to Messrs. P. & P. Santamaria, Rome, whose present to me for use in an earlier book of a complete set of plates from one of their sale catalogues, has once again been of inestimable value.

Finally I should say that I should never have written this book at all without the encouragement and help of my English friends. Mr. P.D. Whitting read the Byzantine chapter in typescript; Mr. Ian Stewart read the whole book, and made many helpful suggestions. To Mr. Philip Grierson my debt is even greater, as a glance at the bibliography might suggest. He directed many of my ideas before ever I put pen to paper and later made a detailed criticism of the whole, thus saving me from a great number of errors of fact and judgment. It goes without saying, however, that the faults in this book are not theirs but mine.

1 The Imperial Foundations

1 Roman Empire; silver denarius *c.* 14 BC, Augustus. The centrepiece of the imperial monetary system [actual size]

2 Roman Empire; gold aureus *c.* 134–8, Hadrian. A typical example of the pure gold coin of the early years of the empire [actual size]

3 *(opposite)* Roman Empire; bronze follis, Diocletian (284–305), London. The large bronze coin of Diocletian's reform, clearly marked with the mint name [enlarged 3.5:1]

In 1965 the government of the United States of America decided in principle to abandon silver coinage and to replace it by silver-plated coins with a base metal core. For twenty years the world price of silver had been controlled by means of sales from the American stockpile, but increasing industrial demand for the metal, powerfully seconded by speculative buying, eventually proved too much for the administration, which found itself compelled to let the price rise at a rate which would soon make it profitable to melt down the United States subsidiary coins and sell the resulting bullion. The decision to give up silver coinage, which followed these events as a matter of course, was probably one of the last occasions in history when a government would be forced into a change of coinage policy by events outside its own control. Coinage, unlike money, is an institution which governments have, in time, learned how to manage. They have done it by degrading it, by depriving it in fact of all its monetary functions except the lowest, that of passing from hand to hand in small retail transactions. It was not always so. At certain periods in the past coinage has been closely identified with money, giving physical expression to money's speculative flights and devaluations; becoming as it were the body of that elusive and wayward abstraction. It is this aspect of coinage, since the collapse of the ancient system in the third century, that this book sets out to examine.

The origins of modern coinage are deeply rooted in the monetary system of the Roman Empire. The emperor Augustus issued coins in gold, silver and copper. The centrepiece of his system was the silver *denarius* [figure 1] in terms of which most prices were quoted and the army and civil service were paid. The gold *aureus* [figure 2] was effectively coined bullion, its value unfixed in monetary terms. The base metal coins on the other hand were fixed fractions of the denarius, their values artificially supported by imperial control of metal prices. The superior pieces were made of brass, the inferior of pure copper. They were theoretically issued by the authority of the Senate and bore the initials SC for *Senatus Consulto* [figure 5].

In the eastern parts of the empire, which were economically much more sophisticated than the west, Greek coinage still flourished. Many eastern cities were allowed to retain their ancient rights to the extent

5 Roman Empire; brass dupondius, Nero (54–68). A fine specimen of early Roman portraiture. The letters SC on the reverse refer to the senatorial authority by which the coin was struck [actual size]

4 (opposite) Roman Empire; five solidi (one reverse), Honorius (395–423), Ravenna; semissis (reverse) and solidus, Galla Placidia, sister of Honorius, Rome; and solidus, Johannes (423–5), Ravenna. A selection of gold coins of the last days of the western empire [actual size]

of striking copper and occasionally silver for local use. Two of the foremost trading currencies of the Hellenistic world were given a new lease of life: silver imperial tetradrachms of cistophoric standard [figure 6] were struck at Pergamum until the reign of Hadrian, while at Antioch and other Syrian mints tetradrachms of Seleucid standard were minted in the name of the emperor until the third century. In Egypt, where silver was never the natural currency, the imperial mint of Alexandria carried on the Ptolemaic tradition of striking heavily debased tetradrachms [figure 7]; these were officially taken at par with the denarius.

Beyond the frontiers of the empire a form of Greek coinage survived in Parthia, where the Arsacid kings struck silver drachmas [figure 8] and occasionally tetradrachms, with inscriptions in Pehlevi and degenerate Greek, until they were overthrown by the Sassanids in 226: this coinage, like that of Antioch, was ultimately derived from that of the Seleucids. In the west the barbarian tribes beyond the imperial frontier struck no coins of their own, but they were familiar with those of the Romans. According to Tacitus, they especially valued the silver denarius.

The economy of the Roman Empire was subject to a growing burden of defence and administrative costs, unmatched by any increase in production. The deficit was met partly by higher taxes and partly by inflation which took the simple form of debasement of the denarius. For about two hundred years this debasement proceeded at a supportable pace, though even then it was enough to leave some of the silver currencies of the eastern empire high and dry, and they disappeared during that time. In the third century the process began to get out of hand as military pressure built up on the frontiers and political disintegration within compelled successive emperors to bid more and more for the army's support. The denarius contained about 40% silver when in 214 Caracalla replaced it as the standard coin by a double denarius intrinsically worth only about one and a half of the current pieces. During the next fifty years matters went from bad to worse. The double denarius became virtually a copper coin, covered with the merest wash of silver which soon wore off. The last of the eastern silver coinages, that of Antioch, though that also had become debased, was left hopelessly undervalued by the progress of inflation and came to an end in the reign of Trebonianus Gallus (251–3). Only the Alexandrian tetradrachms, whose debasement kept pace with that of the imperial coinage, were still issued. The traditional senatorial copper and the multifarious issues of the former city states were all discontinued as even they became undervalued in terms of the miserable coin of which they were meant to represent the fractions. The government tried to avoid the consequences of its own acts by insisting on payment of taxes in bullion and refusing to take its own coin, but that only made matters worse. Finally, in the wake of Valerian's defeat and capture in 260 by the Sassanian king Shapur, the

7 (*opposite*) Roman Empire; billon tetradrachm, Aurelian (270–5), Alexandria. The debased tetradrachms of Alexandria, which were taken at par with the denarius, were the last surviving Greek coins within the Roman system [enlarged 2:1]

6 Roman Empire; silver tetradrachm *c.* 19 AD, Augustus, Pergamum. A Greek silver coin incorporated into the imperial system, this is of the cistophoric weight standard used at Pergamum in Asia Minor during the first century BC [enlarged 4:1]

8 Parthia; silver drachma, Artavasdes (227–8). Another coin of Greek origins, this one struck outside the Roman Empire by the last of the Arsacid kings of Parthia [enlarged 2:1]

emperor Gallienus abandoned all restraint in striking the now wholly debased double denarius [figure 9]. Enormous numbers were issued, the government's credit was destroyed and the currency became worthless.

The inflation of Gallienus's reign was almost as intense as that of Germany in 1923 and far more widespread. Nevertheless it may not have been so grievous in its social effects. The Roman Empire was never a monetary economy in the modern sense. Nearly all wealth was held in the form of land; agriculture was by far the most important economic activity. There was little manufacturing industry and much of that was owned and operated by the imperial government. The class which might have accumulated savings was small. The enormous hoards of double denarii dating from Gallienus's reign suggest not so much savings lost in the crash as the abandoned hopes of currency speculators. It is more likely that the crisis caused an overall drop in the standard of living than that it ruined whole sections of the population. Money ceased to be the prime medium of exchange. Payment of taxes, the remuneration of the civil service and the army, all came to be made in kind. For the taxpayers this meant an increase in the levy to cover the cost of storage, wastage and transport of commodities. On the other hand no number of rations *(annonae)* were likely to compensate such officials as provincial governors for the high monetary salaries which they had enjoyed in former times. Private soldiers ceased to receive any regular pay; they merely got their keep. As for the peasants, the collapse of the currency, by impairing the market for their occasional surpluses, simply brought them nearer than ever to subsistence level. There was some dispersal of population from the cities to the country, but that was probably caused more by the increasing hardship of civic duties than by the decline in trade. Much of the trade in the necessities of life, in bread and wine for example, was in any case carried on by the state.

Whatever the distress caused to the population by the monetary disorder, the soldier emperors who succeeded Gallienus gave low priority to finding a remedy for it. Their first concern was the restoration of the imperial frontiers. The coins of Aurelian, Probus and Carus can have done little to restore confidence in the currency though Aurelian did issue a double denarius of rather better quality. It was not until 295–6 that reform of the currency was firmly taken in hand by the emperor Diocletian as part of a general renewal of the civil institutions of the empire. Diocletian's reform of the currency is still imperfectly understood, for there are no documents to explain it and the coins themselves are enigmatic, but some facts about it stand out clearly.

The Alexandrian tetradrachm, last survivor of Greek coinage within the empire, was discontinued, thus leaving the field absolutely clear for the new coinage. New mints were set up to provide one in theory for each of the dioceses or super-provinces into which Diocletian divided the empire. The practice of marking every coin with the mint

13

9 Roman Empire; billon double denarius, Gallienus (253–68). Excessive issues of these debased coins finally broke up Rome's first monetary system [enlarged 2:1]

name and code number of the issuing *officina* or mint workshop was extended to become a general rule. The mints were thus decentralised and yet made easily subject to central supervision, an arrangement typical of Diocletian's administrative reforms.

As regards the coinage itself, Diocletian's most important change was to make his system revolve round the gold coin. The aureus had not been discredited like the denarius. During the third century it had become rare and had tended to fluctuate somewhat in weight; but it was never to the emperor's advantage to debase it since his own liabilities were rarely expressed in terms of it, whereas obligations to him were often paid that way. It was therefore the one piece which was still worth having. Diocletian stabilised its weight at sixty to the Roman pound and issued it in larger quantities [figure 10]. At the same time he issued a silver coin at ninety-six to the Roman pound, struck very pure and marked with the figures xcvi to encourage public confidence in it [figure 11].

The gold and silver coinage is the good side of Diocletian's reform. His failure, and it was fundamental, was that he did not fix the rate of exchange between the gold and silver on one hand and the bronze on the other. It is this bronze coinage that scholars have found so hard to interpret. In the first instance there were three coins, all containing a slight trace of silver. The largest of these [figure 3] was called the *follis*, a word whose earliest meaning was 'purse', which suggests that it was worth a fair number of denarii. The denarius still survived, not as a coin but as a unit of account, a mere fraction of the lowest coin in circulation, like the *lira* in modern Italy. It is not known how many denarii went to make up the bronze coins, nor how all of these were related to each other, for they underwent a steady diminution in weight during the course of the reign. What is certain, however, is that the government was not prepared either to convert bronze into aurei or to accept it in settlement of payments due to itself. Diocletian and his successors were not, like Gallienus, totally unrestrained in the amount which they issued, but since they were continually adding to a stock undiminished by tax payments, the floating rate of exchange between gold and bronze moved continuously against the latter. Against market forces so powerful even the draconian system of price control contained in Diocletian's *Lex de maximis pretiis* of 301 was quite ineffective. Inflation continued inexorably.

In its details, so far as they can be assessed, Diocletian's coinage was short-lived. The weight of the follis and of the other bronze coins was continually changing. The silver coin with its mark of value was never reissued in precisely the same form. Finally in 312 Constantine the Great found it convenient to adjust the weight of the gold coin from sixty to seventy-two to the pound. He called the new coin [figure 12] the *solidus*, signifying perhaps by that name his intention of consolidating and stabilising the coinage on the basis of this new weight standard. In any case it was the end of Diocletian's standard,

11 Roman Empire; silver, Galerius (292–305). The silver coin of Diocletian's reform, struck at ninety-six to the Roman pound. This one is in the name of Diocletian's junior colleague in the tetrarchy [enlarged 2:1]

10 Roman Empire; gold aureus, Diocletian, (284–305), Cyzicus. The aureus formed the centrepiece of Diocletian's reform of the Roman system [enlarged 2:1]

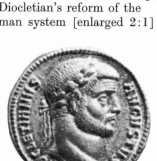

whose coins in all three metals were thus superseded within twenty years. Nevertheless the general principles of his reform stood the test of time. During the later years of the Roman Empire the coinage consisted of the gold solidus, pure and immutable, weighing twenty-four *carats* or *siliquae*; of a small silver coin, also pure but given to fluctuations in weight and value, though frequently corresponding to the siliqua; and finally of plentiful silvered bronze, only too mutable. All three were foreshadowed in Diocletian's coinage.

[The term 'carat' as used here and later needs some explanation. The word comes from the Greek κεράτιον meaning a carob bean. It was originally a weight. At Constantinople it was equivalent to 0.189 grams but in Syria and Arabia it was heavier (0.212 gm.). During the long existence of the solidus as a coin of pure gold weighing twenty-four carats, the carat became a measure of fineness as well as weight. Anything less than twenty-four carats weight of gold put into the solidus became in effect a measure of its debasement, and so, on a similar scale of twenty-fourths, with other gold coins and articles. It is in this sense that the word is most generally used now, though the Syrian carat is still a weight in the diamond trade. In the first two chapters of this book 'carat' is used in either sense according to the context. In the later chapters it is always used as a measure of fineness.]

To modern eyes it is extraordinary that a monetary system so economically unsatisfactory as that of Diocletian should have stood the test of time so well. It did so because it effectively fulfilled its intended function, which was to facilitate the collection of taxes. To the officials who ran the Roman Empire that was far more important than the provision of adequate supplies of reliable currency for general use. Even during the Principate, tax payment was regarded as one of the prime functions of the coinage [figure 13]. Since then the inflation of the 260s had destroyed public confidence in money as a means of exchange. The primitive economy of the empire was managing to rub along without it, except in this matter of tax collection, which, as long as it continued to be made in kind, was burdensome and inefficient.

Late Roman coinage was a dual system providing sound money for the public (imperial) sector of the economy and unsound money for the private sector. It worked tolerably because of the supreme importance of the state in economic life. The public sector included not only the vast army and civil service, but also most of the bigger mining and manufacturing enterprises and the distribution of such essentials as bread and wine. Moreover the emperor was himself by far the largest single landowner. In the private sector the most important activity was agriculture, for the most part not very profitably conducted. For this, coinage was of only marginal use. The one class which suffered therefore from the instability of the lesser coinage was that of the small traders. They were few and poor, even in the eastern cities; they had no claim to political consideration and the government supposed that they could be browbeaten by price controls.

During the fourth century the dual nature of the currency became more pronounced. The two classes of coinage were even issued from different mints. Base metal still continued to be struck at the regular diocesan mints, but the minting of gold tended to accompany the emperor and his *comitatus* or court in their travels. In the west, Milan in 353 and Ravenna [figure 4] after 402 became important mints for solidi; neither was a regularly constituted mint, but each became an imperial residence at the appropriate date.

A simple illustration will perhaps best show the relationship between the two coinages. An official called the *rationalis vinorum* was in charge of the public sale of wine. He was obliged to account for the

12 Roman Empire; gold solidus, Constantine I (306–37), Treveri (Trier). An aureus of reduced weight, the solidus continued to be minted, unchanged in weight and purity, for seven centuries [enlarged 4:1]

proceeds of his operations to the emperor's chief financial officer, the *comes sacrarum largitionum*. Like a nineteenth-century brewer, the *rationalis vinorum* took most of his revenue in the form of small payments of copper. But he was not permitted to pay this into the treasury. He had to go and buy solidi in the open market and pay those over instead. Even the solidi were not taken at their face value, but were melted down and treated as bullion. Indeed they had no face value; they fetched what they could in the market place and were always melted when they were paid over to the treasury. The bullion was then remade into coin when it was required, say for the annual payment of salaries to the palatine officials or for the *quinquennial donative* which was the only regular payment in specie to the rank and file of the Roman army. This repeated process of melting down and reissuing was the chief reason why the weight of the solidus was so well maintained. The coin did not usually circulate long enough to become worn.

The position of silver in the late Roman system is obscure. So far as its position was fixed, it would seem to have been as a fraction of the gold rather than as a multiple of the bronze. Conceivably the government issued silver as a substitute for gold when that was short. That would explain why it was always commoner in the western provinces than in the east, though it may have been demand rather than supply which produced that phenomenon. Sometimes silver was common, as in the last years of the fourth century, but more often it was rare. The fitful absence from the scene of this 'pale and common drudge 'tween

13 A late Roman bas-relief from Noviomagus in eastern Gaul showing payment of taxes. Tax requirements were the key to much minting activity, both in the late Roman period and in the early middle ages

14 Roman Empire; bronze follis, Decentius (351–3). An early example of forthright Christian imagery, used on a coin of the brother and junior colleague of Magnentius [actual size]

man and man' shows how little man and man were considered in the ordering of the late Roman currency.

It is not only the inward content of late Roman coinage that points to a lack of humanity. Its outward appearance shows the same spirit. The coin portraiture of the Principate had been very distinguished, a happy combination of the realistic death mask tradition of republican Rome with the lively naturalism and technical polish of Hellenistic artists. It had reached its highest perfection under Nero's patronage, but the standard was well maintained throughout the Antonine period [figures 2 & 5]. However in the third century, when the coinage became contemptible, coin portraiture sank with it [figure 7], to emerge very different after Diocletian's reforms. The modelling was less subtle and the features were more conventionally rendered than before [figure 3]. On the common run of coins this was perhaps partly because of lack of skill or of interest in portrayal, but even on the presentation pieces and others to which more care was presumably devoted, the artists' aim appears to have been to substitute an official hieratic remoteness for the human personality of the subject. The occasional use of the full face on such pieces enhances that effect. The intensive use of such imagery by Constantine and his successors illustrates how the emperor, having shuffled off his own tarnished state divinity, yet managed to intensify the reverence in which he was held by associating himself with a more transcendent religion. This change of style was accompanied by the adoption of more fulsome titles such as *Dominus noster* and even *Beatissimus*.

There was a parallel development in the reverse types, a decline in technique and invention by comparison with the earlier period. An uninspiring personification of the Genius of the Roman People remained for some years the sole type for Diocletian's folles [figure 3]. Jupiter figured prominently on the same emperor's coins in other metals and Hercules on those of Diocletian's colleague Maximian, for the two Augusti were especially associated with those divinities. Constantine's adoption of Christianity, as revealed on his coinage, was more discreet; just one of his coins, a copper, showed the Christian *labarum* with the Chi-Rho monogram on the shaft. The first bold use of Christian symbolism was made in about 350 by the Emperor Magnentius who adopted the same monogram for the whole of the reverse of a coin [figure 14], but that was premature. It was not until well into the next century that the cross and the Chi-Rho became a normal feature of Roman coins. In the Constantinian period military types preponderated, some of them, notably harsh in conception, showing a Roman spearing a fallen enemy or dragging a captive by the hair [figure 12]. It was more usual however simply to represent soldiers with the standards or a piece of military architecture such as a camp gateway. These types were repeated frequently with little variation.

Along their European frontier the Roman emperors were opposed to barbarian tribes. In Asia they faced a civilised power, the Sassanian

15 Sassanian Empire; silver drachma, Shapur I (241–72). An early example of Sassanian coinage showing the characteristic Zoroastrian fire altar [actual size]

Empire of Persia founded by Ardashir in 226 on the ruins of the kingdom of Parthia. If a regular and plentiful silver coinage is one of the signs of a healthy monetary economy, it is not surprising that the Sassanian Empire proved on occasions to be more than a match for Rome. Lying across the more southerly caravan routes and one of the main sea routes by which the luxuries of the east were transported to the Mediterranean world, the Sassanian Empire lived by trade to a much greater extent than Rome. And from the Parthians the Sassanians had inherited a well-respected system of coinage founded upon the silver drachma of Seleucid origin. For this reason silver dominated the system from the first. Originally the Sassanians issued gold and copper as well, but although, as subsequent events were to show, there was plenty of gold in the royal treasury, their later coinage was almost exclusively silver. It was as if they were deliberately making up for the deficiencies of the Roman system, though the Romans contended that the reason why the king of Persia did not issue a gold coinage was that he was not great enough to sustain one.

In appearance Sassanian coinage showed little trace of its Greek pedigree. The Greek inscriptions which had survived on Parthian coins were eliminated. In other respects the first Sassanian coins were rather like a reinvigorated version of the Parthian, but in the reign of Shapur I (241–72) the portraiture became at once more florid and more stylised [figure 15]. Throughout the four hundred years of the dynasty the normal reverse design was a Zoroastrian fire altar. The weight of the drachma was well maintained, probably because each new king recoined in his own name all the coins of his predecessors which lay in his treasury or which came into his hands. However, in the course of this successive reminting, which, in order to save expense, was carried out without actually remelting the coins, a curious change took place in the fabric: it became thinner and broader until finally the drachma was hammered out to cover an area bigger than that of a Seleucid tetradrachm [figure 16]. The design was not enlarged proportionately so that a wide border appeared, which was left blank except for a few symbols. Of course the thin coins had to be struck in much lighter relief. It is not known why the change in the fabric took place, but it was to have wide repercussions. Ancient coins were generally thick and struck in high relief; medieval ones were thin and in low relief. It was the Sassanian coinage which set the pattern for that fundamental transformation.

During the fifth century the substructure of the monetary system founded by Diocletian and Constantine appears to have disintegrated. The solidus still remained intact, but in the west its survival was more theoretical than practical for there was not enough gold to strike many. Those bearing the names of the last Roman emperors in the west, the shadowy nominees of Odoacer the Goth or of Constantinople, are of good quality but extremely rare [figure 17]. In all parts of the empire the solidus remained essentially the imperial coin, reserved

16 Sassanian Empire; silver
drachma, Khusru II (590–628),
Zirinj. This drachma, struck
by Chosroes, the long standing
enemy of the Byzantine emperor
Heraclius, has the broad thin
fabric characteristic of late
Sassanian coinage [enlarged 3:1]

for payment of taxes, for the emperor's own honorific payments or for his subsidies to barbarian princes, these last now occurring more often than they did. Apart from the solidus and the fractional gold coins, which became relatively commoner as gold was harder to come by, there was no currency except for the lowest of copper coins, known to archeologists and numismatists as *minimi*. To contemporaries they were known as *nummi*, which simply meant 'coins'. They are so mean and so wretchedly struck that they cannot be accurately ascribed to their mints or issuing authorities. Some may be of barbarian origin, but recent scholarship has come to the melancholy conclusion that most of them are Roman. It is hard to say whether they represent the extreme of inflation or deflation. On the one hand the price of the solidus in terms of the lesser coin, if that was the unit of account, must have been very high, probably at least 7,200 to one: to that extent prices appeared to be higher than ever. On the other hand it could be said that, as the logical result of Diocletian's and Constantine's dual system, the lesser coinage had finally withered on the vine and was worth practically nothing. The common people therefore had no valuable currency; gold was all that mattered and supplies of that were diminishing. The true position therefore was one of severe deflation. The extraordinary thing was that the solidus came through all this, for the political and military disasters of the fifth century were enough to destroy any currency system. As it was, in the west the system was shattered, but the fragments of the solidus were left to be picked up and refashioned into new currencies. Meanwhile in the east the solidus, true to its name, served as the foundation for yet another unified system of coinage on the Roman model.

17 Roman Empire; gold tremissis, Romulus Augustulus (475–6), Milan. A coin of the last Roman emperor in the west [actual size]

2 The Unbroken Tradition: Byzantium and Islam

19 Byzantine Empire; copper follis, Justinian I (527–65), Constantinople. A coin of the year 539, when Justinian raised the weight of the copper coinage and revalued it in relation to the gold solidus [actual size]

18 *(opposite)* Byzantine Empire; copper follis, Anastasius (491–518), Constantinople. The centrepiece of the reformed copper coinage of 498, with the prominent mark of value and mint name on the reverse [enlarged 3:1]

In the year 498 the emperor Anastasius instituted a currency reform as part of his general policy of restoring the public finances after a century of disasters. The architect of the reform is thought to have been a distinguished palatine official called John the Paphlagonian, who, as *comes sacrarum largitionum*, was in charge of all matters of public finance. Since the solidus was still intact, in spite of barbarian depredations in the gold-producing Danubian provinces, the restoration centred upon the lesser coinage. John did not venture upon a bimetallic system. Profiting by recent experiments made in western provinces controlled by the Vandals and the Ostrogoths [see page 43] he introduced large copper multiples of the discredited nummus. He revived memories of Diocletian's reform by calling the largest of these, the piece of forty nummi, the *follis*. This coinage consisted originally of the follis [figure 18] and pieces of twenty and ten nummi; the nummus continued for a time to be issued in its old form. The chief feature of the multiples was the mark of value prominently displayed on the reverse, M (40) for follis, K (20) for half-follis etc., together with the mint name and the code number of the *officina*. In Justinian's reign (539) the date was added, expressed in terms of the regnal year [figure 19]. This was evidently a strictly administered coinage.

The reform of 498 set the pattern of Byzantine coinage for five centuries; it was to consist of the solidus, unchanging at the weight of twenty-four carats, supplemented by a substantial copper coinage, with silver intermittently absent. On the face of it, it was like Diocletian's reform in its reliance upon an immutable gold coin and in the creation of a new multiple of a discredited lesser unit. However that reform had shown that the multiple of a discredited coin is itself unworthy of confidence unless it has some other virtue of its own. Now the follis of 498 was a substantial piece of metal; that doubtless made it worth something. If, however, folles were accepted by the treasury instead of gold, or were officially convertible into gold in some other way, or even if the authorities simply exercised strict self-discipline over the amount of copper which they issued, that would have been a major innovation, making the Byzantine coinage a far more reliable monetary instrument than what had gone before. Unfortunately we do not know whether that was so. There are no

Byzantine mint records; all the documentary evidence is fragmentary and much of it comes from Egypt, an exceptional province from which it is unwise to draw general conclusions. The coins, as they evolved through the centuries, must speak for themselves.

The follis was certainly not so stable as the solidus. After Justinian's reign there was a gradual decline in its weight. That this was associated with a fall in its purchasing power is suggested by the virtual discontinuance of the lesser denominations, the nummus in the middle of the sixth century, the five nummi in the reign of Tiberius II (578–82), the ten nummi in that of Heraclius (610–41) and the twenty nummi in that of Constantine V (740–75). Finally Theophilus (829–42) decided to leave off the traditional mark of value, which was superfluous once the follis had become the basic unit. On the other hand the changes in weight, which were not always downwards, look more like the controlled mutations of certain medieval and modern coinages than the runaway inflation of the third and fourth centuries. This suggests at least some control of the amount of copper coinage in issue. The Byzantines were well aware of the relationship between prices and the amount of money in circulation. As to convertibility, the chief evidence for an official rate of exchange is a reference by Procopius to Justinian's devaluation of the solidus from 210 folles to 180. This operation, which is usually associated with the raising of the weight of the follis by thirty-one per cent in the year 539, would have been impossible to carry out effectively unless the treasury was prepared to sell solidi against its own copper coin at the new rate. The frequent occurrence of Byzantine copper coins which have been overstruck on previous issues is clear evidence that, from the last quarter of the sixth century, the treasury was prepared to take in copper.

If the study of the coinage has tended to support the view that the Byzantine economy was static and sterile, it is because attention has naturally been centred upon the gold. The solidus early became a symbol of imperial greatness. In the time of Justinian, Cosmas Indicopleustes wrote: 'The gold money of the Roman Empire is accepted everywhere from end to end of the earth. It is admired by all men in all kingdoms because no kingdom has a currency to compare with it.' Some two centuries later, Bede, writing in Northumbria, where the solidus can have been seen but rarely, ventured to compare the virtue of the princess Earcongota of Kent to that of Byzantine gold. The solidus, unchanged in weight and purity for more than seven centuries, is such a dazzling monetary phenomenon that it is easy to look at the Byzantine economy and to see nothing else. Traditional economists have regarded it as the very pattern of sound money, and therefore beneficial; others have questioned whether it did not cause economic stagnation. However, just as recent studies in the artistic field have shown that Byzantium was a more dynamic society than it was once thought to be, so detailed consideration of the whole Byzantine coinage, not just the gold, suggests that here was a monetary

20 Byzantine Empire; gold solidus, Heraclius (610–41), Constantinople. A light-weight solidus, differentiated by the symbols below the cross on the reverse. The emperor is shown with his son Heraclius Constantine [actual size]

21 Byzantine Empire; gold solidus, Constantine VIII (1025–8). One of the light weight solidi of dumpy fabric known as tetartera which supplemented the issue of full weight coins at this period [actual size]

instrument of surprising versatility. Anyone who has compared Byzantine works of art with those of Carolingian Europe or who has read the excited account which the usually laconic William of Villehardouin gave of the riches of Constantinople at the time of the fourth crusade, will be aware that Byzantine wealth was of quite a different order from that of contemporary Europe. Yet after the Arab conquest of Egypt, the Byzantines had no easy access to gold supplies. Byzantine wealth was created by trade and by skilful economic management, in which an active coinage policy played an important part.

Even the solidus proved adaptable to unusual circumstances. Three groups of light-weight solidi are known. In Italy debased and light-weight gold coins were issued in the name of Constantine IV (668–85) and of his successors during two centuries [see figure 43]. This seems to have been a case of impoverished provinces proving unable to live up to the twenty-four carat coin. The other two groups are more difficult to explain. The earlier, which dates from the century after Justinian, was struck at varying weights between twenty and twenty-three carats. No deception was involved since the weight was clearly marked on the coin and the metal was pure [figure 20]. A high proportion of coins in this group has been found outside the empire, but the attractive theory that they were struck especially for foreign trade cannot be sustained. Private citizens were strictly forbidden to export gold and, although no doubt they often broke the rule, it is inconceivable that the government struck special coins to help them to do so. The third group of light-weight solidi dates from the second half of the tenth century. The coins in it are distinguished by their small module and dumpy fabric [figure 21], all the more remarkable in that the normal solidus was just then becoming broader and thinner. They have been identified with the *tetartera* referred to in literary sources as an innovation of Nicephorus Phocas (963–9), but the earliest surviving specimens bear the name of Basil II (976–1025). There are conflicting theories about their function.

The incompleteness of modern knowledge about Byzantine coinage is most evident in the case of the silver. During the seven centuries of the twenty-four carat solidus, silver coinage was never more than a minor auxiliary. For quite a long period there was none. Justinian and his successors struck silver in the west, but otherwise nothing but ceremonial silver was issued during the sixth century or during most of the eighth. On the other hand there were big issues by Heraclius and his son Constans II, and silver was struck regularly in the ninth century and plentifully throughout the tenth.

The term *miliaresion* was applied indiscriminately to silver coins of different weights and values at different periods. The difficulty is to establish what the values were. For example Heraclius used the abundant supplies of silver, which the church gave him from its treasuries for the expenses of the Persian war, to strike a heavy miliaresion [figure 22]. This was called the *hexagram* on account of its theoretical weight of

22 Byzantine Empire; silver miliaresion or hexagram, Heraclius (610–41) with Heraclius Constantine. There are conflicting theories about the value of this coin, whose issue was connected with the financing of the Persian war [enlarged 2:1]

23 *(opposite)* Byzantine Empire; gold solidi, *(left)* Leo VI (886–912) and *(right)* Leo VI with Constantine VII (908–12), Constantinople [enlarged 3:1]

six *grammata*. Some texts suggest that it was worth two carats, that is to say one twelfth of a solidus. That would make it somewhat undervalued on a gold:silver ratio of 18:1, but the circumstances of its issue and the fact that it was drawn out of circulation as soon as the Arabs started coining silver on a lower ratio, tend to support the valuation. However, other contemporary sources say that the hexagram was issued in order to spare the resources of the treasury and that it was intended that every payment due by the emperor in solidi should be made half in gold and half in silver. Now the issue of an undervalued silver coin in those circumstances would be not a saving but an extravagance. So it has been convincingly argued that the hexagram was officially overvalued at one sixth of a solidus, on a gold:silver ratio of 9:1. Where the authorities differ as to one hundred per cent it is rash to draw any conclusion. It does however appear certain that the later miliaresia of the ninth and tenth centuries were effectively token coins valued at much more than their intrinsic worth on the basis of fourteen, later twelve, to the solidus. These were thin, after the fashion of that time, and weighed less than half as much as the hexagram. As first issued by Leo III (717–41) they appear to have had a ceremonial use connected with the creation by the emperor of an imperial colleague, for such coins are known only in the joint names of pairs of emperors. Theophilus, however, struck miliaresia in his sole name, and thenceforward they were issued on a regular monetary footing [figure 27].

The first great period of Byzantine art, in the reign of Justinian, seems to have left the coinage almost untouched. The style of early Byzantine coinage was essentially late Roman. The designs were modelled in shallow relief and the portraiture was perfunctory, whether the type adopted was the facing bust of the emperor of late fourth-century origin, in armour and plumed helmet, or the profile bust of even earlier antecedents, wearing a diadem. The facing bust was normal on the solidus. Justinian also adopted it for the follis, on the larger flan of which it made a more impressive showing [figure 19]. Aesthetically, however, the most satisfactory feature of sixth-century coinage was the bold figuration of the marks of value on the reverse of the copper [figures 18 & 19].

The first appearance of a specifically Byzantine style of coinage was in the reign of Justinian on an exceptional but not rare follis of the mint of Antioch. This, instead of a mere bust, showed the emperor at full length seated on his throne and wearing a diadem and other rich regalia. In the reign of his successor Justin II the normal type of the follis at all mints was the emperor similarly enthroned, but with his wife, the empress Sophia, beside him [figure 25]. In the following century the appearance of the copper was ruined by overstriking, but the aspect of the gold coinage was much improved by Heraclius, whose later solidi have a neat and subtly balanced double facing portrait of the emperor and his young son, side by side [figure 20]. At this period double and even triple standing portraits of members of the imperial

25 Byzantine Empire; copper follis 565–6, Justin II with Sophia, Constantinople. The full length figure design, supplementing the classical portrait bust, became one of the normal types of Byzantine coinage during Justin's reign [enlarged 2:1]

24 (opposite) Ummayad Caliphate; gold dinar AH 77 and silver dirhem AH 79, 'Abd al-Malik (684–705), Damascus. The gold and silver coins of 'Abd al-Malik's reform of 696–9 which set the pattern of Islamic coinage for seven centuries [enlarged 2.5:1]

family became common on both gold and copper, reminiscent of the long rows of mosaic figures on the walls of Byzantine churches. The relationship between the figures was carefully worked out in terms of precedence.

Byzantine coinage, like every other aspect of life in that society, was deeply imbued with Christian symbolism. At first this tendency was countered by the more restrained traditions of late Roman coinage so that even in Justinian's reign it amounted to little more than the *globus cruciger* which the emperor held in his hand and a small cross on the reverse. Tiberius II, however, made the cross the chief feature of the reverse of the solidus [figure 20], and later, when Byzantium was beset by Islam, Christian imagery dominated the whole coinage.

The earliest use of an icon as a coin was by Justinian II during his first reign (685–95), who with a suitable Latin inscription placed the bust of Jesus Christ on the obverse of the solidus and moved his own portrait to the reverse. It so happened that this innovation coincided with one of the best periods of Byzantine coin engraving when two separate schools were contending, one working in a naturalistic manner, the other in a formal linear style. Both produced solidi of the new type [figures 26]. The use of such a holy icon in connection with the sordid dross of trade and tax paying is an extreme illustration of the traditional Orthodox theory of the inherent goodness of matter. It was to become commonplace in later centuries and, in the hands of inferior craftsmen, totally inoffensive, but the telling image created by Justinian II's engravers still has power to shock us. And it shocked the Byzantines. The iconoclastic controversy was just beginning and these coins were part of the opening barrage by the iconodule party. When the iconoclast Leo III succeeded in 717 everything was changed. For the portraiture of the emperor, the formal school of engravers was encouraged; the simple cross was once again adopted as the reverse type

26 Byzantine Empire; gold solidi, Justinian II, first reign (685–95), Constantinople. Contrasting schools of Christian iconography were at work in Constantinople during this reign [enlarged 2:1]

of the solidus, though with growing frequency Leo and his successors replaced it with portraits of their associates or, failing those, with a second portrait of themselves. On the new silver miliaresia there were no portraits whatever, just a cross on one side and a calligraphic inscription on the other [figure 27]. Usually such inscriptions were in the Greek language, but not altogether in Greek characters. As early as the reign of Justinian I it was evident that the die engravers of Antioch did not understand Latin, for they frequently made nonsense of it. Gradually Greek superseded Latin at all mints, but the Byzantines did not forget that their emperor was the Roman emperor and Latin kept recurring, as for example in the inscription round the bust of Christ on Justinian II's solidus. From the middle of the eighth century Greek predominated [figure 27], but as late as 866 the Pope's taunt that the Byzantines knew no Latin could provoke Michael III into styling himself *imperator*. Latin characters were occasionally used in otherwise Greek legends until late in the eleventh century, when contact with the crusaders at last revealed to the Byzantines how passionately Greek they felt themselves to be.

The figure of Christ reappeared on the Byzantine coinage soon after the triumph of the party of the images in the ninth century. It was reintroduced by Michael III and at once became the standard type for the solidus. As for the copper coinage, it was devoted entirely to the

27 Byzantine Empire; silver miliaresion, Leo VI (886–912), Constantinople. The purely calligraphic inscription and the triple ring round the border of this later Byzantine silver coin point to a connexion with the dirhems of Islam (see figure 24) [enlarged 2:1]

28 Byzantine Empire; gold solidus Michael III (842–56), with his mother Theodora and sister Thecla, Constantinople. A typical coin of the ninth century showing the imperial family, carefully graded according to their relative political importance [enlarged 2:1]

icon of Christ by John Zimisces (969–76). The emperor's portrait name and titles were all withdrawn. The obverse of the follis was given over to the bust of Christ with the title Emmanuel; the reverse to the simple inscription in Greek: Jesus Christ King of kings [figure 29]. It was as if the follis was intended to be the small change of all Christendom. Only the most extreme piety can have prompted this abrupt departure from the thousand-year-old tradition of imperial coinage. This style however was maintained with little variation for more than a century, thus incidentally creating countless problems of classification for numismatists. It was copied by the Normans in southern Italy and Antioch and was through them to have an important influence upon coinage in the west. The bust of Christ was not the only icon to be used in this intensely religious phase of Byzantine coinage. That of the Virgin Orans [figure 23] was introduced by Leo VI (886–912) who was especially devoted to her cult, and although the Virgin did not become a regular feature of the coinage until much later, she reappeared in subsequent reigns, either alone or conjointly with the emperor.

It is of some interest that Justinian II's first experiment with militantly Christian iconography for the solidus coincided almost exactly with the first issue of an uncompromisingly Islamic coinage by the Arabs. For the first years after their conquest, the Arabs, who had had no coinage of their own in Arabia, continued to issue the sort of coins

29 Byzantine Empire; copper follis, John Zimisces (969–76), Constantinople. In this period the Byzantine copper coinage was wholly devoted to the name and image of Christ, with no mention of the emperor's name [enlarged 2:1]

which they found in the conquered territories: in Persia the silver drachma of the Sassanians, which they called the *dirhem*, and in Syria the copper follis of the Byzantines, with the name corrupted to *fals*. At first they changed neither the weight nor the general aspect of these, adding only a short cufic inscription in the wide border of the dirhem [figure 30]. At this stage they struck no gold but used the Byzantine solidi which still circulated in the former imperial provinces, to which they added what more they could get by tribute, plunder and trade. Byzantine merchants, as we know, were forbidden to make external payments in gold, but they probably did so from time to time. Besides, the empire relied upon Egypt for its supplies of papyrus and the imperial trading organisation which monopolised papyrus imports was no doubt exempt from the rule which bound private traders. This curious fact gives some colour to the traditional story of the origin of Islamic gold coinage. The story goes that Justinian II complained to the caliph 'Abd al-Malik that the seal on the papyrus sent to Constantinople was offensive to Christians. The caliph replied that if the Greeks wanted the papyrus they must put up with the seal; Justinian retorted that in that case he would pay in coins no less offensive to Islam. The caliph closed the argument, saying that he did not depend upon the emperor for gold coinage and that he would issue gold of his own. This story is supported by the existence of Justinian II's solidi with the bust of Christ, which must have been particularly obnoxious to Arab sensibilities just when Islamic teaching was hardening against the use of images of any kind. However the truth is that for some years before his reform of the coinage in 696–9 'Abd al-Malik had been experimenting with new gold coins, some of which bore representations of the caliph and

30 Ummayad Caliphate; silver dirhem AH 68 (AD 687), 'Umar bin 'Ubaidullah, governor of the East. An early Arab coin of Sassanian design and weight from the Persian mint of Ardashir Khurra [actual size]

31 Ummayad Caliphate; gold dinar, c. 693, 'Abd al-Malik. An early Arab experiment in gold coinage, copied from a solidus of Heraclius (610–41) but with all the crosses removed and an Arabic inscription [actual size]

other figurative designs [figure 31]. A reform was overdue. Arab rule was now consolidated over an area formerly served by totally disparate currencies. The conquest of such rich civilisations as those of Persia and the oriental and African provinces of Byzantium had released quantities of hoarded treasure. Moreover the Arabs now controlled the flow of bullion from the gold-bearing reaches of the upper Nile to its outlet in the Mediterranean. These economic forces, calling for regulation in terms of a unified currency, were a stronger motive for 'Abd al-Malik's reforms than a quarrel about the seals on papyrus.

The reorganisation of the currency in 696–9 was far-reaching. The new coinage was bimetallic, consisting of the gold *dinar* with its fractions, and the silver *dirhem* [figure 24]; copper coinage also continued. The word *dinar* is a corruption of denarius, a name applied quite generally to Roman coins at that time, including the solidus or aureus denarius of which the dinar was evidently a sort of Arab version. It was about six and a half per cent lighter than the Byzantine coin, a difference which has been convincingly explained in terms of the weight measurements then in use in the Mediterranean world. As against the solidus of twenty-four Graeco-Roman carats, the dinar weighed twenty of the Syro-Arabian variety (see page 15). This was convenient, since the twenty carat multiple was itself a metric unit of long standing in Arabia and it happened also to coincide with the weight of the worn solidi which were circulating beyond the confines of the Byzantine empire. There was no such happy convenience about the weight of the new dirhem. That too represented a break with tradition. It was lighter by a third than the Arab-Sassanian version and, apart from its name, the only characteristics which it shared with its predecessor were its broad, thin fabric and the triple

33

32 Abbasid Caliphate; gold dinar AH 212 ,'Al Ma'mūn (813–33), Medina es Salam (Baghdad). A dinar of the great age of Arab prosperity [enlarged 2:1]

ring and pellets around the rim. Its weight seems to have been chosen without regard to precedent to give it the value of one twentieth of a dinar on the basis of a gold : silver ratio of 14 : 1.

'Abd al-Malik's new coinage coincided with the first high tide of iconoclastic sentiment in Islam and the types chosen for it were therefore entirely epigraphic. In the field of the obverse of both gold and silver was written in Arabic the profession of faith: 'There is no god but God; He hath no associate'. The rest was taken up with sentences from the Koran, the date and, in the case of the dirhem, the name of the mint. The Ummayad caliphs concentrated the striking of dinars at the mint of Damascus, their capital, and it was not thought necessary to name the mint except on those few dinars which were struck elsewhere, at Kairouan in Africa or at Cordova in Spain. Conversely Kairouan and Cordova seem to have been the only mints to strike large numbers of fractional gold coins, thus conforming to the general pattern of gold coinage of lower value on the western Mediterranean; on these coins also the mint was not usually named. For a brief period there was an attempt to concentrate the coinage of dirhems on a single mint in Mesopotamia, but it came to nothing. Ummayad dirhems were issued from more than sixty mints ranging from Balkh in north-eastern Khorasan to Cordova in Andalusia. Stylistic differences between mints have been noted, but the uniformity of the dirhem over this great area is remarkable. It was not shared by the copper coinage. The fals was a token coin and its issue seems to have been left to the discretion of provincial governors. Both in weight and type it varied from mint to mint: in some areas it even escaped the interdiction of figurative designs and, whereas even the name of the caliph was not put on the gold and silver, that of the provincial governor quite often appeared on the copper.

The absence of the caliph's name from the Ummayad dinars and dirhems heightens the impression which they give of having been the universal coinage of Islam. That this is only an impression is suggested by the way that in practice the caliphs were prepared to modify the system in response to local conditions, as for example by striking debased fractional dinars in the west. With the passing of Arab unity, regional variations tended to multiply. Half a century after 'Abd al-Malik's reform, the Ummayads were overthrown by the Abbasids, who established their caliphate at Baghdad. At first they made little change in the coinage apart from rearranging and extending the sacred texts and altering the calligraphy [figure 32]. In spite of the eastward shift of the political centre of gravity and the transfer of the principal mint for gold from Damascus to Baghdad, the period of the great Abbasids, notably Haroun al-Rashid, was the economic heyday of the dinar in the Mediterranean. Byzantium was drawn in on itself, a trading power certainly, but nursing a favourable balance of payments and jealously on guard against the export of gold. The caliphate by contrast was expansive, controlling vast wealth, but paying it out

33 Ummayad Caliphate of Cordova; silver dirhem AH 155, 'Abd al-Rahman I (756–88), el Andalus (Cordova). This western caliph, like his Frankish neighbour, Pepin the Short, struck only silver coins [enlarged 2:1]

freely to support the pace of its development. Though less stable than the solidus, the Abbasid dinar was far more easily obtained and it became the chief gold trading currency of the Mediterranean lands. Further north all gold coins were regarded as rare curiosities and silver was preferred for trading purposes. With that too the Arabs were very free and enormous numbers of Abbasid dirhems have been found in Viking hoards in Scandinavia, presumably carried thither in the course of trade by the eastern routes through Russia.

In the ninth century it became necessary for the caliph to put his own name on his dinars and dirhems in order to distinguish them from those struck by his rivals or by rulers who, while they acknowledged his spiritual authority, had become politically independent enough to issue coins autonomously. Prominent among the former were the Ummayads in Spain. In 756 'Abd al-Rahman I set up an independent caliphate at Cordova and issued dirhems there after the Ummayad pattern [figure 33]. Curiously he struck no dinars, but this was not because he felt any political inhibitions about doing so. Gold was short in the west and 'Abd al-Rahman found himself impelled towards silver monometallism by the same economic forces that moved his contemporary, the Carolingian Pepin I, to adopt the same principle. Whether one of these rulers influenced the other in this we cannot say. Certainly the Spanish Arabs were to make a permanent escape from it much earlier than the Franks, for gold dinars were regularly struck at Cordova from the reign of 'Abd al-Rahman III (929). However this Ummayad coinage still shared other characteristics with western coinage, notably a tendency towards debasement of the silver during the next century; nor is there much doubt that the thin fabric of the Carolingian denier (see page 54) owed something to its influence.

With the sprouting of many different Arab dynasties all issuing their own coins, it became necessary to increase the amount of information given in the inscriptions, which thus became more and more

34 Ayyubid Sultanate of Egypt
and Syria; gold dinar AH 587,
Saladin (1169–93), Cairo. The
concentric circles of inscription
which characterised the dinars of
Egypt were to have an
influence upon the
appearance of Frankish coinage
[enlarged 2:1]

35 Fatimid Caliphate; gold
quarter-dinar or ruba'i in name
of 'Al Mustansir (1035–94), Sicily.
The quarter-dinar issued
gold coin by the Saracen
emirs in Sicily was the
prototype of much south Italian
coinage after the Arabs were
driven out again [enlarged 2:1]

elaborate. Arab calligraphy, however, rarely failed to make an elegant pattern of even the most lengthy texts. The Fatimids, who conquered Egypt in 969 and whose rule extended eastwards into Syria and westwards along the north African coast, emphasised points of the heretical Shi'ite doctrine on their coins, celebrating the name of 'Ali with that of the Prophet. Like other rulers of Egypt before them, they found it impossible to sustain a silver coinage there, and they therefore issued mostly dinars and copper. Their dinars are distinguished from those of the Abbasids by the emphasis on the circularity of the design, a characteristic which was even further exaggerated by their successors the Ayyubids, whose Egyptian dinars were taken up almost entirely with concentric inscriptions [figure 34]. In Sicily, where emirs acknowledging the suzerainty of the Fatimids ruled for most of the tenth century and the first half of the eleventh, the Arabs responded to local European conditions as they did in Spain. Here they struck only the quarter-dinar or *ruba'i*, a piece roughly equivalent to the Lombard *tremissis* [see page 45] but more reliable. This unimpressive little coin became a mainstay of Italian commerce in the critical early phase of its development in the south [see page 59]. The Italians copied it and it was for many years the only gold coin struck in Latin Europe, but it never became a Latin coin, for it was still inscribed in what purported to be Arabic even in the thirteenth century.

The supplanting of the solidus by the dinar as the chief trading currency in the world was not, as we have seen, because of any weakening in the Byzantine coin, but because of the change in the pattern of commerce which took place after the Arab conquest. In the eleventh century, however, when Byzantium came under severe pressure from the Seljuks advancing in Asia Minor, the emperor Michael IV (1034–41), in order to spare the drain on his treasure, took the unprecedented step of debasing the solidus. In the disastrous years leading up to and immediately after the battle of Manzikert (1071) the fineness of the solidus came down from twenty-four carats to eight. Inflation so rapid might soon have destroyed the financial basis of Byzantine prosperity, but it was checked by Alexius Comnenus (1081–1118), whose reign was spent in restoring the broken structure of the empire.

The coinage of the Comneni should properly be considered with that of medieval Europe, but the Byzantine system was so different from that of the Latins that it is more convenient to bring its history to an end here. The Comnenian coinage was in four metals, gold, electrum (an alloy of gold and silver), billon (an alloy of silver and copper), and copper. With the exception of some smaller pieces, mostly copper, these coins were all of about the same size and of generally similar aspect. They were thin and saucer-shaped, usually with a representation of the emperor on the concave side and one of Christ on the other [figure 36]. The copper coins were no longer anonymous. The gold coin was a restoration of the solidus: it was called the hyperpyron, from a Greek word meaning pure, though in fact it was only

36 Byzantine Empire; gold hyperpyron, Alexius I (1081–1118), Constantinople. The solidus as restored by Alexius Comnenus after the debasement of the previous half-century [actual size]

$20\frac{1}{2}$ carats fine. The precious metal content of the alloyed coins was quite consistent. The electrum piece was intrinsically worth one third of the hyperpyron and was no doubt current at that value. The billon piece, which may be identified with the *staminon* which according to the Frankish chronicles was used to cheat the crusaders, was reckoned at one forty-eighth of the hyperpyron and the copper perhaps at one sixth of that. The reference to cheating is interesting since it suggests that some of the coins were token pieces, current for more than their intrinsic value, a sophisticated concept which would certainly have seemed like cheating to the simple Franks.

For most of the twelfth century the Byzantine monetary system was still the best administered in the world. All the evidence suggests that the Comnenian age was the Indian summer of Byzantine commerce. Shorn of its agricultural base by the Turkish advance in Asia Minor, the empire was having to trade for its life and was pursuing a far more open policy than before with regard to the west. Latin Europe, owing to its rising population and standard of living, was a more active trading partner and customer. But already before 1204 the system was showing signs of weakness and the fourth crusade completely broke it up. The Franks and Venetians put nothing satisfactory in its place, contenting themselves with the issue of degenerate versions of the base metal coins. The Greek emperors at Nicaea issued hyperpyra, but these underwent a debasement from which they never recovered. Michael Palaeologus, after his recapture of Constantinople in 1261, continued to issue hyperpyra, curiously ill-struck pieces with the image of the Virgin on the convex side surrounded by the battlements of the reconquered city [figure 37]. But there was to be no second restoration of the solidus. In the fourteenth century merchants who wanted to safeguard the value of their contracts wrote them in Venetian currency, not in hyperpyra. The final epitaph on the solidus was written in 1332 by the Arab traveller 'Ibn Battuta, who said of it: 'The gold of that country is no good'.

In the middle of the fourteenth century Byzantium turned to the silver monometallism from which the rest of Europe was just emerging. This silver period was a curious epilogue to the long predominance of the gold solidus. Gold was provided by the Venetians and the Genoese and western influence was paramount throughout the empire. In Neopatras John II Angelus (1303–18), a prince of the Comnenus family under Frankish tutelage, struck coins of entirely French type. Even at Constantinople the reformed silver coinage of Andronicus II (1282–1328) evidently owed much to a Venetian prototype [figure 37]. However the monetary inventiveness of the Byzantines was not entirely dead. During the reign of John V a last reform of the coinage was made. The coins of this issue were quite different from anything that had gone before. Flat in fabric and made of quite fine silver, they were much heavier than any contemporary coins and so compensated to some extent for the lack of locally struck gold. They were quite degenerate in style [figure 37], but in other respects they curiously foreshadow the heavier silver pieces which the Italian cities were to adopt some ninety years later when they too were faced with a shortage of gold. So, just as the first Renaissance medal, Pisanello's portrait medal of John VIII Palaeologus, harked back to Byzantium, so the last coins of Byzantium looked forward to the first coins of the modern era.

37 Byzantine Empire; gold hyperpyron, Michael VIII (1261–82), silver, Andronicus II and Michael IX (1295–1320) and silver John V (1341–91). Three coins of Byzantium in its decline, the gold looking back to the prestige of the solidus which Michael could not afford to restore, the coin of Andronicus looking towards contemporary Venice, and that of John V, the empire's last monetary experiment, foreshadowing the heavy silver coins minted in western Europe some seventy years later [enlarged 2:1]

38 Trebizond; silver asper, Manuel I (1238–63). During two centuries of independence of both Byzantium and the Seljuks, this empire on the Black Sea issued a plentiful silver coinage [enlarged 2:1]

The Byzantine tradition of coinage was upheld in one area which did prosper during the late middle ages. Just before the Latin conquest of Constantinople, a member of the Comnenus family set up an independent orthodox state at Trebizond on the Black Sea and this remained separate even after Michael Palaeologus recaptured the metropolis. By a policy of tactful submission towards its Moslem neighbours, the empire of Trebizond managed to stay in being until 1461. Its coinage was initiated by John I (1235–8) but it was during the reign of his brother Manuel I (1238–63) that it came into prominence. As a result of the Mongol devastation in the caliphate culminating in Hulagu's sacking of Baghdad in 1258, much of the trade between Europe and the east was diverted northward through Asia Minor. Trebizond became an important entrepôt on the new route, for it was there that the caravans came to the sea and the merchandise was transferred to Genoese and Venetian ships. Since the little empire had its own silver mines, the large coinage required for this market was made of that metal. The principal coin was called the *asper*. Manuel's aspers, which were struck in great profusion, had on one side the standing figure of the Grand Comnenus, as the emperor was always called, wearing imperial regalia, and on the other the patron saint of Trebizond, Eugenius, also standing [figure 38]. The Greek inscription consisted only of the names of the two figures, but it incorporated a sophisticated system of secret marks and pellets, which doubtless related to the administration of the mint.

In outward appearance the asper was the last vigorous offshoot of Byzantine coinage. From the beginning, however, it had oriental characteristics. It was of the same weight as the dirhem. At Iconium, not far from Trebizond, the Seljuks of Rum, who likewise profited from the diversion of the eastern trade route, struck dirhems of similar fabric to that of the asper. The Seljuks were exceptional among Moslems in preferring figurative designs for their coinage. The most celebrated of these is perhaps the lion and sun on the dirhem of Kai Khusru II (1234–45). This device is said to have represented the horoscope of the sultan's beautiful Georgian wife, which was as far as he dared go towards putting her portrait on the coins. Not that the Seljuks were inhibited from representing the human figure, since an equestrian portrait of the sultan was in regular use. Eventually this equestrian type was adopted also for the aspers of Trebizond. On the aspers of Alexius II (1297- 1330) both the Grand Comnenus and St Eugenius were provided with horses. This supersession of a well-tried design on a trading coinage of high repute is unusual. It is telling evidence of the strength of Turkish influence in the tributary empire. The change marks Trebizond's final break with the Byzantine tradition, but it was by no means the end of the coinage, which continued for at least another century. Its weight slowly declined, but it survived as an important trading currency for long enough to influence the early coinage of the grand dukes of Muscovy.

3 The Fragments: Coinage in the Barbarian Kingdoms

39 *(opposite)* Ostrogothic kingdom of Italy; silver half-siliqua, Totila (also called Baduila) (541–52), with the name and portrait of the emperor Anastasius (491–518). Totila preferred to put a dead emperor on his coins rather than Justinian, with whom he was at war. His own name is on the reverse [enlarged 4:1]

40 *(opposite below)* Vandal kingdom in Africa; silver fifty denarii, Gunthamund (484–96). An early instance of autonomous coinage in the Roman manner by a barbarian king [enlarged 4:1]

None of the Germanic peoples whose invasion in the fifth century brought about the collapse of the imperial authority in the west had a coinage of their own. In Britain, where the Anglo-Saxons effaced what remained of Roman civilisation, the last Roman issues were made in about 406; those circulated for some twenty years after that, but then coinage seems to have disappeared altogether until it was reintroduced from the continent in the seventh century. In Gaul, Italy and Spain the invaders were received by the Romans as allies. Unlike the Anglo-Saxons they were always a minority in the lands which they settled; their kings acknowledged the suzerainty of the emperor and, having no civilisation of their own to offer, they did not impose a way of life, but learnt one. The Roman currency, with its mints and the profits from them, was but one of the institutions which they took over. At first they altered nothing, not even the name in which the coins were issued. This was usually that of the emperor with whom they were last in contact, or whose coins still commonly circulated. As long as an emperor remained in the west, they coined in his name. After 476 those who were in touch with Constantinople changed to the name of the emperor reigning there though sometimes, for political reasons, they would favour an earlier emperor. Thus in the middle of the sixth century the Ostrogothic kings Totila and Theia, at war with Justinian, reverted to the name of Anastasius, who had died in 518 [figure 39].

The persistence of Roman coinage after the invasions is evidence of the continuing economic unity of the empire after its political disintegration. However, a difference between the Byzantine and western currencies soon emerged. In the east the solidus was still struck in large numbers, its weight and quality unimpaired. In the west, while it remained the basis of the accounting system, the coin itself began to give place to a piece of one third of its value, the *tremissis* or *triens*. This had first been introduced at Constantinople by Theodosius the Great in 383 but there it always remained the fractional coin that it was originally intended to be. In the west it had become more common than in the east even before the invasions [figures 4 & 17], and from the beginning of the sixth century there were more tremisses than solidi in circulation there. After about 550 it was exceptional for

western rulers to strike solidi at all except at Marseilles, the chief emporium of eastern trade, and, much later, in the Lombard duchy of Benevento whose links with Byzantium were especially close.

The main cause of the change to a smaller coin was shortage of gold. The Spanish mines were nearly worked out and there was no longer any important domestic source of supply. The west was reduced to accumulated stocks and to the diplomatic subsidies of the Byzantine emperors, traditionally paid in solidi. Slaves were the only major export to be set against the costly and varied goods imported by Syrian and Jewish merchants, but they were not enough and there was still a persistent outflow of gold. Thus while the continuance of the Roman monetary system in the western kingdoms points to the maintained economic unity of the Roman world, the diminution of gold coinage among them shows how that world had lost its balance.

Several reasons probably contributed to the readiness of the western kings to go on issuing coins in the emperor's name rather than their own. Habit may have been one. Their peoples had been acquainted with Roman coins when they had lived beyond the imperial frontiers and some may have believed that a piece not struck in the name of an emperor was no coin at all. If so, they got over that idea quickly enough, since the Ostrogoth Odoacer (476–93) and the Vandal Gunthamund (484–96) both issued autonomous silver and bronze [figure 40]. It was essentially with gold that the old tradition stuck and that the invaders' self-assertion was limited to the monogram or initial of the issuing king added as a difference beside the emperor's name. Some have deduced from that a sacred imperial monopoly of gold coinage, but there is an economic explanation. Silver and bronze were for local circulation, for which the name of a local potentate was enough guarantee. Gold on the other hand was the currency of merchants trading extensively, and the name in which it was issued had to be widely known.

The economic argument seems to be borne out by the earliest exception to the rule. When at last a Frankish king, Theodebert of Austrasia (534–48), who had conquered Justinian's armies in Italy, ventured to issue solidi in his own name [figure 41] the reaction of the Byzantine historian Procopius was not so much indignation at an infringement of an imperial prerogative as surprise that a barbarian should think that he could make his own gold coinage succeed, when even the king of Persia, with great stocks of the metal at his command, reckoned that he could not. The doubts of Procopius were well-founded. Theodebert's solidi, of standard imperial type but with the provocative legend DN THEODEBERTUS VICTOR, were not enough of a commercial success to circulate far beyond his own territories or to encourage his successors to follow his example.

The barbarians, who had at first imitated everything, seem early to have discriminated between what was worth copying and what was not. The gold coinage evidently was: silver and bronze were another

41 Austrasia; gold solidus, Theodebert (534–48). The first coin in the name of a Frankish king and the first gold coin struck anywhere within the old Roman Empire in the name of anyone but an emperor [actual size]

matter, since the late Roman silver currency, though of good quality, was sparse, while the bronze was plentiful but trash. However, in two areas those two metals soon came briefly into their own again. In Africa, the Vandal Gunthamund issued a silver coinage [figure 40]. With its system of marks of value this was in some respects a reformed coinage, as it needed to be, since the Vandals minted little gold and the rôle of their silver was correspondingly larger. Similarly silver figured increasingly in the currency of Italy under the Ostrogoths, though they made plentiful issues of gold also. It is noteworthy that Justinian, who struck silver at Constantinople only in minute quantities for ceremonial purposes, felt impelled to issue an extensive silver coinage for Africa and some silver also for Italy after his reconquest of those countries.

As regards bronze coinage, there was an important reform, if not by the Vandals and Ostrogoths themselves, at least by the senates of Carthage and Rome acting under their suzerainty [figure 42]. Carthage issued a series of quite original pieces with new designs and a system of marks of value. The largest, the piece of 42 nummi with a horse's head on it, was bigger than any bronze coin struck in the Roman world for nearly a century. The coins issued by the Roman Senate are no less curious. The earliest are even bigger than the Carthaginian pieces and bear the name of the emperor Zeno (474–91). But Zeno himself never issued coins like that: not only the module but the style and portraiture seem to be intended to recall the sestertii of the first and second centuries, while the letters sc for Senatus Consulto on the reverse are an explicit reminder of that earlier time. A slightly later issue, with no emperor's head but a personification of Roma Invicta on the obverse and an eagle or a wolf and twins on the reverse is less imitative but just as nostalgic. This conscious antiquarianism may have had the serious political purpose of reasserting for the Roman Senate its ancient minting rights in the absence of a proper bronze coinage issued by the emperor. However, the special interest of both Roman and Carthaginian issues lies not in their retrospection but in their anticipation, by perhaps as much as twenty years, of the great reform of the Byzantine bronze coinage by Anastasius in 498 [see page 23]. It was apparently in centres where imperial authority no longer operated that the first steps were taken to fill the inconvenient gap which had opened in the late fourth century between the bronze nummus on one hand and the gold tremissis, which was worth 2,400 times as much, on the other.

The reformed bronze coinage of Rome was copied to a limited extent at Ravenna and lasted intermittently for a number of years. Its last appearance was in the reign of Theodahad (534–6) whose pieces carry his portrait and repeat the sc cypher on the reverse. It is the portrait which makes these remarkable, for it is the product of a rare fusion of Roman realism and Gothic invention [figure 48]. It shows that the Ostrogothic kingdom of Italy was much closer to the

42 Carthage under the Vandals; bronze forty-two nummi. Rome under the Ostrogoths; bronze forty nummi (folles) in the name of Zeno and in the name of the city, all *c.* 480. With these issues the senates of the two cities appear to have attempted to restore the bronze currency of the invaded empire. The types are consciously antiquarian and seem intended to recall better days [enlarged 2:1]

ancient world than any other of the barbarian successor kingdoms.

Africa and Italy were both brought back into the imperial fold by Justinian's reconquest and, for a time, the coinages of both were typical of those of Byzantine provinces. In Africa and Sicily that situation persisted until the Arab conquests in the seventh and ninth centuries. In Italy an earlier but less complete change followed the Lombard invasion. The Lombards penetrated but did not entirely subdue the country; the direct authority of the emperor was still

44

acknowledged at Rome, Naples and Ravenna, at Rome until not many years before Charlemagne's coronation there in 800 and at Naples a little later even than that. The exarchate of Ravenna lasted until 751. A scanty imperial coinage was issued from those three centres. Among the coins was the *solidus mancus* [figure 43], a light-weight solidus devised especially for the poor economic conditions of the west. Denoted simply as the gold mancus in the accounts of Frankish and Anglo-Saxon treasuries, the identification of this coin was to baffle historians for many years.

The coinage of the Lombards themselves had borne an imperial stamp when that people had still lived by the Danube and it remained characteristically imitative after they came to settle in the Po valley. The use of the imperial name persisted until late in the seventh century and the designs usually followed changes at Constantinople. However, the crude execution of Lombard coins [figure 44], so different from the sophisticated copying of imperial prototypes practised by the Ostrogoths, shows how much more Italy was barbarised by this latest invasion. In the Lombard kingdom proper the tremissis was the typical coin, as elsewhere in the west, but in the duchy of Benevento, the only one of the four Lombard duchies of Italy to which a distinctive coinage can be ascribed, the solidus was the normal piece until as late as the ninth century [figure 45]. The persistence of the larger gold coin there long after gold coinage had stopped altogether in the rest of Europe shows how close and exclusive were the links of southern Italy with the east.

As Byzantine influence faded, three distinct coinages of tremisses were developed in western Europe. That of the Lombards was the least original but, since the seeds of economic revival lay in Italy, the coin types evolved there were to be of some international importance later. The coinage of the Visigoths in Spain was the one which in its own day attained the highest degree of sophistication, but it led nowhere because it came to a sudden end when the kingdom was overrun by the Arabs after 711. The coinage of the Franks was the crudest and most fragmentary of the three; but it was the most important since it was pregnant with the whole of the future monetary system of Europe.

The Visigoth Leovigild was the first western ruler to assume the diadem and the purple, that is, to proclaim himself a sovereign prince. In about the year 575 he abandoned the old style of coinage derived from imperial prototypes and issued gold tremisses in his own name. By the end of his reign the distinctive Visigothic coinage was established in all its essentials as it was to be until the end; that is, exclusively royal and wholly consisting of more or less debased gold tremisses bearing the king's effigy and a mint name. Visigothic coins of this period are rare: the total number extant has been estimated at less than four thousand and about a quarter of those come from a single hoard. Yet of the nineteen kings who reigned between 568 and about

43 Byzantine Empire; gold solidus mancus, Constantine v (740–75), Rome. One of the debased solidi issued in Byzantine Italy to suit the depleted conditions of western trade [enlarged 2:1]

44 Lombard kingdom of Italy; gold tremisses in the name of the emperor Maurice Tiberius (582–602) and King Liutprand (712–44). Coins which show the increasing barbarity and poverty of Italy under Lombard domination [enlarged 2:1]

714, the coins of eighteen are known for certain, as well as those of four pretenders. The coins are distributed between about eighty different mints from Narbonne to Malaga. More of these mints are in Galicia than in any other province, but they account for only a small proportion of the surviving coins. This fragmentation among many small mints was the natural consequence of the difficult communications of that region. The reason why coins were issued at all in those remote valleys was that there was alluvial gold there. The Visigoths, in maintaining these obscure mints, were continuing a practice established by their predecessors in Galicia, the Suevi, whose rare late sixth-century tremisses, some of which bear no name except that of the issuing mint, point to a similar decentralisation. It is dangerous to draw economic conclusions about the Visigothic kingdom from such a small and perhaps unrepresentative sample of the coinage as has survived, but the nature of the coins and their consistency throughout the kingdom presupposes a high degree of royal control and administrative efficiency. The fabric of all Visigothic coins is thin and broad. Their design is curious, derived ultimately from Byzantine types but handled with great originality to produce a sort of abstract portrait [figure 47].

If the regularity of the Visigothic tremisses suggests efficient civil organisation, the dispersion of the Frankish coinage among a multitude of issuing authorities reveals the dissipation of the powers of the Merovingian kings. The solidi of Theodebert I show that the Frankish coinage was royal in its beginnings. There is also quite an extensive series of gold tremisses in the name of Chlothaire II (613–22). However, although a few coins are known in the names of most of Chlothaire's successors until about 711, these are exceptional and a high proportion of them come from the Marseilles area where the idea of royal or imperial coinage persisted, like the solidus, longer than it did elsewhere. For the rest, coinage in seventh-century France seems to have fallen into other hands. The Church was prominent among the new mint authorities. Coins were struck in the names of bishops, perhaps in right of their position as chiefs of their municipalities. Abbeys such as St Martin of Tours and St Martial of Limoges appear even more frequently as issuing authorities. However, as the seventh century proceeded, it became the usual practice for coins to carry no personal name at all except that of the moneyer who had issued them. More than 1,400 moneyers are given for the Merovingian coinage and no less than a thousand mints. The organisation and indeed the purpose of Merovingian coinage is still a matter of controversy, but it seems probable that like Roman gold coinage it was primarily directed to tax payments. The Merovingian moneyers, who were not mere mechanics but men of some standing, were perhaps tax farmers who were empowered to collect the tax in whatever form was convenient, whether bullion or old coin, and then obliged to coin it themselves, and so accept responsibility for its payment in due form. This would

45 Lombard duchy of Benevento; gold solidus, Grimoald III (788–806). Under Byzantine influence the solidus survived in southern Italy longer than elsewhere in western Europe. The suzerainty of Charlemagne is acknowledged in the inscription on the reverse [enlarged 2:1]

explain how mints arose at all points where taxes might be gathered, not only royal fiefs and palaces, but also fortresses, local capitals, maritime and river ports and toll places.

Although the types of Merovingian coinage were various, two main classes may be distinguished and some idea of the contemporary pattern of trade may be drawn from their distribution. The first came from Marseilles and spread up the Rhône and the Saône to Chalon [figure 46] and then into the areas of the Meuse, the Rhine and the Moselle; the other was centred on Paris and Orléans and spread westwards in Neustria along the Seine and the Loire. Marseilles itself declined in importance as the Arab conquest of North Africa and Spain reduced Frankish trade in the Mediterranean early in the eighth century. Primacy in the first group of mints passed to the northern end of the trade route whose focal point was Duurstede, a Frisian community on the banks of the Rhine.

The commerce of Duurstede extended not only along the northern shores of continental Europe but also to England, and this contact was the genesis of the English coinage. Enough Merovingian coins have been found in Kent to suggest that in that area at least the Anglo-Saxons were familiar with coinage in the early part of the seventh century. It is impossible to establish exactly when they began to mint coins of their own. The coins in the Sutton Hoo ship burial (c. 650–60) are all Merovingian tremisses, but East Anglia was a backward area and the absence of Anglo-Saxon coins need not necessarily mean that mints were not operating in Kent at that time. The Crondall hoard, thought to have been deposited in about 670, consists mostly of Anglo-Saxon gold pieces. All of these are thought to have been minted in Kent or in London and they show the native coinage already fairly well developed. In weight and also by their anonymous nature the English coins clearly reveal their Merovingian ancestry. The designs, however, are less derivative. After the long break in coinage tradition it appears that English die-engravers were prepared to go back much further for their models and to draw on such antique specimens as they happened to see [figure 46]. That remained a firm characteristic of English coinage until the Norman conquest.

Anglo-Saxon gold coinage had only a brief existence, for within a few years gold coinage in western Europe came to an end. It is not certain that the severance of contact with Byzantium which followed the Arab incursion into the western Mediterranean hastened the change, since in spite of imperial subsidies, Byzantium was more of a drain than a tap for western gold supplies, as it was to be again when intercourse was renewed later. During the seventh century the persistent accumulation of treasure by the Church was probably the most important single factor in the withdrawal of gold from circulation. But, whatever the cause, the gold stock in the west, if not quite exhausted, was proving inadequate for the growing volume of trade

46 *(opposite)* Merovingian and Anglo-Saxon gold tremisses from the Crondall hoard, deposited *c.* 670. The top four are Merovingian from the following mints (left to right) Rodez (rev.), Chalon sur Saône, Metz and Amiens. The rest are Anglo-Saxon: the coins of Roman style in the middle are obverse and reverse of similar coins and the bottom left pair are obverse and reverse of identical coins from the London mint [actual size]

47 *(overleaf left)* Visigothic kingdom of Spain; gold tremissis, Sisebut (612–21), mint of Ispali (Seville). A typical example of the barbarous but well ordered coinage of the western kingdom [enlarged 5:1]

48 *(overleaf right)* Ostrogothic kingdom of Italy; bronze follis, Theodahad (534–6), Rome. An exceptionally beautiful example of Ostrogothic coinage in Italy [enlarged 3.5:1]

on the North Sea coast. There was consequently a change towards a greater quantity of coin but pieces of lower value in that area. The transformation took the form of a gradual debasement of the gold and the emergence of a silver coinage. The process began in about 680 and was completed by the virtual disappearance of gold from circulation in the early years of the eighth century. The new silver piece was called by an old name, the *denarius*. On both sides of the Channel the new denarii were much more plentiful than the old tremisses had been, for the change was in more than the metallic content of the coinage. What had previously been a moneyers' coinage intended primarily for fiscal purposes was superseded by an anonymous coinage intended for trade.

The new development was not wholly confined to Merovingian France and Anglo-Saxon England. In the last years of the Visigothic kingdom of Spain there was a further deterioration in the alloy of the gold which suggests that there, as in France, a silver coinage might have evolved if time and the Arabs had permitted. In Lombard Italy the reduction in the gold content of the currency was later and less marked, but the coinage of Lucca, which flourished in the latter part of the eighth century, was of very debased gold and its success seemed to point in the same direction. In general however it must be said that it was only after Charlemagne's conquest and the introduction of his monetary reforms that Italy conformed to the new practice, and even then it was only the north which changed.

According to the Salic law the solidus was equivalent to forty denarii. There is some evidence, however, that when the original twenty-four carat solidus all but disappeared in the west, the term was transferred to the tremissis. This in theory would give $13\frac{1}{3}$ denarii to the eight carat solidus/tremissis. But by the seventh century the Franks had abandoned the Mediterranean weight system of the carat for one better suited to their own economy based upon the barley grain. The consequent adjustment in the weight of the solidus/tremissis made this coin equivalent to twelve denarii instead of $13\frac{1}{3}$. Since two hundred and forty denarii were struck to the Roman pound, at some point in the transition of Frankish coinage from gold to silver a new accounting system emerged: one pound (£) = 20 solidi (s) = 240 denarii (d). Changes in the weight of the denarius soon obliterated the relationship of the coin to the pound weight and within a generation the solidus/tremissis had disappeared, but the accounting system stayed. It may seem paradoxical that a monetary arrangement so enduring should have been conceived at such an obscure point in economic history. It may be however that this point was the turning of the tide, that the end of gold coinage in the west and the blocking of the western Mediterranean by the Arabs closed the economic epilogue of the ancient world and that the nascent commerce of the North Sea, in which the new coinage and the £ s d system originated, was the first stage in the development of the modern economy.

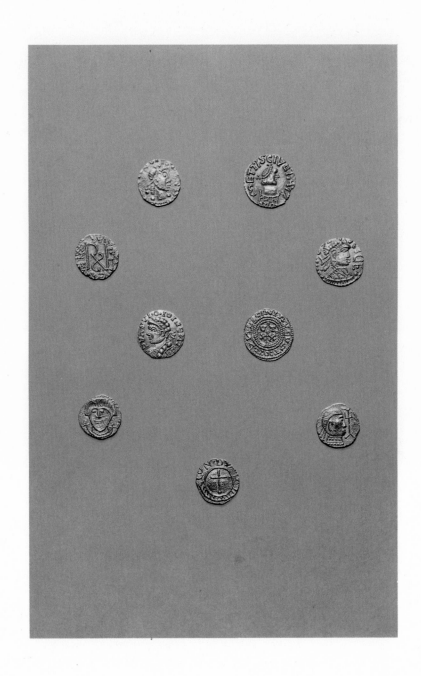

4 The Penny in Carolingian and Feudal Europe

49 *(opposite)* Mercia (incorporating the kingdom of Kent); silver pennies, Offa (757–96) Canterbury (one reverse) and Coenwulf (796–819). London; Kent, silver penny, Cuthred (786–805), Canterbury [enlarged 3.5:1]

In the year 768 a moneyer of Lucca called Grasolfo bought some land for 28 solidi. He paid fifteen in coin and settled the balance by delivering a horse. This is one of the few cases where it is known how a payment was made in the eighth century. Grasolfo, as a moneyer, must have had readier access than most to coined money, yet even he settled nearly half his debt with a horse, and that was at Lucca, then one of the richest cities of Europe. Most of western Christendom was then settling into what is known as a manorial economy, whose typical unit was a small self-contained rural community. The most common obligations were those arising between lord and vassal, which were normally expressed in terms of services and goods, or between lord and villein, which were usually paid if not stipulated in kind. Even in the other processes of economic life, coined money was only one of the means by which payments might be made. Between people of standing, and especially between the monastic institutions which were among the foremost creators of wealth and capital in feudal Europe, the process of gift exchange played an important part. As for that other function of money, the storage of movable wealth, a king's crown jewels and an abbey's church plate were more important items in the treasury than coin, since they were hardly less liquid and produced a better return in terms of prestige if of nothing else.

The main function of coin in the eighth century was to provide a means of exchange for a peasant population which might in some years manage to produce a small surplus, and for trade in towns, which were neither large nor numerous. For those purposes the small silver coin, the new denarius developed by the trading communities of the north, was well suited. It might not however have so quickly become the monetary unit of nearly the whole of western Europe if it had not been for the rise to eminence of the Carolingians. Their hereditary lands and therefore the source of their power lay in Austrasia, where the denarius was most firmly established. The idea of the mint as a function of royalty disappeared in Merovingian France, but not in Visigothic Spain nor in the Lombard kingdom where, in spite of an extensive issue of anonymous coins in the seventh century, the laws of Rothari (636–52) had emphatically restated the principle of royal control. The vigorous new dynasty in France was not disposed to leave unasserted such an important and profitable royal prerogative. In the reign of Pepin the Short (751–68) anonymous coinage was stopped and thenceforward every piece was stamped with the king's name or initial. The weight standard remained the same, but the fabric was a little broader and thinner than before.

The re-establishment of royal control was only the first of the Carolingian reforms. In 793–4 Charlemagne increased the weight of the denier by about a third, probably as part of a general reform of weights and measures. At the same time the practice of putting the name of the mint on the reverse of the coin, which had begun in Pepin's reign and had become more frequent since, was made a rule. An effort was made to reduce the number of mints. In 805 the capitulary of Thionville declared that no mint should operate 'except in our palace' but this could not work in the prevailing conditions of economic fragmentation and the number of mints actually increased during the ninth century. The Carolingian project of a single mint was not achieved in France until 1879.

The importance of Charlemagne's reign for the development of Europe's monetary system lay not so much in his reforms as in the fact that his great conquests, combined with his interest in coinage and his determination that it should be accepted by all his subjects, meant that the Carolingian denier became the uniform currency of a wide area. Within the Frankish empire this was subject to only one limitation: Charlemagne's new German subjects did not take readily to coinage and for most of the Carolingian era there was only one not very prolific mint, usually Regensburg, east of the Rhine. In the south the Lombard duke of Benevento, Grimoald III, who acknowledged Charlemagne's suzerainty for a time and put Charlemagne's name with his own on his gold coinage [figure 45], introduced a silver denaro into the Beneventan monetary system. Charlemagne's domination in the matter of currency can be judged by the reform of 793–4 which was totally effective in mints from Treviso to Duurstede and from Mainz to Toulouse.

The adoption of a monometallic silver currency in the west was helped by the increasing quantities of that metal which appeared during the eighth and ninth centuries. It is not certain where all the new supplies came from. One source may have been Spain, where the Ummayad caliph 'Abd al-Rahman I struck quantities of silver dirhems [figure 33], but no gold. Another was certainly the silver mine at Melle in Poitou, where there was an active mint in Carolingian times. However they would not account for the whole of the increase. A coin of Charlemagne with the legend METALL GERMAN and yet others reading EX METALLO NOVO point to a German source of silver. 'German Melle' has not been identified. The Harz mines were not opened until 968, but it is possible that the product of other German mines came to the Franks, perhaps by way of tribute, as a result of Charlemagne's German conquests.

50 Frankish Empire; silver denier, Charlemagne (768–814), Milan. The typical coin of Charlemagne's reform of 793–4 with the mint name and Karolus monogram on the reverse [actual size]

Charlemagne's earlier coins differ little in type from those of his predecessor Pepin the Short; the king's name is written across the field on one side and the mint name usually appears on the other. There are a number of local varieties. The reform of 793–4 introduced a uniform type for all mints, on the obverse a cross within an inner circle with the royal title around it and on the reverse the Karolus monogram, the same as was used to authenticate documents, with the mint name [figure 50]. This was to be one of the standard types for European coinage and, with its derivatives, it continued in use for centuries. In 805, five years after Charlemagne was crowned emperor at Rome, a new type was introduced with the imperial title and a portrait. The best executed of these coins [figure 51], which have no mint name but carry the legend XPICTIANA RELIGIO on the reverse with a representation of a Roman basilica, are perhaps those issued at the palatine mint in accordance with the capitulary of Thionville. The other imperial coins of Charlemagne must date from the time when the single mint project was abandoned, for they all have local mint names. The die engraving of these is less accomplished than that of the palatine coins, but the various designs on the reverse are interesting: the mining towns Melle and 'German Melle' have coining instruments, the ports of Duurstede and Quentovic a ship and other towns a city gate. The representation of the emperor is entirely Roman, not Byzantine, in spirit, and on the palatine coins at least it seems to be a true portrait, since it is very like the head of the contemporary equestrian statue of Charlemagne, formerly in the Metz cathedral treasury and at present in the Louvre.

England, which had closely followed the continent in changing from gold to silver, was not slow to copy the new coinage policy of the Carolingians. Within twenty-five years of Pepin's first coinage, two minor kings of Kent, Heahbert and Ecgbert, issued pennies like Charlemagne's deniers. Offa, king of Mercia, after he conquered Kent in 783–4, developed a substantial penny coinage. Offa's coins differed from Charlemagne's in that they followed the older fashion of carrying the moneyer's name and not the mint name. This was presumably because at first Canterbury was the only mint issuing pennies in England and responsibility for each coin could thus be brought more nearly home. Offa's coins are far more varied and fanciful than those of Charlemagne; the Anglo-Saxon die engravers seem to have been given greater freedom than their Frankish counterparts. Some pennies from the Canterbury mint are among the prettiest coins ever made in England; imaginatively conceived and exquisitely worked in detail [figure 49]. After Offa's death there was a rapid falling off in design and execution.

While Kent was following the monetary innovations of the Franks and the penny coinage was spreading over southern England, the kingdom of Northumbria, whose days of greatness had been before coinage was introduced into England, still kept to the old-fashioned coins of thick fabric. These are known for a number of Northumbrian kings from the middle of the eighth century but, progressively debased, they were almost pure copper by the early years of the ninth. It was not until the Danish kingdom of York was set up on the ruins of Northumbria late in the ninth century that the new style of penny was introduced and northern England was brought into the mainstream of European monetary development.

In the ninth century, silver monometallism was still not quite complete in the west. Louis the Pious (814–40), possibly in vindication of what he deemed to be his imperial right, struck a regular series of gold solidi [figure 52] which found ready acceptance in Frisia and were much imitated there later. Nevertheless that period was un-

52 Frankish Empire; gold solidus, Louis the Pious (814–40). One of the last gold pieces struck in northern Europe for four centuries [enlarged 2:1]

doubtedly the heyday of the Carolingian denier, which was struck in large numbers, its weight and fineness well maintained. It was then that the types were established which were to last through many evolutions until late in the middle ages. The basilica on Charlemagne's rare portrait coins reappeared on an enormous issue of Louis the Pious which was to be the prototype of much German and French coinage. Another issue of Louis, which reverted to the device of the mint name written across the field, was the pattern for many north Italian and some French issues during the next four hundred years. The Karolus monogram was revived by Charles the Bald in 864 for a new coinage intended to supersede all previous French issues; Dane-geld payments were beginning at that time and many mints were engaged in striking the great quantities of coin which were needed. The Karolus monogram and the simpler monogram of Eudes (888–98), transformed into a variety of unlikely figures, constantly reappeared on French coins throughout the feudal period.

The Carolingian coinage was administered for the king by his counts. Late in the ninth century, as royal authority was relaxed, the counts became more independent. There was still no indication of this in 864 when Charles the Bald's edict of Pitres decreeing his new coinage was obeyed throughout his kingdom, but by the end of the century local variations in the coinage suggest that some counts were issuing coins independently. At the same time the king began to make grants of minting rights to other subjects who were not royal officers, especially to abbeys and bishops. The licence so given was to issue coins at will and to receive the seigneurage, the fee which was charged on bullion brought for coining. It did not give the right to issue coins except in the king's name, nor was that done at first; but just as five hundred years earlier some Ostrogothic kings had put their initials beside the emperor's name, so in the tenth century some feudal lords put their names or initials beside the king's, and if later they sometimes left out the king's name altogether, there was nobody to stop them.

Although neither Offa nor his successors as masters of south-eastern England made any change in the weight of the penny corresponding to Charlemagne's reform of 793–4, it is still fair to say that for most of the ninth century Europe from the Tiber to the Trent formed a single monetary area. Although it was broken up among many mints, as economic conditions required, those mints were mostly subject to central control. During the next century that unity was broken. The fundamental reason for the change was the disintegration of the Carolingian empire, but at the same time economic factors were taking the different parts of Europe along divergent paths. In the north, the Viking raids at first disrupted trade and destroyed both Duurstede and Quentovic; but later, when those enterprising sea-farers had become more settled in the lands around the North Sea, trade sprang up again with renewed vigour. In the south, the Italian

53 Mercia; gold dinar, Offa (757–96). A copy of a dinar (774) of the caliph 'Al Mansur with the name and title of Offa upside down on the reverse. A coin which provides startling evidence for commercial links between Islam and north-western Europe in the eighth century [enlarged 2:1]

cities began to grow prosperous. Coinage in different areas changed to meet local conditions and it became necessary to stipulate pence of Verona or pence of Pavia when the price of a contract was fixed. Of course the whole £ s d system changed with the change in the value of the penny, so that men referred to the pound *(lira)* of Pavia, meaning 240 denari of Pavia, and the shilling *(soldo)* of Verona, meaning twelve denari of Verona, although no such coins as the lira pavese or the soldo veronese actually existed.

The growing prosperity of the Italian cities may be partly ascribed to a monetary cause. The Islamic conquests had temporarily diminished Christian trade in the western Mediterranean, but this trade had been adverse to the Latins. The more permanent effect of the conquests was to release gold to the Mediterranean world through several channels. First the Arabs conquered the tribes of the upper Nile, whose hostility to Byzantium had blocked the flow of Nubian gold to Alexandria. The conquest of Syria and Egypt restored to circulation the contents of many rich church treasuries and perhaps, since the Arabs were notorious tomb-robbers, some pharaonic gold as well. The conquest of Persia released even more. The Sassanians, with no gold currency of their own, had for many years hoarded in their treasury the gold from their trade with Byzantium; all this was now freed by the Arabs. Finally their conquests in Asia gave the Arabs control of the gold from the Urals and the Caucasus, while their African conquests opened a way to the Mediterranean for the gold of the Sudan and the upper Nile. The Arabs, unlike the Byzantines, bought not only slaves from the Latins, but also timber, iron, tin and furs. On the other hand the Latins did not buy direct from the Arabs on a big scale. When trade in the Mediterranean was reopened they went to Byzantium for oriental products and the Byzantines in turn bought them from the Arabs of Syria and Mesopotamia. In this way gold began to circulate from the Arabs to the Latins, from the Latins to the Byzantines and from the Byzantines to the Arabs. The balance of trade was still unfavourable to the Latins and at first not much gold stuck to their fingers. It was enough however to give them a clear impression that a gold coin was essentially an Arab coin. One of the

54 Norman duchy of Apulia; gold tarí, Robert Guiscard (1059–85), Salerno. A coin of Arab inspiration, though the inscription means nothing except for the two Latin initials R(obertus) D(ux) [enlarged 2:1]

three known gold coins of Offa's reign is a copy of a dinar of the Abbasid caliph 'Al Mansur with the words OFFA REX upside down in the middle of the cufic inscription [figure 53]. In 798 a poet writing in Provence about the bribery of judges explains how it is done with Latin silver and Saracen gold coins. In Scandinavia a hoard has been found containing Abbasid dinars, some with runic inscriptions scratched on them, which probably reached the north by the eastern trade route established by the Norsemen along the great rivers of Russia. The remains are scanty, but widespread enough to suggest that, if Byzantium was more immediately enriched by the new pattern of trade, the Latin world was greatly stimulated by it.

Southern Italy, which had never lost touch with Byzantium and was nearest to the Arabs of North Africa and Sicily, was the first part of western Europe to share in the increasing prosperity. Amalfi, whose citizens were to be granted a wharf at Constantinople some fifty years before the Venetians, and Salerno both grew rich in spite of perpetual wars. There the last Lombard dukes and their Norman successors issued quarter-dinars copied from the coins of the Fatimid caliph Al-Mu'izz (953–75) with curiously mixed Latin and Arabic inscriptions. These gold coins, called *tarís* by the Italians, were to be the staple currency of the area until nearly two centuries after the Normans had expelled the Saracens from Sicily [figure 54]. However, the revival of trade was not confined to the south. The north Italian cities also increased in size and wealth in spite of the political disruption of the tenth century. Pavia, Verona and Lucca were the foremost mints, together with Milan which gradually came to replace Pavia as the chief town in northern Italy after the Ottonian conquest of 961. In this area the increase in trade outran the increase in the supply of silver. To maintain trade at the new rate more money had to be struck from the same amount of metal; there was a steady debasement and reduction in the size of the coins of all the north Italian mints in the tenth century which was accelerated in the next two hundred years as new mints were opened and the area became more active economically. Early in the twelfth century the denari of Pavia (known as *brunetti* on account of their high copper content) were still

the main currency of a commercial centre as important as Genoa, whose own mint was not opened until 1139.

In Italy economic considerations overrode political ones in determining the shape of the coinage. In France it was the other way round. There the early evolution of the feudal coinage was shaped by political forces. By the end of the tenth century it was a well established feudal principle that the mint belonged to the count and not to the king. Coinage in the king's name was quite exceptional outside the royal domain. In the days of Hugh Capet (987–96) only two lords, the bishops of Laon and Beauvais, put the king's name on their coins and that seems to have been an expression of their own special status as spiritual peers of France. They held their mints neither by special grant nor by usurpation, as other bishops did, but by right: and of all the French bishops they stood closest to the throne, supporting the king at his coronation. Later, as the Capetians extended their power, a few more feudatories acknowledged them on their coins, but the practice never became common.

As for coinage within the royal domain of France, it was essentially feudal in its type and scope. If the deniers of Robert II (996–1031), for example, gave his title as ROTBERTVS REX, this was because any feudal magnate described himself by his grandest title as a matter of course; their main territorial reference was to the mint of Paris. When Philip I (1060–1108) opened new mints at Château Landon and Orléans, he issued coins of local types at each; and, when he confiscated the county of Dreux, he struck coins there of the same type as the dispossessed count had done.

Politically the royal domain was the most important part of France but economically it was not, and the coins of many of the French king's subjects had a wider circulation than his own. Such for example were the deniers of the counts of Champagne [figure 56], struck at the mints of Troyes and Provins. Fairs had been founded at those two cities and, with the other fairs of Champagne, played an important part in the expansion of European commercial life during the next two hundred years. The fairs took up most of the active part of the year and filled the country with merchants of Italy, Provence and Catalonia, who came to trade with those of Flanders, the Rhineland and England. Consequently the deniers of Troyes and Provins, which were the natural currency for transactions at the fairs, were much in demand and figured largely in the accounts of the money-changers of Bruges and Milan. They were known in Italy as *provisini* and the Roman Senate in the thirteenth century even went so far as to issue a Roman version of them. There were other feudal issues as successful as those of Troyes and Provins. On the same trade route from Flanders to Italy the deniers of the archbishops of Lyons and Vienne enjoyed a high reputation. In the west the counts of Poitou controlled the mine and the mint of Melle; the one kept the other busy. Farther south the coins of the dukes of Aquitaine and the counts of Toulouse circulated

55 *(opposite)* A capital from the Norman Abbey of St Georges de Boscherville (11th century) showing a moneyer at work

56 Champagne; silver deniers, Counts Thibaut II (1125–52), Troyes *(above)*, and Thibaut IV (1201–54), Provins. The trade fairs of Champagne made these among the most widely used of all French feudal coinages [actual size]

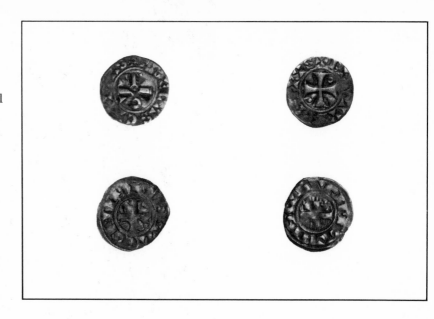

57 Poitou; silver denier, twelfth century, Melle. The name on this coin from the silver mining town in western France is that of the ninth century king Charles the Bald, but it was probably issued by Richard Coeur de Lion [actual size]

over wider and more prosperous areas than the Ile de France.

It was a feature of medieval coinage that types and rulers' names sometimes remained unchanged for long periods. Nowhere was this more marked than in the feudal coinage of France. The counts of Poitou continued with the type and the name of Charles the Bald without changing the name until Richard Coeur de Lion became count in 1169. The name of Louis IV of Outremer (936–54) was perpetuated on the coins of the counts of Angoulême, and in Maine the monogram of Count Herbert I, the Watchdog (1016–36), after remaining unchanged for more than two centuries, was adorned with fleurs de lys and transformed into a crown in honour of Charles of Anjou, who was granted the fief as an appanage in 1246. Such changes as there were took place gradually. The comb (peigne) on the deniers of Provins [figure 56], regarded in its later years as a canting device on the last syllable of Champagne, evolved from a part of the monogram of Eudes; on the deniers of Nevers the word REX written across the field of the coin in the days of Louis of Outremer eventually turned into a sickle and cross. Some feudal mints did however adopt new types during the twelfth century. The patron saint of an abbey or city became a familiar type especially in central France. The bust of St Martial appeared on the coins of his abbey at Limoges, the Virgin on deniers of the bishops of Clermont, and St Maieul [figure 59] on the coins of the Cluniac priory at Souvigny; all three look as if they were taken from reliquaries or statuary in the church treasuries.

The plentiful issues of Souvigny and the comparative rarity of the coins of the mother house of Cluny illustrate an interesting point about the nature of feudal coinage. Success or failure did not much depend upon the political prestige of the issuer. The coins of Cluny had to

58 A contemporary capital in the abbey church showing the monks at their minting activities

59 Souvigny; silver denier of the Cluniac abbey, twelfth century [actual size]

circulate in an area where there was much competition from those of the dukes of Burgundy, the counts of Mâcon and the bishops of Autun. In the Bourbonnais, an isolated area, the priory of Souvigny had a head start over all others and by the time the lords of Bourbon were powerful enough to bring pressure to bear on the priory, the St Maieul deniers were established as the currency of the area. All the secular lords' attempts to promote a rival currency failed and, in the end, the best that the lay power could achieve was to co-operate with the priory and take a share in the profits. The kings of France found themselves in a rather similar position. It was only when Philip Augustus, having confiscated the county of Touraine from John of

60, 61 France; silver denier tournois, Philip II (1180–1223), Tours; and silver denier Parisis, Louis VII (1137–80), Paris. Only when they adopted as their own the well established feudal deniers of the abbey of St Martin of Tours did the Capetians manage to achieve a national as distinct from local coinage. Their first attempt to do this with the denier parisis was only partially successful [actual size]

England in 1203, adopted for his coinage in the west the popular feudal type of the deniers of the abbey of St Martin of Tours [figure 60] that the royal coinage was provided with a broad enough economic base from which to expand its influence. For all their increasing political power, his and his predecessors' attempts to extend the scope of the royal coinage on the base of the denier of Paris [figure 61], which with its legend FRANCO(rum) written boldly across the field seems to have been intended as a national coin, were only partly successful.

Two reasons may be given for the extreme conservatism of the French feudal coinage: first the natural unwillingness on the part of any coin-issuing authority to change something which is successful as it is and secondly the feudal theory that if something is not done according to precedent it may not be legal to do it at all. This did not however prevent debasement; the need for more money in circulation was ever more pressing, though less than in Italy, and the profits to be made from debasement were an obvious and continuing temptation. As early as 1164 we find a creditor trying to protect himself against it by stipulating repayment in money as good as he gave.

Except for the *provisino* mentioned above, French feudal coinage did not have much influence outside France. Although Frankish barons made an important contribution to the Spanish Reconquista, the Visigothic tradition of exclusively royal coinage was not lost south of the Pyrenees, except in Carolingian Catalonia where, after the Frankish manner, there were mints in the hands not only of the counts of Barcelona but of two bishops and two other counts as well. South-western French influence is discernible in the style of some

64

63 Norman duchy of Apulia; silver ducatus 1156–60, King William I of Sicily (1154–66) with his son Roger. A coin of Byzantine inspiration whose name, taken over by the Venetians, was to have a long history [actual size]

64 Norman county of Calabria and Sicily; copper follaro, Roger I (1072–1101), Mileto. An unusual example of the Normans using an original and not a derivative coin type in conquered territory [actual size]

62 Aragon; silver dinhero, Sancho Ramirez I (1063–94). The little kingdoms of northern Spain preserved almost intact the Visigothic tradition of exclusively royal coinage [actual size]

Spanish coins, but the king's head which appears on most is a native type [figure 62]. There was no Moorish influence except on the gold coins, called *marabotins*, which, following the existing practice at some newly captured Moorish mints, the kings of Castile, Leon and Portugal all issued from time to time during the twelfth century.

By the time of the Norman conquest late in the eleventh century the coinage of southern Italy was already too sophisticated economically to absorb much of French influence. It was in any case the Normans' practice to leave coinage as they found it wherever they conquered, from England to Antioch. In Sicily, Apulia and Calabria they issued gold, silver and copper. Saracenic influence was uppermost especially on the gold tarís, but many copper *follari*, coins based originally on the Byzantine monetary system, were inscribed in both Latin and cufic and so showed all three elements of south Italian culture. Other coppers and the silver *ducats*, so called because they were first minted in the duchy *(ducatus)* of Apulia, were of wholly Byzantine inspiration [figure 63]. One especially prolific issue of follari by William II (1166–89) was evidently derived from the ancient Greek. Another exceptional issue of Roger I (1072–1101) showed the count, mounted and armed with longshield, lance and pennon, thus for once giving expression to the chivalric aspirations of the Normans themselves [figure 64].

The Holy Land of the crusaders was the only part of the Mediterranean where the influence of French feudal coinage was strongly felt. The political and economic complexion of the states set up by the Franks after the first crusade is illustrated by their coinage. The

65 Edessa; copper, Count Baldwin I (1097–1100). One of the earliest and rarest coins of the crusaders. This coin is overstruck on or by another which reads, in Greek, 'Lord help Richard'. Richard has been identified with Richard lord of Marash (*c.* 1111) whose fief lay on the borders of Edessa and Antioch [actual size]

66 Principality of Antioch; copper, Tancred, regent for Bohemund I (1104–12). A typical coin of the Normans in Syria, Byzantine in general style and with a Greek inscription which reads 'Lord help thy servant Tancred'. The head is of St Peter, patron saint of Antioch [actual size]

rare issues of the first two counts of Edessa, Byzantine copper over-struck with a representation of the count in armour, reflect the military preoccupations and the instability of the precarious Frankish salient in Mesopotamia [figure 65]. At Antioch, a Norman principality with a predominantly Greek population, Bohemund and Tancred in typically Norman fashion adopted the Byzantine type of copper coinage with which the inhabitants were familiar [figure 66]. Antioch was by far the most prosperous place conquered in the first crusade and the only one where much coinage was issued in the early years of the twelfth century. Later when it came under the regency of Raymond of Poitiers (1136–49) and Norman influence had waned, Greek coinage was replaced by Frankish deniers with Latin inscriptions. In Tripoli, Provençal influence was as strong as Norman was at Antioch and the county remained in the hands of the family of the counts of Toulouse until 1187. The earliest coins of Tripoli, struck by Count Bertrand (1109–12), were deniers. His and his successors' coins are of a style reminiscent of the feudal deniers of Languedoc: Raymond II (1152–87) actually copied the star device introduced a few years before by his cousin Raymond V of Toulouse for the deniers of Provence [figures 67 & 68].

The kings of Jerusalem, although nominally the first of the four great barons of the Holy Land, seem to have come last in the matter of coinage, both in time, since no surviving coins of theirs date much before 1150, and also in point of sovereignty. Within the territories of the other three princes, only they had mints and they managed to retain their sole authority until the end. The kings of Jerusalem exercised a less exclusive right. Even before Saladin's defeat of King Guy of Lusignan at Hattin in 1187, there was one instance of a vassal of the king striking coins in his own name. This was Renald, lord of Sidon, who was despoiled of his fief and captured after the battle. He never recovered his city and the rare deniers with the legend RENALDVS on one side and SYDONIA on the other [figure 69] must therefore have been struck before 1187, maybe within a few years of the beginning of the king's own coinage. After Hattin the king's position was much weakened and in the thirteenth century more vassals ventured to issue their own coins. Foremost among them were the lords of Beirut, of the Ibelin family which played an illustrious part in the later history of the kingdom. There are deniers also of the princes of Tyre, Philip de Montfort (1246–70) and his son John (1270–83). It is not known by what right, if any, these mints were established. French feudal theory was distinct from French practice, and the rules of the model feudal kingdom of Jerusalem, as set out in the Assizes of Jerusalem, did not give minting rights to any vassal. The extreme rarity of the feudal coins and the fact that none were issued when the kingdom was strongly governed point also to their illegality. On the other hand the close personal relationship between the Montforts and the Lusignan king Hugh III argues, in their case at least,

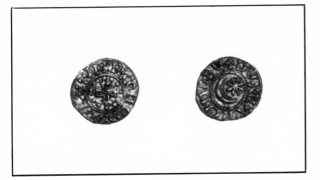

67 Marquisate of Provence; silver denier, Count Raymond VII of Toulouse (1222–49). A common coin of Provence, which since many of the crusaders came from there, had some influence on their coinage in the Holy Land [actual size]

68 (above right) County of Tripoli; silver gros, Bohemund VI of Antioch (1251–75). A coin of tournois weight and standard whose design shows the extent of Provençal influence in this crusading principality [actual size]

69 Sidon; silver denier, Renald (c. 1165–87). A rare example of a coin struck by a vassal of the king of Jerusalem before the kingdom was broken up by Saladin in 1187 [actual size]

against the minting rights having been simply usurped. All the coins of the kingdom of Jerusalem, whether royal or feudal, were debased silver or copper deniers; their designs were often proper to the Holy Land, representing such monuments as the Holy Sepulchre or the Tower of David [figure 70], but their general style was Frankish.

The cities of Outremer naturally attracted a large part of the western trade which had formerly gone to Constantinople and all the currency needs of those rich but precarious settlements could not be met by the scanty copper and debased silver issues of the crusading princes. Among the Franks themselves an important part was played by the Italian, Provençal and French deniers brought out in the scrips of successive waves of pilgrims. The local inhabitants doubtless continued to use the Byzantine copper in circulation, to which the issues of Antioch and Edessa added a proportionately tiny amount. For important mercantile transactions gold dinars and besants (the Frankish name for Byzantine hyperpyri) provided the chief means of exchange. Dinars must have predominated for it was those which the crusaders copied when they themselves struck gold coins. They evidently began to do this quite early, since an Arabic text ascribes imitations to Tyre in 1124. It is believed that this refers to dinars struck by the Venetians at Tyre and it is probable that most of such issues were put out by the Italian mercantile communities. Later they became a cause of scandal. Newcomers thought it improper that crusaders, of all people, should issue coins proclaiming the doctrine of Islam and, at the instance of the papal legate who accompanied the fifth crusade, Innocent IV promulgated a bull excommunicating those men of Acre and Tripoli who persisted in the practice. Thereafter the dinars of the crusaders were distinguished by the sign of the cross and Arabic statements of Christian belief [figure 71]; which may have restricted their circulation farther east, but at least appeased western opinion. The episode illustrates the fanaticism of those who were new to Outremer and their indignation at the orientalised attitude of those who had long been settled there.

Unlike the later Carolingians, the kings of England kept their coinage rights intact. They even managed to extend them. In the

70 Kingdom of Jerusalem; silver denier, Baldwin III (1143–62). A typical coin of the crusading kingdom showing the Tower of David [actual size]

71 Acre; gold dinar, c. 1252. Struck probably by one of the Italian trading communities in Acre, this coin is Arabic only in its general aspect. The reverse legend is a statement of Christian doctrine and the obverse bears a cross [actual size]

ninth century the archbishops of Canterbury and York had issued coins in their own names, but during the tenth it was established that, although ecclesiastical mints might continue, the coinage was the king's, issued in his name and complying with his decree. 'It is our will', the laws of Aethelstan (924–39) stated, 'that there shall be one coinage in the whole kingdom'. This strict royal control was originally a matter of political history. In the critical years 871–939 the kings of England, Alfred, Edward the Elder and Aethelstan were the three most capable men who have ever sat in succession on the English throne. By the time the incompetent Aethelred II succeeded late in the tenth century, the principle of royal coinage and the efficient administrative machinery to uphold it were too well established to be easily upset. This was to have important economic consequences. The king's firm hand kept English coinage on a different path of development from any followed by the less managed currencies of continental Europe. The rigid sense of justice which characterised Anglo-Saxon kingship prevented him from debasing the coinage for reasons of private profit, while England's geographical situation as a rich primary producing country, economically unsophisticated as compared with Italy or Flanders, but with a favourable balance of trade, isolated her to some extent from inflationary pressures elsewhere. Debased foreign coin could be kept out and there was enough silver from the mining areas of Wales, conquered by Aethelstan, to meet the growing needs of the people.

Anglo-Saxon coinage was remarkable in its time for its consistent fineness and its uniformity throughout England. The only rival coinage was issued in some Viking areas in the north which for brief periods in the tenth century were independent of the English kings [figure 72]. The economic fragmentation of the country, common to the whole of medieval Europe, was provided for in England by the great number of mints. Aethelstan laid down that every borough should have one and in the later period, for which mint signatures on the coins themselves provide evidence, it appears that that was, with little exception, the actual state of affairs. Control of the mints was exercised through the die-cutting centre which alone might issue dies to the local moneyers and did so on a regional basis against payment of quite a heavy fee. This fee, which the moneyer in turn recouped from those who brought silver to the mint for coining, provided the king with his coinage revenue. Late in Eadgar's reign, in about 975, a means was found of increasing this revenue without recourse to debasement. All coins in circulation were demonetised and pence of a new type issued in their place. This process, which of course involved a complete change of dies, was found so successful as a means of raising revenue that thereafter it was repeated quite regularly, normally every three years. It accounts for the great variety of coins issued by the later Anglo-Saxon and Norman kings which contrasts so strongly with the long production runs of continental Europe. As

72 Danish kingdom of York; silver penny Anlaf Quaran (c. 930–50), moneyer Aethelferd. An exceptional example of English coinage issued by one other than an English king. The raven on the obverse was the standard of the Danes [actual size]

73 England; silver penny c. 980, Aethelred II, moneyer Aethelric of Bath. A coin typical of those in which Danegeld payments were made to the Viking invaders [actual size]

74 England; silver penny c. 1066, William I, moneyer Colswegen of Hastings. Like the Normans in other parts of Europe, William made no essential change in the coinage of the land he conquered [actual size]

medieval taxes went, it was less burdensome and expensive to collect than most and, if somewhat random in its application, at least it could only fall upon those who had means to pay it. The system, which seems to have borne without strain the additional burden of minting coin for the enormous Danegeld payments of Aethelred II [figure 73] and his successors, testifies to the remarkable efficiency of Anglo-Saxon administration. It incidentally provided a safeguard against debasement since, although demonetisation was probably not wholly effective, the repeated withdrawal of the older pence prevented the currency from getting into the worn and clipped condition which elsewhere was often given as a reason for issuing new coins of lower intrinsic value.

In fact intrinsic value does not appear to have been of so much importance for the internal currency of Anglo-Saxon pence as it was for other medieval coins. There were quite considerable differences in weight between one issue and another and even between coins of the same issue. These were most marked in the reign of Edward the Confessor (1042–66), whose issues varied in average weight between seventeen grains and twenty-seven. These unexplained changes were not progressive, as they would have been if the currency had been subjected to the inflationary pressures which were operating elsewhere. There is no evidence about their effect upon prices, but the fact that they could be carried through without causing serious economic upheaval suggests that in England it was the king's authority as much as intrinsic worth which gave the penny its value.

The variations in the types of English pence after the reign of Eadgar are mostly on the single theme of the king's portrait on the obverse and a cross on the reverse. Roman coins were the prototypes for most of the portraits [figure 73], but in the middle of Edward the Confessor's reign some German influence appeared and the portraiture was touched with more realism. All coins had the king's name on the obverse and the name of the moneyer and his mint on the reverse.

The coinage of Normandy was one of the worst of feudal France and Duke William after his conquest of England in 1066 showed no disposition to substitute that for the profitable and well-ordered English currency. Like Robert Guiscard and Bohemund of Antioch he took over the local coinage without making any essential change [figure 74]. So far as can be judged from the moneyers' names, even the personnel continued in office unmolested; not until the next generation, towards the end of the reign of Henry I (1100–35), did the Norman Richards and Rogers first appear as moneyers among the English Aelfgars and Godrics. One change, however, William did make. With perhaps a greater awareness than his predecessor of the overseas repercussions of the erratic weight changes of the penny, he fixed it at 22½ grains, where it stayed for two centuries. This stabilisation of the penny earned it an even better reputation abroad than it had had before and a new name, sterling, which means in Old English

75 England; silver penny,
Stephen (1135–54) and Matilda.
Remarkable coins were produced
during the wars of Stephen's reign.
This penny, ascribed to York and
the period of Matilda's capture of
Stephen in 1141, has an
interesting parallel in
contemporary German coinage
(see figure 85) [enlarged 5:1]

76 England; silver penny or sterling, 1180–9, Henry II (1154–89), moneyer Reinier of Winchester. The short cross penny in the name of Henry was the only type of coin struck in England for sixty-seven years [actual size]

the fixed or the strong thing, much the same in fact as the word solidus means in Latin. Under that name the English penny was much used and later imitated abroad, and sterling is still the name for English currency in the foreign exchange markets of the world.

The French influence implicit in the Norman conquest only affected English coinage during the reign of Stephen (1135–54) and then not at all for the better. 'Castles sprang up in every country', wrote William of Newburgh, 'and England had as many kings (or rather tyrants) as there were lords of castles: each struck his own money and usurped the royal powers of justice'. No doubt some of the shabby pence which bear Stephen's name were issued by the barons for their own profit, and a few coins survive in the names of the more important barons and of his rivals the Empress Matilda and her son Henry of Anjou. Besides those there are pence for which the name of the issuing authority has been deliberately obscured or defaced. Conditions in fact were far worse than in France, since there at least feudal coins were established currency. Nor probably was it any comfort to contemporary Englishmen to find among the baronial pence some of the most curious and pleasing designs in twelfth-century coinage. Some of these have much in common with German coins of the same period and later [figure 75]. It is tempting to ascribe this to the presence of the Empress Matilda in England, but a common origin in baronial seals is a more likely explanation.

Although the baronial mints were suppressed in the last years of Stephen's reign, the restoration of English currency was left to Stephen's successor, Henry of Anjou. Henry's coinage policy provides good evidence for the contention that the Angevins were more destructive of Anglo-Saxon institutions than the Normans ever were. Henry much reduced the number of mints, thus bringing to an end the old equation between mint and borough. He also abolished the system of periodical type changes. His first penny, introduced in 1158, was continued until 1180. His second, the 'short cross' penny [figure 76], went on, without even any alteration in the king's name during the reigns of Richard I and John, until Henry III introduced the 'long cross' penny in 1247. This reversal of policy aligned English practice with that of western France where Henry II, as count of Anjou, still issued deniers in the name of Fulk, his tenth-century ancestor. Consistency of type added to the consistent fineness of the Anglo-Saxon penny and the consistent weight of the Norman sterling made the English coin the most satisfactory trading currency in northern Europe. This was greatly to help the Angevin policy of reopening English trade in the North Sea, which had dwindled during the previous century.

It was only after the introduction of the 'short cross' penny that continental imitations of English coins were issued on a big scale, but the Anglo-Saxon penny had nevertheless played an important part in the earlier development of coinage in some places. During the tenth century the Vikings took home great quantities of English pennies

77 Bohemia; silver denar, Dukes Boleslas II (967–99) and Jaromir (1002–12). The coin of Boleslas is a copy of an English penny of Aethelred II. The first of Jaromir's coins is of German type but carries the name of King Aethelred on the reverse; the other shows barbarised Byzantine influence. The three illustrate the many strains which contributed to the early coinage of the Czechs [enlarged 2.5:1]

which they had got by piracy, by trade and by way of Danegeld payments, and they copied them both in Scandinavia and in their Irish settlements. The earliest regal coinage of the Northmen was of this type: the only coins of Sweyn Forkbeard of Denmark (985–1014), the chief persecutor of Aethelred II, are closely modelled on those of his victim. The union of the crowns of England and Denmark in 1016 under Sweyn's son, Cnut, naturally strengthened the economic connexion between England and Scandinavia, although it put an end to the plundering of one by the other. However, about ten years after the death of Harthacnut and the re-separation of the kingdoms in 1042, a change in Edward the Confessor's policy reorientated English trade towards Normandy. From that time few English coins were buried in Viking hoards and the Scandinavians looked elsewhere for their prototypes, particularly to Byzantium whose influence came both directly along the trade routes of eastern Europe and indirectly through Germany.

It was no doubt the English pennies carried eastward by the Vikings which inspired the imitations of coins of Aethelred II by such distant rulers as Boleslas Chrobri (992–1025) of Poland and Duke Boleslas II (967–99) and Queen Emma (d. 1006) of Bohemia. No Anglo-Saxon pence have ever been found in Bohemia but coins of Boleslas and Emma dating from about the turn of the century are closely modelled on Aethelred's type of 979 [figures 73 & 77]. A coin of Duke Jaromir (1002–12) combines the type of a south German pfennig with the name of Aethelred [figure 77] and an even more curious piece of the same type actually carries the name of Aelfsige, one of Aethelred's moneyers at Winchester, instead of the name of the Bohemian ruler. Other coins of Jaromir show a strong Byzantine influence [figure 77] and most of the smaller pence which were issued after Bretislas I debased the Bohemian coinage in about 1050 are purely local in type. As might be expected, however, the most persistent foreign influence in medieval Bohemian coinage from its start in the reign of Boleslas I (936–67), the murderer of St Wenceslas, was that of Germany.

The beginnings of German coinage are to be found in the Carolingian mints of the Rhineland. It was no part of Carolingian policy that these should be the only mints in Germany. As early as 833 Louis the Pious granted minting rights to the abbey of Corvey on the Weser because of the shortage of currency in that area; but the people of Corvey evidently did not mind the shortage, since no mint actually came into operation there until the eleventh century. There was nearly always one outlying mint in the south, usually Regensburg or Augsburg, and that was to be important as a base from which coinage spread in and around Bavaria as the province grew in wealth and political importance during the tenth century: it was the early Regensburg pfennig of Charlemagne's basilica type which Jaromir of Bohemia copied for his Aethelred coin. For northern Germany,

78 Cologne; silver pfennig, Archbishop
Pilgrim (1021–36) in the name of the
Emperor Conrad II (1027–39). The coinage
of Cologne was always one of the most
important in Germany and was the original
type of several coinages in other parts of the
country [enlarged 4:1]

79 Holy Roman Empire; silver pfennig,
Conrad II (1027–39) with his son the future
emperor Henry III, imperial mint of Speyer.
Showing the Byzantine influence that
sometimes made itself felt in the imperial
coinage of Germany [enlarged 4:1]

80 Holy Roman Empire; silver pfennig,
Henry II (1002–24), imperial mint of
Regensburg, moneyer Anno. Augsburg;
silver pfennig, Bishop Bruno (1006–29).
Contemporary coins whose similarity
illustrates the close relationship sometimes
existing between imperial and episcopal
mints [enlarged 4:1]

however, the Rhenish mints, particularly Cologne [figure 78], provided the starting point of a gradual eastward push of German coinage. It was at Cologne that the stylised basilica of the Carolingian denier was first transformed into a no less stylised 'holzkirche' (wooden church) thus taking on the familiar helmet outline of so much German medieval architecture. The type was adopted by the towns of the middle Rhine and Main and spread thence to Saxony where, serving for the prolific issues which followed the discovery of the Harz silver mines near Goslar in 968, it took a new lease of life. Another Cologne type, originally Carolingian, with the mint name written across the field, spread into Westphalia and was later crossed with Anglo-Saxon strains as the inland cities there grew rich by supplying the Viking traders along the North Sea coast.

There was a remarkable unity about the coinage of Germany in its earliest stage, the consequence of its single origin in Carolingian coinage and the political control exercised by the Saxon line of Holy Roman Emperors. However, the central political control was soon lost and Germany's geographical position exposed the country to influence from all directions. Throughout the second half of the tenth century the emperors Otto II and Otto III were making grants of minting rights to great feudatories both clerical and lay. In the next century, under the Salian emperors, the practice grew more common [figure 82] and, during the investiture dispute with the papacy, many who had not already been granted minting rights usurped them. The position was the reverse of what happened in France. There the king persistently tried to assert the paramountcy of his coinage but issued it only in his own demesne. In Germany the emperor's right to issue coins was nowhere disputed, but he continually granted the right to others. In some places an imperial mint subsisted beside the feudal mint and the two issued coins of very similar pattern [figure 80].

By the twelfth century the administration of German coinage was almost completely dispersed and the different parts of the empire had adopted quite distinct coinages. One such area was the Low Countries whose growing industrial importance called for a big increase in the money supply. As in northern Italy this was met by a rapid diminution in the intrinsic value of the denier. There was less debasement than in Italy, but by the end of the century the deniers of such rulers as the counts of Flanders, Namur and Holland, the bishops of Liège and Utrecht were much reduced in size [figure 81]. In the Low Countries as elsewhere, some imperial mints continued to operate but they were not commercially significant. In Germany proper, the most important issue was still that of Cologne. There was an imperial mint in the city, but that was now completely overshadowed by the archbishop's establishment across the river in the suburb of Deutz. The archbishop's pfennigs had on the obverse a representation of the prelate enthroned as it was customary for spiritual lords to appear on seals. For the reverse, late in the eleventh century the Carolingian

81 Holland; silver penning, Floris v (1256–96), Dordrecht, typical of the small deniers which were the normal currency of the Netherlands in the twelfth and thirteenth centuries [actual size]

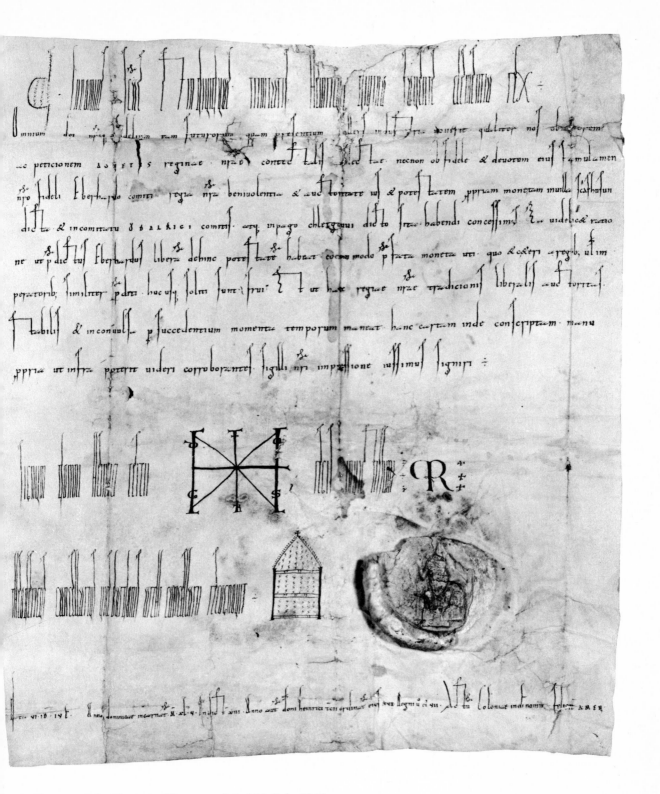

82 Charter of the Emperor Henry III dated 10 July 1045
granting minting rights at Schaffhausen to Count Eberhard
in reward for his faithful and devoted service

83 Cologne; silver pfennig, Archbishop Philip von Heinsberg (1167–91). The standard coin of the Rhineland in the twelfth and thirteenth centuries [actual size]

basilica type was again reinterpreted to give a detailed picture of a romanesque church [figure 83]. Variously adapted this realistic architectural motive was to be very influential all over Germany and, even before the eleventh century was out, it was copied by the Normans in southern Italy, so far and so fast was Rhenish commercial influence carried.

The most important division in German coinage was that which grew up between east and west during the twelfth century. In the west the fabric of the pfennig was the same essentially as that of the Carolingian denier. East of the Elbe and in Swabia, in those areas in fact where there had been no Carolingian mints nor any extension of coinage in the immediate post-Carolingian period, a new fabric was adopted, much broader but thinner, so thin that the coin could take only one impression and the design appeared in intaglio on the reverse. The chief characteristic of *bracteates*, as these coins are now called, was their fragility, and consequent unfitness for circulation. Probably they were not much used for that purpose but, like Merovingian coins, were issued in connexion with tax payments; like Anglo-Saxon coins also, they were a means of taxation in themselves, since they were frequently demonetised and reissued. There is some evidence that mint charges were higher in the bracteate area than elsewhere. Viewed in this light bracteates were less impractical than they looked; their fragility might even provide an excuse for frequent recoinage. From a non-monetary point of view they had one great advantage. Their broad fabric gave scope for imaginative design and careful workmanship by the die-engraver. Some are among the most beautiful of all medieval coins and they are the only class of pieces which are a worthy expression of romanesque art [figures 85, 86 & 88]. The ecclesiastical ones have much in common with German romanesque bas reliefs, an effect which is often heightened by the architectural framework of the design, though this feature may well be derived from the humbler but more useful pfennig of Cologne. The secular pieces commonly show a heraldic device or a representation of the issuer. Contemporary seals were no doubt the prototypes for many of them. Bracteates were issued not only by feudal authorities but also by the emperor himself. Outside Germany they were only struck in the countries on the eastern march, namely Poland, Bohemia and Hungary, where they are associated with a period of strong German influence: for example the reign of the later Přemyslids in Bohemia.

The bracteate area formed a belt across Germany running northeast from Swabia and Augsburg through Franconia and Thuringia to the mark of Brandenburg. In Swabia the bracteates were smaller than in the north, less spectacular but also less fragile and far more suitable for trading purposes, as befitted the currency of the area lying between Italy and the Rhineland. Their influence was felt south-east of the bracteate line, further into Bavaria, in Austria and in the lands of the archbishops of Salzburg. There the coins were a

84 Brunswick; silver pfennig, Duke Henry the Lion (1139–95) [enlarged 2:1]

85 Brandenburg; silver pfennig, Margrave Albert the Bear (1142–70). A bracteate which shows the margrave and his wife Sophia in a pose similar to that adopted by King Stephen and the Empress Matilda on an English penny [enlarged 2.5:1]

86 Thuringia; silver pfennig, Landgrave Ludwig II (1140–72), Eisenach. A coin type which illustrates the harsh way of life in the east German frontier provinces [enlarged 2.5:1]

87 Hungary; silver denar *(below)* and copper, Bela III (1173–96). A strong Islamic and Byzantine influence may be seen in the coinage of twelfth-century Hungary [actual size]

hideous compromise, nearly as thin as Swabian bracteates but weakly struck with obverse and reverse dies so that some of each impression shows through on the opposite side. In some areas the coins were struck on square or polygonal flans, which made their appearance even worse, as the corners were often uneven and the dies badly centred. However, they made up in economic importance what they lacked in aesthetic appeal. The opening in the twelfth century of silver mines at Friesach in the eastern Alps led to a very prolific issue of pfennigs from that mint in the years 1200–30 by Archbishop Eberhard II of Salzburg and to an associated issue at the neighbouring mint of St Veit by the dukes of Carinthia. Apart from silver mining, there was little economic activity in the immediate area of those mints, but the Friesach coins, because of their number and high silver content, soon became a staple currency of south-eastern Europe, most of them finding their way eastwards towards lower Austria and Hungary.

The coinage of Hungary itself was originally oriented towards Byzantium and Islam. It was part of the achievement of St Stephen in making a western kingdom of the country early in the eleventh century to institute coinage along Carolingian lines, but in the twelfth century some remarkably oriental coins were still issued, Islamic type gold and Byzantine type copper [figure 87]. Even the silver took on an Arabic appearance from time to time. However Hungary had this much in common with the west, that by the thirteenth century the silver coinage was much debased and in need of reform. In the more sophisticated economic era which was just about to begin, Hungarian currency was to play a more important part.

88 *(opposite)* Halberstadt; silver pfennig, Bishop Ulrich I, (1149–60 & 1177–80). One of the finest of east German bracteates of the twelfth century showing the stoning of St Stephen [enlarged 4.5:1]

5 The Commercial Revolution: Groats and Florins

90 Aquileia; silver denaro, Patriarch Gregory of Montelongo (1251–69). The patriarchs of Aquileia were exceptional among the prelates of Italy in keeping their minting rights in and after the thirteenth century [actual size]

89 *(opposite top to bottom)* Brindisi; augustale *c.* 1231, Emperor Frederick II, Barletta; augustale *c.* 1266, Charles I of Anjou; Venice, ducat Doge Giovanni Dandolo (1280–9); Florence, florin *c.* 1252, obv. and rev. Some of the earliest gold coins of medieval Italy, including the first ducat and the first florin [actual size]

In Italy as in Germany the minting rights of the emperor passed out of his hands during the twelfth century. Usually they were transferred to the bishops, who in some places, notably those nearest to Germany, such as Trent and Aquileia [figure 90], succeeded in holding on to them. Most mints, however, soon fell into the hands of the communes, which were already the main economic force in northern Italy, and after the treaty of Constance were emerging as the foremost political force as well. The lay nobility had mostly taken to the cities by the end of the twelfth century and so did not enter the competition as it did in Germany. At the beginning of the twelfth century there were eight mints in northern Italy; by the end of it the number had nearly trebled. Some cities, especially those which favoured the Ghibelline cause, acknowledged the emperor on their coins, not in most cases the reigning one, but the original grantor of the minting right: thus thirteenth-century Pisa commemorated Frederick Barbarossa and Bologna Henry VI. Later this practice fell into disuse, but Genoa still honoured Conrad III (1138–52) in this way until the seventeenth century.

The rapidly increasing wealth and economic sophistication of twelfth-century Italy was not reflected in the currency. The single unit of coinage introduced by Charlemagne had been reduced to an absurdly low value by repeated debasement and was proving inadequate for the needs of the money economy which had developed in the cities. The position was made worse by the gradual impoverishment of the Byzantine empire and consequent weakening of the coinage which had formerly played such an important part in the transactions of Italian merchants.

The first move towards a solution of the problem was made during Frederick Barbarossa's contest with the Lombard communes. Sometime between 1155 and 1161 Frederick closed the mint of Milan and at his own mint at Noceto issued *denari imperiali* at double the weight of the current coin. He thus effectively revalued the denaro by one hundred per cent. Since of course only half as many of the new coins were required to make payments, they were well received by the mercantile community. By 1175 at the latest, the reopened mint of Milan found it convenient to issue similar coins and other Lombard mints,

91 Venice; silver grosso or ducato, Doge Enrico Dandolo (1192–1205). Issued in 1202, this was the first important coin of multiple value struck to meet the growing demands of trade in western Europe [actual size]

including Pavia, followed suit. Politically Frederick's experiment failed, since Guelf and Ghibelline mints alike thrived on the issue of imperiali. Economically it was a qualified success; by the twelfth century debasement of the denaro had gone so far that a revaluation of one hundred per cent provided only partial relief.

It was left to the Venetians to institute in 1202 the currency reform which was really needed. The timing was decided by the fitting out of the fourth crusade and the physical problem of meeting the heavy expenses involved by enormous payments of denari. Significantly it was this crusade which decisively broke the economic primacy of the Byzantine empire in the eastern Mediterranean and so left the Venetians more than ever in need of a satisfactory coinage of their own. The Venetian solution of the problem was an entirely new coin of good silver [figure 91]. In its earliest days it was called the ducat, which suggest that it was inspired by that other Adriatic coin, the ducat of Apulia. The similarity of the design of the coin supports the theory, but the identity of name may have been no more than a coincidence, since constitutionally Venice, like Apulia, was a duchy or *ducatus:* as for the design, though both ducats were ultimately Byzantine in inspiration, the immediate prototype of the Venetian one was not a coin at all but the doge's seal. Later this coin came to be known as the *grosso* or the big coin, though it was big only by comparison with the denaro since it weighed only 2.2 grams.

The Venetian grosso was the first large multiple coin to be issued as part of the Carolingian system of £ s d. Its primary advantage was that it reduced the number of coins required for each transaction without involving revaluation of the existing currency. But it went further than that. It put into the hands of the authorities a new financial weapon, the full scope of which even the Maggior Consiglio at Venice did not fully appreciate at first. Although it was originally current for 24d. or two soldi, the grosso bore no mark of value, nor did its name relate it to the £ s d scale. It was open to the government further to debase the currency while leaving the grosso physically unaltered, simply by writing up the value of the larger coin in proportion to the debasement of the denaro. Thus the whole monetary system of the ancien régime, whereby accounts were kept and prices expressed in £ s d while the coins in circulation, except the lowest in value, were allowed to rise or fall against it, as foreign currencies still fluctuate against one another today, all this was inherent in the first issue of the grosso at Venice.

The Venetian experiment was an immediate success. Early in the thirteenth century the chronicler Martino da Canale wrote of the silver ducat 'qui cort parmi le monde por sa bonte'[1]. It was not long before the initiative was followed elsewhere in Italy: within a few years Genoa, Bologna and Verona all issued grossi of similar weight to the

[1] Which is current throughout the world on account of its good quality

92 Genoa; gold genovino, 1252 or later; one of the first gold coins of the modern era [actual size]

Venetian, but variously valued in terms of local currency. The cities of Tuscany were slower off the mark, since they were experimenting with the Lombard device of a revalued denaro, but Siena issued grossi by 1220 and Pisa and Florence a little later. The Florentine coin was originally current for one soldo, but it was not known by that name; it was called *fiorino*, which, like the device of the lily *(fiore)* which it bore, was a play on the name of the city. Finally even the Lombard cities of Pavia and Milan, proclaimed as republics after the death of Frederick II, conformed to the new pattern of Italian coinage.

In 1231 Frederick II, who had inherited the kingdom of Naples and Sicily through his mother Constance, issued a new gold coin at his mints of Brindisi and Messina. Known as the *augustale*, it is chiefly remarkable for its design, with the profile bust of the emperor in high relief, a careful reinterpretation of antique models which, while not quite achieving realism, still foreshadows the portraiture of Renaissance coinage [figure 89]. It is tempting to look upon the augustale as the forerunner of the gold coinage of modern Europe, but except that it was copied later at the same mints by Frederick's eventual successor, Charles of Anjou, it found no imitators. It is probably more correct to see the augustale as the last of the sporadic early medieval issues of gold in those areas which were subject to Islamic influence and to class it, in spite of its appearance, with the marabotins of Spain and the tarís of Sicily.

The first of the north Italian cities to introduce gold coinage was Florence in 1252, followed very closely by Genoa. The Florentine gold piece, like the other coins of the city, bore the lily on one side and St John the Baptist on the other, 'la lega sigillata del Batista' as it was described by Dante. It was current originally for one lira, but it was called the *fiorino d'oro*, later to become simply *fiorino* or florin [figure 89]. The Genoese coin, which bore the city's traditional gateway *(Janua)* device and of course the titles of Conrad, was called the *genovino* [figure 92]. The importance of these two was that they were the first gold coins to be issued as part of the regular currency of that part of Europe which counted in £ s d. In immediate practical effect they were even more beneficial to the mercantile community than the grosso had been fifty years earlier, since the scale of business already required a coin of substantial value. However, the new coins introduced for the first time the complications of bimetallism. Both the grosso and the florin were useful instruments of currency manipulation, but whereas changes in the current value of the grosso took place only as and when the government willed, in the florin's case changes in the relative market prices of gold and silver would sometimes take the matter out of the government's hands. Thus the florin and the genovino brought a new element of instability to the monetary system.

The reappearance of gold coinage in Europe in the thirteenth century coincided with, and was a direct consequence of, a change in the balance of trade between east and west. The reason why Florence and Genoa were the first Italian cities to strike gold coins was that they, as the chief exporters of European products, were the first to accumulate large reserves of gold. These reserves were the basis not only of the coinage of the two cities but also of their lead in the development of banking. The position of Venice was different; her prosperity was founded on the import of oriental goods which were then sold at a big profit north of the Alps. Most of her payments were made in the Levant, where Byzantine gold, as long as it remained of tolerable fineness, was the required currency. Only when the Byzantine hyperpyron collapsed [see page 37] did Venice find it necessary to strike her own gold coinage. For this, the discovery of gold in Hungary late in the thirteenth century proved timely. In Hungary the Venetians were exporters and creditors and they received a large part of the output of the Hungarian mines by way of payment; the word Hungarian became synonymous with bullion merchant in the Venetian dialect. The decision to issue gold coinage was taken by the Venetian Maggior Consiglio in 1284 [figure 93]. This was late indeed, for by then even France and England had experimented, though unsuccessfully, with gold coinage, and before the end of the century the Papal camera was demanding payment of dues in gold. The new Venetian coin, of pure gold like the florin, but weighing just a little more at 3.56 grams, was called the *ducato d'oro*, but like the florin it soon commanded such a position in the market that the adjectival *d'oro* was dropped and the name ducat ceased to be applied to any but a gold coin. Its design was to remain essentially unchanged until the end of the republic: on the obverse it showed the doge kneeling before St Mark [figure 89] and on the reverse Jesus Christ surrounded by stars in a mandorla. The reverse legend SIT T'XPE DAT' Q'TV REGIS ISTE DVCAT (May this duchy which thou rulest be given to thee O Christ) was later thought to be the origin of the name ducat, but the pedigree of the word, going back to the coin's silver predecessor which had no such legend, shows that this was not so.

Until the end of the fifteenth century the florin and the ducat were the most important coins in European trade, playing much the same part as reserve currencies do today in international transactions. They owed this position to their reputation for purity, to their convenient size and value, and above all to the great economic strength of Florence and Venice. Their purity and weight were maintained throughout a period of inflation and debasement of the *moneta piccola*, as the small silver coinage based on the denaro was called; their value in monetary terms simply rose, the florin for example which had been current for one lira (i.e. 20 soldi) in 1252 rising to 29 soldi during the first century of its existence. In due course merchants grew wise to the inflation and, for contracts in which they wished to escape its effects, adopted a new system of accountancy based not on the *moneta piccola* but on the gold coin. Florentines, for example, accounted *a fiorino* on the basis of a florin whose value was theoretically

93 Minute of the Maggior Consiglio of Venice recording the decision to mint the first gold ducat, dated 31 October 1284

94 Milan; silver grossi, Henry VII, king of the Romans and emperor (1311–13). Two of the last imperial coins struck in Italy. Both show St Ambrose on the reverse. The larger, tariffed at two soldi, shows saints Gervasius and Protasius side by side in the Venetian manner. The imperial title is used only on this later coin, whose gothic appearance illustrates the influence of Henry of Luxemburg in bringing the foreign style to northern Italy as the Angevins brought it to Naples. Naples; gold saluto, Charles I of Anjou (1266–85) [enlarged 2:1]

fixed at 29s.; the figure was arrived at during a period of economic stagnation after the Black Death when the florin did actually hold steady at that rate in terms of *moneta piccola* for a number of years. Thereafter a debt of say £29 *a fiorino* was settled by payment of twenty florins, however the florin was valued. Systems differed elsewhere, but all adopted the same principle of what we now call the gold clause to provide a refuge from the uncertainty of medieval money. It was a great advantage to the capitalist to be able to pay his wages in the depreciating *moneta piccola* and to have his trade debtors owe him the hard currency of gold florins.

In the years 1274–93 the trade of Genoa, stimulated by the introduction of gold coinage, is estimated to have increased fourfold to a figure that was no less than ten times the value which the trade of the leading Hanseatic city of Lübeck attained in its mid-fourteenth century heyday. This comparison goes some way to explain the dominant influence of Italy in the monetary developments which took place elsewhere in Europe in the hundred years after 1252.

The first development was the striking of larger coins after the example of the grosso. One of the earliest of these was minted in 1258 at Merano, on the very borders of Italy, by the counts of Tirol. Silver had been minted in the Tirol since about 1170 and a new coin was found to be a useful means of putting it on the market. There were two distinct varieties of this, both of the same weight and fineness as the *grosso veronese*. The first, known as the *tirolino*, or, in German, *kreuzer*, had a spread eagle on one side and a double cross on the other [figure 95]; on the second coin, called the *grosso aquilino*, the eagle was more naturalistic and the cross was single. The fortunes of the two were quite dissimilar.

The kreuzer enjoyed its greatest vogue in the reign of Meinhard II (1271–95), a period when silver was in short supply elsewhere, to judge from the statutes prohibiting its export then in force at several German cities including Vienna, Augsburg and Cologne. Such was the success of the coin in southern Germany that its type was immobilised, even to the name of Meinhard, for more than a century; the kreuzer became an important small change denomination in the Austrian coinage and survived as such until well into the nineteenth century.

The briefer career of the grosso aquilino lay in Italy. In 1319 its issue was taken up at Treviso by Meinhard's nephew, Henry II, count of Gorizia, who was appointed imperial vicar of the city. This was a natural extension of its range, but a year or two later, as a matter of simple imitation, the same type was adopted at Padua when that also was won by the imperial or Ghibelline party. At this point the eagle seems to have become identified as a Ghibelline type, for the successive reappearance of the aquilino at other cities provides a commentary on the party's progress in northern Italy. It was adopted by Vicenza when that city was under the control of Cangrande della Scala, lord of Verona. Verona itself abandoned its traditional grosso

95 Cortemiglia (Piedmont); silver tirolino or kreuzer, Manfred, marquis of Carretto (c. 1270). An early example of a grosso copied in another Alpine principality from the kreuzer of Tirol [actual size]

96 Mantua; silver grosso aquilino, c. 1328, of the type which became the mark of the Ghibelline cities of northern Italy. The little shield of arms in the obverse legend could belong to either of the families which disputed the lordship of the city, the Bonacolsi or the Gonzaga. The name commemorated is Virgil's [actual size]

for the aquilino under Cangrande's joint successors, Alberto and Mastino; Mantua adopted it some time before 1328 under the rule of the Bonacolsi [figure 96] and finally Parma likewise, during a short period of Scaliger rule there in 1341–4. However, the identity of the aquilino with the Ghibellines set a limit to its period of influence, for it did not survive the downfall of the Scaligers who had inspired the party's revival in the fourteenth century.

In France both large silver and gold coins were introduced by Louis IX towards the end of his reign. In 1266 he instituted a general monetary reform, intending to complete the Capetian policy of establishing the royal coinage at the expense of the feudal. It will be recalled that that policy, which had been begun with the introduction of the denier parisis by Louis VII, had achieved its first real success when Philip Augustus adopted as royal coinage the already well-established denier tournois of the abbey of St Martin of Tours. The special position of the denier tournois was strengthened during the next two reigns and Louis IX was at pains to protect the distinctive châtel type from imitation by feudal mints. His brother Alphonse, who as count of Poitou and Toulouse was responsible for the prolific coinages of those provinces, was the chief offender in this respect, but Louis obliged him to change his coinage in 1262. Nevertheless the king was still flouted by his brothers. Both Alphonse and Charles of Anjou had conquests outside the kingdom, in the Venaissin and Provence, and the most that Louis could do about their imitations of the tournois type in those territories was to forbid their import into France. Within the kingdom itself, however, the supremacy of the royal coinage was vindicated and Louis was even able to declare in 1262 that while his own coinage was current throughout the realm, feudal deniers might be tendered only in the domain where they were issued. The final step was to issue a new coin, the gros tournois, to be current for twelve deniers or one sou tournois [figure 100]. The right to issue this was to be exclusively royal. Italian precedent showed that there was a good demand for such a coin. For the king it had the special merit of reducing the denier, and so the whole of feudal coinage, to the level of small change.

97 A thirteenth-century window
in Le Mans cathedral showing
money changers

98 (opposite) County of Tripoli; silver gros,
Bohemund VII of Antioch (1275–87). Coins
of the same specification as the gros tournois
were struck in this crusading state in the last
years before the Franks were driven out
[enlarged 4:1]

100 France; silver gros tournois 1266–70, Louis XI. Hainault; silver gros, Count John II of Avesnes (1280–1304). Holland; silver gros, Count John II of Avesnes (1299–1304), Dordrecht. The French version of the grosso, which finally established the ascendancy of royal coinage in France and signalled the commercial revolution in northern Europe, with two early imitations from the Low Countries [actual size]

99 (opposite) England; gold penny c. 1257, Henry III, moneyer William of London. England's first but unsuccessful experiment with gold coinage [enlarged 4.5:1]

The *gros tournois*, the biggest silver coin in Europe when it was first issued, was an immediate success not only in France but internationally. In the north Floris V, count of Holland (1256–96) and John II, duke of Brabant (1294–1312), each produced identical coins thus foreshadowing a whole host of imitations, some of them exact, others with a local device substituted for the distinctive châtel tournois [figure 100], which appeared in the Low Countries and the lands of the Rhine and Moselle during the early years of the following century. In the south, Charles of Anjou in Provence capped his version of the denier tournois with a copy of his brother's gros. This likewise was the forerunner of a series of gros tournois imitations issued by the principalities along the Rhône valley. Before the end of the century the influence of the gros tournois spread even to the far end of the Mediterranean: in the expiring county of Tripoli the last two counts, Bohemund VI (1251–75) and Bohemund VII (1275–87) issued coins of the same standard and weight as the gros tournois and evidently based upon it, though of different designs [figures 68 & 98]. This oriental connexion is doubly interesting since it has been suggested that the concentric design of St Louis's gros tournois may have been inspired by the Ayyubid coins which the French king and his court must have seen during the disastrous crusade of 1249 [figure 34].

The success of the gros tournois finally established the livre tournois as the normal accounting medium of France, particularly for international transactions. The livre parisis, four of which were worth the same as five livres tournois, was still favoured in northern France and the dual system persisted actively for another century, perhaps causing as much confusion to contemporaries as it still does to economic historians. By the fifteenth century however the livre parisis seems to have become restricted to such special purposes as keeping the accounts of the royal almonry. No parisis coins were struck after 1593 but the system was not formally abolished until 1667.

A little after the gros tournois was first issued, Louis IX reinstituted gold coinage in France. His gold coin, the *écu d'or*, was of the same weight as the gros and was to be current at 10 sous tournois; which put the value of gold at ten times that of silver. Gold was plentiful in the second half of the thirteenth century but, even so, a ratio of ten to one almost certainly undervalued it. That probably explains why the écu never seems to have got into general circulation. Very few specimens have survived and references to it in contemporary texts are rare. When Philip III succeeded Louis in 1270 he did not proceed with it.

The episode of the écu illustrates the difficulty which the northern kingdoms experienced in establishing gold coinage. It repeated almost exactly the pattern of events in England where in 1257 Henry III introduced a gold penny [figure 99] weighing twice as much as the silver penny and tariffed on the same 10:1 ratio at 1s. 8d. Nearly all of them were melted down at once and all the English merchants who held gold bullion considered the experiment to be a fraud. The truth was that the kings of England and France, unlike the commercially experienced governments of the Italian cities, were not prepared to allow free play to the forces of the market. They were accustomed to fix the value of their own coins and to regulate the trade of their own kingdoms. It was usually a temptation to them to overvalue silver, since they had supplies of that from their own mines and made most of their own payments in it, whereas they had to buy gold from the merchants who imported it. They did not at first realise, as they came to later, that bimetallism brought a new element into their coinage policy which they could not themselves regulate without a system of exchange control. Even when they came to institute such a system, and the exchange control regulations of the fourteenth and fifteenth centuries were the most rigorous that ever existed until the present century, the kings were not able to enforce it. Whenever, by accident or design, they fixed an artificial ratio between gold and silver they always ran into the same trouble at the mint, namely too much of one metal or none of the other.

The successful establishment of gold coinage in France was the work of Philip IV (1285–1314). The variety of his issues, their different weights and standards of fineness, is some evidence of the difficulty which was found in fixing the right rate for gold in France. It is remarkable however that although each new coin had a different name, usually referring to the type, in practice they were all known as florins, a name which was by then applied indiscriminately to gold coins in western Europe. They were handsome pieces [figure 101], mostly of the same generic type as contemporary seals, which was a new development in France. Philip however is not remembered in French monetary history for his beautiful gold but for his bad silver. He was the first king to depart from 'la bonne monnaye du tems sainct Loys', a concept which played the same part in the economic mythology of the late middle ages as the franc of Germinal in nine-teenth-century France. He replaced the denier by the *double*, a coin of slightly greater intrinsic value but current for two deniers, and then increased the tariff of the higher value coins accordingly. In 1303, in the aftermath of the French defeat by the Flemings at Courtrai, the gros tournois rose to as much as $26^1/_4$ deniers tournois, but before the end of the reign the position was partially restored and the gros brought back to 15 d. t. as compared with the 12 d. t. of 1266. Philip, who never actually tampered with the fineness of the gros tournois, followed a more restrained monetary policy than many of his Valois successors and it is arguable that the deflation at the end of the reign caused more hardship than the inflation during the Flemish wars. However, as the first king to manipulate the currency by exploiting the new and more complex system of coinage, Philip IV incurred most of the odium of the policy and his nickname of 'le roi faux monnayeur' is still remembered against him.

101 France; petit royal assis
c. 1290, Philip IV. French gold
coinage was first successfully
established with this coin of the
same weight as the florin of
Florence [enlarged 2:1]

When the gros tournois was introduced into the Low Countries in the closing years of the thirteenth century it had to be fitted in to a system which already comprised one large silver coin, namely the sterling. To such an extent had the English penny maintained its value while the equivalent coins on the continent had declined, that early in the thirteenth century it was not only circulating but being copied in northern Europe, playing something of the same rôle there as the grosso in Italy. It has already been noted how its international reputation was enhanced by the long continuation of the short cross type introduced by Henry II. When King John lost his lands in Normandy and Anjou, English commercial and foreign policy turned towards the Empire. Sterlings of the short cross type are found in Rhenish hoards after 1207, possibly connected with John's subsidy to Otto IV in that year. Later, between about 1228 and 1245, when Henry III was in close diplomatic relations with the Emperor Frederick II and was granting generous trading privileges to German merchants in England, quantities of sterlings circulated in Westphalia in common with local imitations struck by, among others, the bishops of Osnabrück and Münster, the abbots of Corvey and the lords of Lippe. Some of these, notably the Münster coins [figure 102], combined the seated bishop obverse type from Cologne with the short cross reverse of the sterling, thus neatly illustrating the interaction of Rhenish and English influence in that region where the sterling and the pfennig of Cologne were taken at par.

It was in the Low Countries that the influence of the sterling was in the end most pervading. John I, duke of Brabant (1268–94), and Gui de Dampierre as count of Namur (1263–97) were the first in that region to issue coins of the same weight as the sterling. These, which were first struck in about 1270, had the distinctive obverse type of a shield displaying a lion rampant, but their reverses were based upon the long cross type of Henry III [figure 103] first issued in 1247. Within a few years the development was taken a stage further by the countess of Hainault, Margaret of Constantinople (1244–80), who struck a double sterling at her mint at Valenciennes. This was not an imitation in the strict sense of the word since there was then no such coin in England.

102 Münster; silver pfennig, Bishop Ludolf von Holte (1227–48). Some coins of Westphalia combined features of the English sterling and the pfennig of Cologne [enlarged 2:1]

103 England; silver penny or sterling, *c.* 1248, Henry III, moneyer William of Northampton. The long cross penny of 1248–79 was much copied by mints in the Low Countries and northern Germany [enlarged 2:1]

Rather it was a hybrid, inspired by the gros tournois and with an obverse design rather similar to that of the French coin, but conforming to an English weight standard. Two of its several names confirm this: on the one hand the petit gros, on the other the double sterling. Its commonest name, however, was *cavalier* or in Dutch, *ridder*. This referred to its reverse design of a mounted knight in armour [figure 104], a representation which to the modern eye seems singularly inappropriate for a woman but which was traditional on the seals of the nobility. The cavalier was a popular coin and, as modified slightly in design by Margaret's successor John II of Avesnes, was copied, not only in the neighbouring principalities, but also in Lorraine and the Rhône valley during the early years of the next century. As countess of Flanders, Margaret also struck a double sterling of different design at her mint of Alost and John I of Brabant likewise struck one at Brussels, the latter an exceptionally pretty coin with a representation of St Michael on it [figure 104]. Neither of these, however, had the same wide success as the cavalier, perhaps because the initial issues were not quite as big, and in the next century both mints turned to the cavalier type.

104 Hainault; silver cavalier, Countess Margaret of Constantinople (1244–80), Valenciennes. Brabant; silver petit gros, Duke John I (1268–94), Brussels. Two examples of the double sterling struck in the Netherlands. The cavalier was the first coin of this value and was much copied by other Dutch princes. England; silver penny or sterling 1280–1, Edward I, Lincoln. Guelders; silver sterling, Count Reinald I (1271–1326), Arnhem. The English sterling of the period when, as the strongest currency in northern Europe, it was most copied on the continent and an imitation made by a Dutch prince in about 1310 [enlarged 2:1]

105 England; silver groat, 1279, Edward I, London. England's first, and unsuccessful, experiment with a silver coin bigger than the sterling [enlarged 4:1]

106 Flanders; silver sterling, Count Gui de Dampierre (1280–1305). One of the near imitations of the English sterling of the 1280s, known in England as pollards or crockards [enlarged 2:1]

In 1279 there was a great recoinage in England. Edward I called in all the long cross pennies of Henry III and issued coins of a new design [figure 104] with a beardless crowned representation of the king full face on the obverse and a plain cross with pellets in the angles on the reverse. This was to be the pattern for English silver coins until 1500. The head was a purely symbolic portrait, since Edward had a beard, and so did many of his successors. This coinage, for the first time in England, included farthings as well as pence and halfpence, and to keep up with French fashion, also a groat of fourpence [figure 105]. This was an exceptionally large and beautiful coin but it was not a success and was withdrawn. The reason for this appears to have been that the original specification for the groat allowed the moneyers no profit on it. Moreover England, though rich, was still backward economically and the penny still met the requirements of a conservative public. More than 107,000 lbs of silver were minted at the Tower in 1279, a great quantity by contemporary standards. This was a time of prosperity for the English wool trade, whose exports to the Low Countries formed the basis of Anglo-Flemish monetary interchange.

The relationship between the currencies of the two regions reached its greatest intensity during the next fifty years. Soon after 1280, Gui de Dampierre, who was by then count of Flanders as well as Namur, and John I of Brabant both issued sterlings [figure 106] differing from the new English ones only in that the facing head on the obverse was not crowned. These circulated locally with the sterlings of the shield type and they were also much used for making wool payments to England, where they were known indiscriminately as *crockards* or *pollards*. Both these words take their origin from the uncrowned head which was their distinguishing feature. 'Pollard' was derived from 'poll' meaning head and 'crockard' from 'crocket' meaning curl, a word which survives as an architectural term but has lost its hair-dressing connotation.

Several neighbouring princes followed this new lead, among others the counts of Hainault and Luxemburg and the bishops of Liège and

Cambrai as well as lesser lords. This situation was tolerated in England until 1300, but by then the pollards and crockards were suspected of debasement. The king of England reverted to the traditional policy of a strict embargo on imports of foreign coin and there was a renewed period of activity at the English mints which had been relatively quiet for nearly twenty years. The Flemings were quick to produce counter-measures. Led by the new count of Flanders, Robert de Béthune (1305–22), they issued a new type of sterling which copied the English type exactly, even to the crowned head [figure 104]. Only the legends on these coins excused them from the charge of forgery, and at a time when most people were illiterate that excuse was flimsy. Later even the legends were manipulated. The worst offender in this respect was John the Blind, king of Bohemia who, as count of Luxemburg 1309–46), adopted the curious spelling EIWANES for his own name on some of his later and more debased sterlings, which was evidently intended to be mistaken for the English king's EDWARDVS. These coins were called 'lushbournes' in England, a corruption of their place of origin, but the count of Luxemburg was not their only perpetrator. There were several others including Robert de Béthune, William I of Namur (1337–91) and the bishops of Toul as well as some who cannot be identified; the count of Ligny even went to the elaboration of copying the distinctive Irish type of sterling with the king's head set in an inverted triangular frame. To their credit it may be said that the dukes of Brabant and the counts of Hainault did not join in the last and most deceptive phase of sterling imitation, but reverted to issuing sterlings of local types.

The sterling area of the thirteenth and fourteenth centuries was not confined to England, the Low Countries and Westphalia. The special sterlings struck in Ireland have already been briefly mentioned. Edward I struck sterlings for his other overseas territory of Aquitaine, where they were mingled with his deniers of the traditional feudal variety. In Scotland pennies were first issued after the English

107 Scotland; silver sterling, King Alexander III (1249–86). The Scottish version of the English penny, struck in large quantities in the 1280s when wool exports were thriving [enlarged 2.5:1]

108 Barcelona; silver croat, 1336–45. King Peter IV of Aragon. The first of the large silver coins of Spain, its reverse design shows traces of the influence of the English sterling [enlarged 2.5:1]

manner by David I (1124–53). For the next hundred years the sparse Scottish coinage closely followed the English, copying all the main reforms but distinguished by the constant use of a profile portrait of the king instead of a full face one. A period of prosperity based on the wool exports of Galloway and the borders is reflected in the relative plenty of the sterlings of Alexander III (1249–86). These coins [figure 107], closely related to those of Edward I in England, were even considered to be worth copying by some of the princes in the Low Countries.

Some of the coins of the Scandinavian kings at this period were closely related to the English sterling in type. Even Philip IV of France, in whose kingdom the sterling was worth one third of a gros tournois, found it worthwhile on two occasions to strike a fractional gros, the *maille tierce*, of the same weight; it is the only silver coin which he has never been accused of debasing. The most remote of the coinages related to the sterling was that of Barcelona. There the weight standards were different, but the type, particularly of the reverse, was evidently copied from the English coin. It is tempting to relate this similarity to the fact that Catalonia was second only to England in the volume of its exports of wool to Flanders. The sterling type, transferred to the *croat* of Barcelona in the reign of Peter III of Aragon (1276–85) thus played a part in the vigorous trade of the western Mediterranean [figure 108].

6 Expedients in Adversity

109 Vlassky Dvůr, the Italian court, a view of the fourteenth-century mint building at Kuttenberg (Kutná Hora), Bohemia, before its twentieth-century restoration

110 (opposite) A banker in his counting house. A miniature of the school of Jean Fouquet from the 'Livre intitulé de richesse', French, c. 1475

Unlike the thirteenth century, the fourteenth was not a time of economic invention and advance, but a stern and practical age in which the monetary ideas of the previous century were put to the test of hard usage in many parts of Europe and were exposed to the harsh economic conditions of the Hundred Years War and the Black Death.

One of the few positive achievements of the century was the extension of the economic frontiers of Europe in the east. For the first time Bohemia and Hungary emerged as forces to be reckoned with. In the monetary field their impact was especially strong, since both were mining areas. Hungarian gold has already been mentioned in connexion with the Venetian ducat. Bohemian silver mines had been a source of raw material for European coinage for many years. In the fourteenth century it was the native coinage of these areas which came into prominence.

The starting point of the new development was the discovery, during the second half of the thirteenth century, of silver at Kuttenberg (Kutná Hora), some fifty miles east of Prague. This was a richer mine than any which had yet been found in Europe and, to exploit it to the full, Wenceslas II opened a mint there in 1298. The building still stands [figure 109] though it has been much restored. It is known as Vlassky Dvůr, or the Italian court, for in its early days it was manned largely by Italians, a feature for which there were parallels elsewhere at that time, notably in England where Edward III appointed Italians to supervise his first issue of gold in 1344. It was perhaps on Italian advice and certainly following Italian precedent that, for his coinage at the new mint, Wenceslas abandoned the traditional Bohemian bracteate for a grosso or groschen. The *Prager groschen*, as it was called (the legend reads GROSSI PRAGENSES although the mint was at Kuttenberg), was a handsome coin [figure 111] in its early years, with the lion rampant of Bohemia on one side and a crown in two circles of inscription on the other. It was struck in great quantities by Wenceslas and his successors of the house of Luxemburg and may be said to have financed the extraordinary flowering of Czech culture in the late gothic period, the great building projects of Charles IV and, less fortunately, the extravagant knight errantry of John the Blind, which ended on the field of Crécy. It circulated widely in Europe and was

Cy commence le liure Intitule de dune acquise que vng riche nentir
Richesse. Et premierement come oit ou Royaume du ciel. Translace
Richesse en riche souuent le sau

Ces deux auctoritez icy ont bien
mestier de exposicion pource que
quant a la premiere il est bien a
noter que mon sauueur ne dist
mie que ce soit impossible dung
riche homme estre sauluez mais dist
que cest difficile. Car cest bien diffi
cile de posseder richesses et de trop es
en lamour dicelles occupez et detenuz
et non estre en lamour dicelles deceu
et pource dist saint augustin en le
pistre quil escripst ad paulini. Les
choses terriennes sont plus aimees

OStre sauueur ihu
crist en son euuan
gile ou viie chapitre
de saint mathieu
Je vous dy veablemt
que vng riche homme difficilement
ou a peines entrera ou Royaume
des cieulx. Et en cest mesmes cha
pitre dit il consequemment que
vng chamoie entreroit plus legie
rement ou passeroit par le trou

111 Bohemia; silver Prager groschen, Wenceslas II (1278–1305). The first of the larger silver coins to be made in central Europe, this was issued to exploit the new silver discovery at Kuttenberg. The coins were minted at Kuttenberg, though they were known as Prager groschen [actual size]

much imitated, particularly in the Saxon margravate of Meissen [figure 112] on the German side of Erzgebirge, where there were rich silver mines, and in Hesse. Its influence also spread beyond the Carpathians, where Casimir the Great (1333–70) reformed the Polish coinage on similar lines and issued a groschen of Cracow differing only from that of Prague in the substitution of the spread eagle of Poland for the Bohemian lion [figure 113]. It appears however that Poland, with its backward economy and no native source of silver, could not really support a coinage of groschen and in practice the currency consisted of halves and quarters.

The personnel of Vlassky Dvůr and the Tower mint at London represent only one aspect of Italian dominance in fourteenth-century monetary affairs. It runs through the whole development of European coinage, especially in gold. This was the great period of imitation. Something of that has already been seen in the history of the sterling in Flanders, but the most copied coin of all was the florin. The earliest example was the *petit royal assis*, the first gold coin of Philip IV of France issued in 1290 [figure 101]; all Philip's gold coins were loosely called florins, but this one really deserved the name as it was of the correct weight and had the same intrinsic value as the Florentine piece. Later there appeared a whole series of transalpine gold coins which copied not only the weight but the type of the florin. The coins of this class are not easy to arrange chronologically, but the first appears to have been issued by Pope John XXII (1316–34) at Avignon. The transfer of the Papacy to Avignon made that city a natural focus of Italian influence and it was well able to exploit its new wealth, for its position on the Rhône was a point of transhipment on the main trade route between Italy and northern and central France. From there, the practice of striking imitations of the florin quickly spread along the Rhône and Saône to be taken up by the archbishops of Arles, the princes of Orange, the dauphins of Vienne, the counts of Savoy and Valence and the dukes of Burgundy as well as the lords of Montélimar and the bishops of Saint Paul Trois Châteaux.

112 Meissen; silver groschen, Frederick II, margrave of Meissen and landgrave of Thuringia (1323–49). The earliest of the German versions of the Prager groschen struck in the mining district of Saxony [actual size]

113 Poland; silver grosz, Casimir the Great (1333–70). A rare variant of the Prager groschen with the Polish eagle substituted for the Czech lion [actual size]

The Rhône valley group was the most concentrated and the coins from it were most like the Florentine originals in workmanship. However, many florins were issued elsewhere and their distribution reveals the whole pattern of Florentine trade north of the Alps. There was a sprinkling of them in Languedoc reaching round to Béarn and Navarre and to the Atlantic coast, where they were struck by Edward III as duke of Aquitaine; across the Pyrenees they were issued in great numbers by the kings of Aragon. In the north they followed the extension of the Rhône-Saône trade route into Flanders: they were struck by dukes of Bar and Lorraine and in the Low Countries by the duke of Brabant, the counts of Flanders and Hainault and the bishops of Liège and Cambrai, to name only the leading princes.

In Germany the issue of florins began rather late, but by 1340 the coin was familiar enough to the merchants of the Hanseatic League for Lübeck to choose it for its currency when the city was granted the right to mint gold [figure 114]. In the Rhineland the issue of florins did not begin until the second half of the century when the Hundred Years War drove the Florentines to take a more easterly route for their trade with Flanders. Then within a few years the count palatine, the count of Nassau and the three archbishops of Mainz, Trier and Cologne all began to strike florins and the practice was taken up down the river by the dukes of Jülich and Guelders and the count of Cleves. This became one of the areas in which the florin rooted itself most deeply. The cities and principalities of southern Germany only began to issue the coin in the last quarter of the century when it had become, as it were, naturalised in Germany and local variants were common.

In the mining areas to the east the florin sprang to prominence quite early. Charles Robert of Hungary struck the first gold coins of central Europe, coins of exactly the Florentine type [figure 126], in 1324–5 at his newly opened mint in the mining town of Kremnitz. Within a year or two John the Blind, afraid of losing the predominance in the metals market which his kingdom had enjoyed for twenty-five years since the introduction of the Prager groschen, issued a similar coin for Bohemia. There followed a brief period in which Hungary and Bohemia competed in each other's markets, but in 1327 they reached a *modus vivendi*. Hungary produced about ten times as much gold as Bohemia and Bohemia about twice as much silver as Hungary; in co-operation they could and did control the central European bullion market and cut out the duke of Austria who had taken a share of both metals as they passed through his lands on the way to Italy. After 1338 however, when Hungary abrogated the agreement with Bohemia, enough gold seems to have stuck to the fingers of Albert II of Austria (1330–58) to enable him also to issue florins. The mint for these was probably Judenburg, a Styrian town lying half way on the direct route from Kremnitz to Venice.

The furthest extent of Florentine influence in the mining areas of eastern Europe was Silesia. The first Silesian princes to strike florins were Boleslas II, duke of Schweidnitz (1326–68) and Wenceslas I, duke of Liegnitz-Brieg (1348–64). The immediate protoype for these was probably the Hungarian rather than the Florentine florin, though Wenceslas is known to have employed an Italian at his mint at Niklas-dorf. The issues of both dukes were quite heavy, for Silesia produced at least as much gold as Bohemia.

In Italy itself there were no copies of the florin except in Savoy and along the Ligurian coast in areas which economically formed part of the Rhône valley trade route. Nearer home Florence was in a position effectively to discourage imitations. In Rome, for example, she was able to put pressure on those of her own citizens who controlled the senate's finances to ensure that it was the Venetian ducat which was copied, not the florin. For, as the English had found with the sterling, imitation, though flattering evidence of a currency's international standing, was ultimately damaging, because the imitators did not have the same inhibitions about debasement. In the case of the florin, the kings of Aragon were notorious for their debased copies and in the fifteenth century numerous German issuers were to bring the florin into disrepute. Thus Venice was lucky in that, apart from the Roman copy, the ducat escaped imitation in the west. It seems surprising at first that it did so, for Venetian merchants were better known even than the Florentines in southern Germany; after 1319 their galleys sailed in annual convoy to Bruges and they traded regularly with the English and the Hanseatic cities. In all this commerce, however, Venice was on balance a seller. It was Florence, the industrial and banking city, which paid out coin. It was the rôle of Venice to receive it, as she received the gold bullion of Hungary, in return for the goods which she brought from the Levant. The converse of this was that in the Levant Florence received payment for her industrial products whereas Venice was paying out in specie for western imports of oriental goods. The coinage of the area reflects this position. By the 1320s even the Byzantines were tariffing their own coinage in terms

114 Lübeck; gold florin, mid-fourteenth century. The florin of Florence was the type adopted by the great Hanseatic city when granted the right to strike gold by the Emperor Louis IV in 1340 [enlarged 3.5:1]

115 Bohemia; gold florin, the Emperor Charles IV (1346–78). The florins issued in Bohemia, as befitted coins struck in the name of an emperor, were of wholly independent type [enlarged 3.5:1]

116 Serbia; silver grosso, King Stephen IV Milutin (1275–1321). A special office was set up in Venice to deal with these imitations, which only the legends distinguished from grossi of Venice (see figure 91) [actual size]

116 Serbia; silver grosso, King Stephen IV Milutin (1275–1321). A special office was set up in Venice to deal with these imitations, which only the legends distinguished from grossi of Venice (see figure 91) [actual size]

of the ducat and later in the century it was the ducat that came to be imitated in the east; scarcely ever the florin.

The earliest imitations of Venetian coinage were made in Serbia where Stephen Urosch (1242–72) and Stephen Milutin (1275–1321) marketed the prolific output of their silver mines in the guise of Venetian grossi [figure 116]. Like some Flemish sterlings these differed from their prototype only in their legends: though the name of St Stephen replaced that of St Mark, the Serbian engravers felt in no way bound by the rules of iconography to substitute the martyr's palm for the evangelist's gospel. In Venice the coins were thought to be a great nuisance and a special office was set up to deal with them as they were brought to the city; its officials doubtless deplored as Dante did 'quel di Rascia che mal ha visto il conio di Vinegia' (Paradiso XIX. 140–1.)[1]

The Serbian kings, whose realm was one of the strongest in Europe in the early years of the fourteenth century, could perhaps afford to brook the displeasure with which the Venetians regarded those who counterfeited the coinage of the republic; but not all of those who ventured to strike gold ducats in the years which followed felt equally self-confident. Consequently many of these imitations were anonymous and some, including the commonest which is a Greek imitation of the ducat of Andrea Dandolo (1343–54), have never been satisfactorily attributed. The grand master of the knights of St John of the Hospital at Rhodes was one authority, however, who struck ducats of the Venetian type and openly acknowledged them. The first of these, a distinctive variant of the Venetian coin [figure 117], was issued during the grand mastership of Dieudonné de Gozon (1346–53). The series continued intermittently until the island was lost in 1522. In the fifteenth century the Hospitallers found that a closer approximation to the Venetian type made the coins more acceptable and on their later ducats the grand master appeared dressed

[1] The Serbian, who in an ill hour saw the coin dies of Venice

117 Rhodes; gold ducat, Dieudonné de Gozon, Grand Master of the Knights of the Hospital of St John (1346–53). Phocaea (Asia Minor); gold ducat, Dorino Gattilusio, lord of Mytilene and Phocaea (1400–49). Two Levantine copies of the Venetian ducat, the earlier an original variant, the latter a more slavish copy made by the Genoese [actual size]

118 Venice; billon tornesello, Doge Andrea Contarini (1368–82). The successor of the Frankish denier tournois in Greece and the Levant, this was made in Venice for export to Venetian colonies. An early example of a coin minted for export to colonies [actual size]

in the robes of a Venetian doge. The knights continued to strike similar ducats after they transferred their headquarters to Malta in 1530 and only stopped in the eighteenth century.

Another fraternity which copied the Venetian ducat was the Mahona, the Genoese trading company at Chios. The Genoese were not at first as bold as the Hospitallers about putting their name to these coins and the earliest attributed to them are arrant forgeries of Venetian coins, distinguishable from the originals only by their workmanship and debased metal. Issues after about 1420 were more frankly acknowledged. Related Genoese issues of ducats were made by the Gattilusi at Mytilene and Phocaea [figure 117] and by the trading community at Pera. All are rarer than might be expected; the Genoese outposts were prosperous emporia or production centres for the medieval chemical industry, but the debasement of the surviving coins suggests that the Venetians, anxious to preserve the ducat's reputation, would have melted down as many as they could find.

While the gold coinage of the Levant was determined by economic circumstances and the prestige of the ducat, the silver coinage was more local in character and political considerations played a more important part in its development. In Greece for example, the coinage of the Frankish baronies which were set up after the conquest of Constantinople in 1204 consisted of deniers tournois of precisely the type which the feudal mints were forbidden by the king to strike in France. Two mints were especially active, that of the dukes of Athens at Thebes and that of the princes of Achaea at Chiarenza on the western coast. Their output of debased deniers was enormous. After the collapse of these principalities in the middle of the fourteenth century, the Venetians moved in to meet the demand among the local population for a continuation of the coinage. Replacing the châtel tournois by the lion of St Mark, they minted *torneselli* [figure 118], as they called them, at Venice and shipped them to Greece and the islands. This is the earliest instance of a mint striking a special coinage for overseas use, a practice which was to become common two centuries later in the period of European colonial expansion, and which continues to this day. It is interesting that, where silver coinage was concerned, Venice, so far from imposing her own currency, found it convenient to adopt one which, by mere political accident, was basically French.

Another silver coin which played an important part in Levantine trade was the *carlino* or *gigliato*. This was originally an Italian grosso issued at Naples in 1303 by Charles II of Anjou to replace the lighter *saluto* which had been introduced by his father. It was bigger than the grossi of northern Italy and it was of a design [figure 119] hitherto more favoured for gold than silver and more French than Italian, as was appropriate to the Angevin dynasty; the name gigliato was derived from the profusion of fleurs de lys on the reverse. Charles's son Robert (1309–43) struck the coin in enormous quantities to finance his political adventures in Italy. He introduced a version of it in his county of Provence, where it was promptly copied by the Pope at Avignon and by some of the princes of the Rhône valley.

The subsequent history of the gigliato is diverse and curious. From Avignon it was introduced to Rome by Urban V (1362–70) where, shorn of its lilies and, known by its original name of *carlino*, it became the standard papal silver coin in the years after the ending of the Great Schism. For purely dynastic reasons it was transplanted from Naples to Hungary by Charles Robert of Anjou when he established Kremnitz as a rival to Kuttenberg in 1324–5 and began to strike large silver coins there [figure 119]. A coin derived from the Hungarian version was even struck on the shores of the Baltic by Winrich von Kniprode, grand master of the Teutonic Order (1351–82). But the most important area of the gigliato's circulation, apart from Naples and Provence, was the Levant. Hoards of Neapolitan gigliati have been unearthed there and imitations were minted by the Turcoman emirs of the Ionian coast and by the Mahona at Chios; the latter transformed the seated figure on the obverse into the semblance of a Genoese doge and, like true Genoese, commemorated Conrad king of the Romans in the inscription. The weight standard and reverse design of the gigliato were also adopted at Rhodes [figure 119] when the grand master of the Hospitallers, Hélion de Villeneuve (1319–46), reformed the essentially Greek coinage of the island to meet the requirements of Latin trade. He was a Provençal and it has been noticed that he copied the Provençal variety, although Neapolitan gigliati undoubtedly circulated in greater quantities in the eastern Mediterranean. The obverse design of the gigliato of Rhodes was peculiar to the Hospitallers and was derived from the seal of the order. Finally the influence of the gigliato can be seen in the coinage of the Lusignan kings of Cyprus. The Lusignans had struck deniers of Frankish type ever since they gained possession of the island in 1192, but their large silver coins and indeed their whole monetary system were basically Byzantine. During the long and interrupted reign of Henry II (1285–1324) this coinage was gradually Latinised in appearance if not

110

119 Naples; silver gigliato 1303–9, Charles II of Anjou. Rhodes; silver gigliato, Hélion de Villeneuve, Grand Master of the Knights of the Hospital of St John (1319–46). Hungary; silver groschen, Charles Robert (1308–42), Kremnitz. Naples and Sicily; silver gigliato, Alfonso V of Aragon (1435–58). Versions of the Neapolitan gigliato, showing some of the variations which arose when the coin was imitated by trading partners or cadet branches of the Angevin dynasty [actual size]

121 Sicily; silver pierreale, Peter of Aragon and Constance (1282–5). A heraldic challenge by the house of Aragon united with Hohenstaufen, the pierreale was a specifically anti-Angevin coin. It was first issued after the Sicilian Vespers and the expulsion of Charles of Anjou [actual size]

120 Cyprus; silver gros, Henry II (1310–24). An example of the influence of the Neapolitan gigliato upon a coinage of Byzantine origins [enlarged 2:1]

in content and the traditional silver besant was replaced by a silver gros whose obverse design was a crude but vigorous imitation of the gigliato [figure 120].

One area where the gigliato might have been expected to flourish, but where it was not much favoured at first, was Sicily. The reason for this was probably political. The detachment of Sicily from Angevin Naples after the Sicilian Vespers in 1282 was so complete as to include such incidental matters as coinage. Peter of Aragon (1282–5) seems even to have used the Sicilian coinage for his own propaganda, since the foremost feature in the design of the new gold and silver was the Hohenstaufen eagle which he displayed in right of his wife Constance, through whom he claimed the island. His coins were thus a sort of heraldic challenge to the Angevin usurpation [figure 121]. Later, when the gigliato appeared in Naples, Frederick of Aragon made no equivalent change in the Sicilian coins and the silver grossi with the eagle on one side and the arms of Aragon on the other continued in the names of his descendants until well into the fifteenth century. Only when Alfonso V of Aragon reunited the kingdom of the two Sicilies in 1435 could an Aragonese prince afford to be magnanimous and, by adopting the gigliato for Sicily, admit that in respect of currency at least, the house of Anjou had had the better of the contest. This coin of Alfonso was the last gigliato; but the lilies were gone from the reverse and the heraldry which replaced them showed clearly enough which side had won in the end [figure 119].

Although much of the western Mediterranean coast was subject to kings of the house of Aragon during the fourteenth and fifteenth centuries, no one currency predominated in the area as the gold ducat and silver gigliato did in the east. The florins of Aragon and the sterling-like croats of Barcelona have already been mentioned as well as the coinage of independent Sicily. Majorca and Sardinia were both Aragonese possessions. Each had a separate coinage. That of Majorca included gold, for the island was an important entrepôt in the seaborne trade between Spain, Provence and Genoa. Sardinia's importance lay in its silver mines and its coinage was only of that metal. The diverse history and economic function of the two islands made

122 Valencia; silver real, Martin (1395–1410). A distinctive coinage was issued for each of the separate kingdoms ruled by the kings of Aragon [actual size]

it only natural that their coinages should be quite distinct. However, even on the Spanish mainland there was no homogeneity. Nor did the kings of Aragon make any attempt to unify the coinage of the different parts of their realm, for when in the reign of Martin (1395–1410) a new *real* or gros was required for Valencia, the area of most rapid economic growth, the coin provided bore no relationship whatever to the coinages of Barcelona [figure 108] or Aragon. The type of the new piece was highly distinctive [figure 122], showing the king full face wearing a curious high pointed crown and on the reverse the same crown surmounting the arms of Aragon on a lozenge. The abundance and variety of these coinages are eloquent testimony both to the wealth which was the strength of the Aragonese kings and to the provincial separatism which was their undoing.

The coinage of Castile was the very antithesis of that of Aragon. Castile was poor but united, its coinage therefore was sparse and often of indifferent quality, but it was uniform. The conquest of Andalusia was the making of the economic as of the political greatness of Castile, and the mint of Seville, which Ferdinand III took over when he conquered the city in 1248, almost at once supplanted Toledo as the most prolific in the kingdom. Gold coinage, reintroduced in the reign of Alfonso XI (1312–50), seems to have presented fewer problems than in most European countries, perhaps because it was already a Moorish tradition. It appears to have been at first a virtual monopoly of the Seville mint, which suggests that the metal was coming from African sources. Alfonso XI also struck the first large silver coins, but the pattern for late medieval Spanish coinage was set in the reign of his successor, Pedro the Cruel, who issued the gold *dobla* with its handsome profile portrait [figure 123] and the silver real whose non-figurative calligraphic obverse design, like that of the gros tournois, evidently owed much to Arabic inspiration [figure 123]. Pedro's coinage, of consistent quality, serviceable, reasonably plentiful and, in silver at least, well distributed throughout the kingdom, reveals something which his personal vices have tended to obscure; that for Castile his reign was a period of unwonted economic prosperity. But it was no more than an interlude. His successors of the house of Trastamare,

123 Castile and Leon; gold dobla and silver real, Pedro the Cruel (1350–69), Seville. Pedro's reformed coinage, plentiful in gold and silver of good quality, suggests that his reign was a period of unwonted prosperity for the kingdom [enlarged 2:1]

124 Portugal; silver grave, Ferdinand I (1367–83). A rather debased silver coin worth three dinheiros, this was typical of the poor coinage of Portugal in the fourteenth century [enlarged 2:1]

obliged to buy their support from a rapacious aristocracy, resorted to a serious debasement of the coinage. For the next century Castilian coinage was characterised by the wretched quality of the everyday currency, thrown into relief by the occasional issue of enormous gold coins, presumably for presentation purposes [figure 129]: a telling symbol of an overprivileged nobility and an overtaxed people.

If the coinage of Castile in the Middle Ages was poor and provincially remote from the mainstream of European monetary development, that of Portugal was even more so. It was in truth born debased, for the kingdom only came into existence in the middle of the twelfth century by which time the dinero of Castile, which was the natural pattern for it, had already degenerated into a wretched piece of billon. The similar coins of Sancho I (1185–1211), the first king of Portugal to strike money, were perhaps the most unpromising beginning which any national coinage ever had. Nor was there much improvement during the next two and a half centuries. Apart from the occasional gold marabotin, nothing except the *dinheiro* was struck until the reign of Peter I (1357–67). He and his successor Ferdinand I made a number of changes, following Castile in the introduction of new gold and larger silver coins. But there was nothing to correspond to the brief period of prosperity in Castile under Pedro the Cruel. Both gold and good silver coins were rare and the currency of Ferdinand's reign, for example, consisted largely of the *barbuda* and the *grave*, coins of pleasing design [figure 124] but of moderate weight and indifferent alloy. During the long reign of John of Aviz (1383–1433) no gold whatever was issued and the main coin was a real of Castilian pattern but of very debased silver. Within a few years the situation was to be transformed, but for the time being the coinage of Portugal developed slowly and in isolation from everywhere but Castile, betraying nothing, either in its design, weight or metallic content, of the country's Atlantic trading connexions.

The coinage of France in the fourteenth century presents a sad contrast with that of the preceding fifty years. The Hundred Years War disrupted the trade and destroyed the real wealth of the country. At the same time it increased the king's own need for money and he naturally turned to debasement of the currency to relieve his indebtedness. Philip IV had shown the way in this and Charles IV had followed it during the English war of 1324–7, but their monetary policy seemed like financial rectitude when compared with that of the hard-pressed Valois.

125 France; silver gros à la couronne, *c.* 1337, Philip VI. A variant of the gros tournois whose appearance marks the beginning of debasement of the major silver coinage by the Valois kings [enlarged 2:1]

All was well until the great war began. Indeed there was more than a hint of the court's extravagance in the great variety of beautiful gold coins struck by Philip VI in the early years of his reign when gold was plentiful [figure 128]. Soon after the war began, however, the shortage of silver for the army and daily needs of civilian life began to make itself felt. The Capetians only debased the lower value silver coins, but Philip VI did not stop at that. The fine silver gros tournois was replaced by a series of gros of inferior alloy. This did not of itself make the weakening of the currency any more serious, but as issue succeeded issue, sometimes at intervals of only a few weeks, each one slightly inferior to the one before and differing from it only by the addition of some small privy mark, the coinage in circulation became so chaotic that it was impossible to restore it to order. The variety of coins gave many opportunities for defrauding the ignorant and the frequency of the changes gave great scope for dishonest speculation by those who were close to the authorities. Like all too rapid inflations however, this one soon defeated itself. People began to stipulate payments in gold, which, although debased by Philip VI, was not tampered with so often or so seriously as the silver [figure 125], and the army anticipated the fall in the purchasing power of money by demanding higher pay. To meet this John II on two occasions at least, in 1351 and 1358, resorted to a secret debasement.

Men might argue whether admitted debasement of the coinage was justifiable; most twentieth-century economists would join issue with Nicolas Oresme, the great fourteenth-century exponent of sound money policies, and agree that it was, especially in war time. John's expedient, however, was an undoubted fraud on his own subjects and made nonsense of the usual claim which the king made when

126 *(opposite)* Hungary; gold florins, Charles Robert (1308–42) *(below)* and Louis I (1342–82), Kremnitz. Two stages in the florin's development in a country of its adoption: first a straight copy with changes only in the mint mark and legend, and second with the arms of the ruling house substituted for the Florentine lily [enlarged 3.5:1]

127 *(overleaf left top to bottom)* Aquitaine; leopard, *c.* 1344, and guiennois, 1360, King Edward III as duke, and the following gold coins of Edward the Black Prince (1362–72): pavillons, La Rochelle and Figeac (reverse), chaises, Bordeaux and Limoges (reverse), and hardi d'or, Limoges [actual size]

128 *(overleaf right top to bottom)* France; agnel, Charles IV (1322–8), and parisis d'or (reverse), lion d'or, pavillon, couronne, ange d'or and écu or chaise (reverse) all of Philip VI (1328–50). A view of the magnificent variety of French gold coinage on the eve of the Hundred Years War [actual size]

he debased the coinage that 'les causes qui nous meuvent a fere tele monnoie sont pour ce que nostre peuple, qui estoit et est a soufrete et povrete de monnoie … puisse plus habundament … estre rempli de monnoye coursable'.[1] Instead, on these secret occasions, the king's order referred baldly to 'le tres grant besoing et necessite que nous avons a present de finance'.[2] Even so, in spite of the frauds and monetary confusion to which it gave rise, the inflation caused less public distress than the spasmodic attempts to correct it with which it was interspersed and the rather longer period of deflation by which it was followed.

The deflationary period more or less coincided with the reign of Charles V. Politically Charles stood for the retrenchment and consolidation which were needed to restore France after the disasters of the previous two reigns. In the economic sphere this meant a return to stable money. Charles's first attempt to achieve this, as regent after the battle of Poitiers, failed in the face of fierce popular opposition and the rising in Paris led by Etienne Marcel. His second attempt, made when he became king in 1364, was more successful. By then the conditions for it were more favourable. The treaty of Brétigny had brought peace. All over Europe there was a contraction in trade caused by the recurrence of plague, the consequent depopulation and the exhaustion of the more accessible veins of the European silver mines. All the same it is not surprising that Charles's reform was unpopular, for his policy was to strike finer but fewer coins and to reduce the value of those in circulation. Prices, of course, came down, but not so fast as wages, and borrowers for once found themselves obliged to repay in appreciating currency. For about twenty years the theories of Nicolas Oresme were applied in France and the value of money was stable. The gros tournois, the symbol of 'la bonne monnaye du tems sainct Loys' was struck once again, lighter than it had been in the old days but of good silver as before. However the situation did not last. War broke out again and inflationary pressures from outside the economy also began to mount. Bullion was withheld from the mint and the undervalued coin began to leave the country, thus causing even greater shortage. Within a year of Charles's death his policy was abandoned and the old process of inflation and debasement began again, to continue, off and on, until the end of the war.

The twenty years of stability left a curious mark on the French coinage. It happened that at the very beginning of this period a new gold coin was issued of the value of one livre tournois. It was struck in great quantities to pay King John's ransom and its type [figure 137] which, unusual for a king, showed him mounted and in full armour, may have been intended to symbolise his restoration from captivity

[1] The reasons why we are issuing such coins are so that our subjects, who were and are suffering from a great shortage of cash may be more plentifully supplied with current coin

[2] The great and pressing need which we now have of money

129 *(opposite)* Castile and Leon; gold four doblas, Henry IV (1454–74). One of the enormous gold presentation pieces which relieved the poverty of Castilian coinage in the fifteenth century [actual size]

to the head of his chivalry. Its name had similar overtones for it was called the *franc*. Now the franc à cheval and its successor, the less showy franc à pied of Charles v, were stable at the value of one livre for long enough for the words *franc* and *livre* to become inseparably connected in Frenchmen's minds. Later, whenever the authorities wished to inaugurate a period of stable money and to issue a coin to be worth one livre, they called the coin a franc. Henry III did this in 1577. Finally, when money of account was abolished in 1793, the franc was once again called in aid and the name of the coin became also that of the currency.

The coinage of fourteenth-century France is interesting not only in its economic but also in its political aspects. During the thirteenth century the power of the king had been enlarged at the expense of that of the nobility and it has been noted how the coinage reform of 1266 had the effect of downgrading the feudal coinage. This process continued, reaching its furthest point in coinage matters in 1315 when Louis x claimed the right to regulate and tariff the issues of feudal mints. Some thirty-one barons still claimed the right to strike coins, but not all of them exercised it. During the reigns of Philip vi and John the Good there was a reaction, fed partly by the new fashion of granting extensive appanages to princes of the blood. There was no increase in the number of those who operated their own mints, but a few of those who were left now became more powerful and independent, keeping almost royal state, developing an almost royal administration and issuing an almost royal coinage, not scrupling to strike both large silver and gold. The new feudalism was the very reverse of the old. The deniers of Hugh Capet or even Louis vi had been just like feudal deniers. Now the coins of the dukes of Brittany and Aquitaine had become like royal coins. It was those two dukes who led the way. The dukes of Burgundy and counts of Flanders [figure 137] had similar coinages, but they were able to dodge the issue with France for they had mints on imperial territory, the counts of Flanders at Ghent and the dukes of Burgundy at Auxonne. All four princes struck coins closely related to the regal issues in type and weight but, since each had trading connexions which were not shared with the rest of the kingdom, they also developed specifically local coinage. This was especially true of Flanders, whose coinage was typical of the Netherlands rather than of a French fief.

Aquitaine provides a good example of the complicated interaction which took place in the coinages of the great fiefs. The kings of England had possessed it since 1154 but, until the time of Edward III, the coins which they had struck there had been quite unrelated to their English ones and were just like those of any other lordship in south-western France. Edward I struck sterlings for Aquitaine as well as the customary deniers but Edward III was the first who radically departed from former practice. Within ten years of his declaration of war on Philip vi, he had issued a gold *chaise* and silver *gros* and

130 Aquitaine; silver demi-gros, Edward the Black Prince (1362–72), Figeac [actual size], and a view of the fourteenth-century Hôtel de la Monnaie at Figeac where this coin was minted

doubles copied from his antagonist, another gros copied from his ally the count of Flanders, and also a gold *leopard* [figure 127], which was local in type but was made to conform to the weight standard of his recently issued English gold. The debasement of his French silver, which contrasts so strongly with the fineness of his English coins, suggests the difficulty of isolating one part of France from the inflation which was taking place at the centre; it also implies that more than their fair share of the cost of the war was carried by Edward's Gascon subjects.

In 1362 the Black Prince was created Prince of Aquitaine. His ten years of rule fell within the period of monetary stability in France and his silver coinage consisted largely of gros, demi-gros [figure 130] and sterlings all of fine alloy and closely related in weight and type to contemporary English coins. Later the sterling was superseded by the *hardi d'argent*, a coin of about the same value but of distinctive type showing the prince full face, holding a drawn sword. This was the only coin to survive the French reconquest; it was still minted in Aquitaine as late as the reign of Louis XII (1498–1515). However, the interest of the Black Prince's coinage lies less in the coins which he struck than in his mint organisation. The apportionment of one mint to each of the eight provinces of Aquitaine and of a distinctive mint-mark to each, the detail of the mint accounts and the hierarchy of mint officials under the superintendence of a peripatetic general master all tell of the high level of administrative competence which was the mark of the new feudalism in France [figure 131].

The stable money policy of Charles V did not long outlast his reign; in 1385 the government of the infant Charles VI dispensed with the

131 France; gold écu à la couronne, c. 1389, Charles VI, Tournai. An early issue of what became the standard French gold coin for more than two hundred years [actual size]

two coins which had symbolised it, replacing the good silver gros tournois by a *blanc*, the traditional name for a gros of inferior and variable silver content, and the franc by the *écu à la couronne*. The écu took its name from the shield of arms beneath a crown prominently displayed on the obverse [figure 131]. Its initial value was 22 s. 6 d. tournois, but the important thing about that was that it could easily be changed. The écu lasted almost as long as the franc, the two representing in some ways opposing schools of thought in French monetary theory. The franc, born of stability, stood for a fixed monetary value and only secondarily for a coin, while the écu, born of instability, stood for something more concrete than money, namely for a coin of a certain standing. The antithesis is not perfect, for both were inconstant in purchasing power. Moreover the issue was complicated for a period after 1576 when franc and écu were combined in a single system designed to stabilise the currency after the great inflation of the sixteenth century. However it may be fair to see in the predominance of the écu during the fifteenth and sixteenth centuries a surrender by successive French kings to the principle of frequent mutations of the currency. It was virtually the only gold coin struck for much of that period. Its weight was gradually diminished and its nominal value not so gradually increased.

The reign of Charles VI saw changes in mint organisation as well as in the coinage. Since the accession of Louis VIII in 1223 the king's coins had rarely carried a mint signature. In 1389 a code was devised to enable the king's officers or those of the Cour des Monnaies, which exercised ordinary jurisdiction in matters of coinage, to identify the product of the different mints. This consisted essentially of a system of points or similar marks placed under numbered letters in the inscription: thus a point below the eighth letter indicated Poitiers, below the sixteenth Tournai [figure 131] and so on. This system continued until 1540.

The depreciation of the currency heralded by the introduction of the écu and the blanc in 1385, gradual at first, became precipitate after the disaster of Agincourt. In the years which followed the coinage fell into utter disorder, reflecting the political disarray caused by the triumph of Lancaster and Burgundy. Charles VI struck more or less debased coins at Paris and the mints loyal to him; by 1419 his écu, though reduced in weight and fineness, was tariffed at 30 sous tournois. The Dauphin Charles, in even more straitened financial circumstances after setting up his alternative government at Bourges, struck coins similar in appearance to his father's but still more debased at the mints south of the Loire. In Normandy Henry V, first as a usurper, then after 1420 as acknowledged heir of the kingdom, struck his own version of French royal coinage in his own name. Meanwhile the duke of Burgundy took over the administration of all the royal mints within his own duchy.

The position improved somewhat after the deaths of Charles VI and

132 France; gold salut, *c.* 1446, Henry VI of England, Rouen. The rival to the écu à la couronne favoured by the Lancastrian administration in France [actual size]

Henry V in 1422, but in a manner galling to the French, for during the next ten years at least the coinage which was best administered, of best quality and most plentiful was that issued in the name of Henry VI by the regent John, duke of Bedford. This differed from that of the Valois in several particulars. The mints, which included Paris and were spread all over northern France and Burgundy, were indicated not by the numbered letters system, but by little heraldic symbols. The gold piece was not the écu but the *salut*, first issued briefly by Charles VI in 1421, but now taken up with vigour by the English government because of its parity with the English half-noble. The most prominent feature of both gold and silver was the juxtaposition of the shields of England and France, a device copied from the Netherlands where it came to symbolise the tacking together of separate dominions under a single dynasty. On the salut this barefaced political statement contrasts oddly with the delicate religious sensibility of the Annunciation scene which gave the coin its name [figure 132].

The decline in English power in France can be traced in the gradual falling away of Bedford's mints. The last to issue coins in Henry's name was Rouen, which stopped in 1449. In 1436, however, after the recapture of Paris, Charles VII instituted a major recoinage and the Henry VI coins were demonetised as hateful reminders of foreign occupation. It was necessary to make a fresh start, and a recoinage was part of the process. French political and economic policies, the latter for a time under the guidance of Jacques Coeur, were reorientated towards the Mediterranean. Plentiful issues of écus of the new coinage, particularly from the mints of Lyons and Montpellier, signalled a new era of commercial prosperity.

The economic strains of the Hundred Years War were more apparent in the French than in the English coinage. There were several reasons for that: the war was fought on French soil, for the greater part of it the English were winning, and the Plantagenets were able to throw a large part of the cost on to their French subjects, Edward III on to the people of Aquitaine and Henry V and his brother on to the people of Normandy and Paris. England, not yet a mercantile nation, but one to which Italian and Hanseatic merchants came eagerly to buy primary products, was still economically unsophisticated but rich. At the beginning of the war she was without either gold or large silver coinage, but the silver content of the penny, which was the basic unit of account, was still what it had been in 1087. Early in the war this was changed. In 1344 gold coinage was introduced, under the supervision of Italian mint-masters [figure 133].

It was a bad time to choose. King Louis of Hungary had been accumulating reserves instead of releasing the production of his mines and there was a gold shortage. Edward III, to encourage English merchants to disgorge what they had, tariffed his new gold florin at 6s. which put the gold:silver ratio at nearly fifteen to one. But that year Louis sent his mother to Italy with 17,000 marks of gold

133 England; gold half-florin
1344, Edward III, London.
Ravishing heraldry but an
economic failure. This weighed
the same as the florin of Florence
but was over-valued at 3s.
[enlarged 4:1]

to further his dynastic ambitions in Naples; later he followed this up with a further subsidy of 4,000 marks. All at once he released some six years of Hungarian production or an estimated two years of world production; his florins are to this day among the commonest of medieval gold coins [figure 126]. Of course the price of the metal fell so sharply that the new English florins were left hopelessly overvalued and nobody would take them. They were promptly withdrawn (at the bullion price) and only two have survived. Nevertheless a new attempt was made in the same year, this time with a *noble* tariffed at 6s. 8d. The gold: silver ratio was put at just under twelve to one, but that involved a small adjustment in the weight of the penny: even the king of England was finding that bimetallism could sometimes force a ruler's hand in currency matters. It was not until 1351, after two more adjustments in the weight of both penny and noble, that a true balance was struck. From that year the noble was an assured success. Its design, showing the king, armed, in a ship [figure 134] may have helped in this a little. Whether or not it was intended to refer to the naval victory of Sluys, it aptly symbolised the aggressive insularity of the English and appealed to their growing nationalism.

The recoinage of 1351 included a silver groat of fourpence as well as the penny and the gold. The reduction in the weight of the penny since 1344 had perhaps made the larger coins more acceptable than it was in 1279. This time it came to stay and the pattern of English coinage was set for the next century and a half. Quite a high proportion of it was struck not in England but at Calais [figure 134]. After Edward III established the Staple there it naturally became an important centre for the receipt of foreign coin and bullion in exchange for wool exports. As long as England controlled the narrow seas it was both convenient and, if foreign coin was to be kept out of the country, politic, to have a mint there. The relative activity of the Calais and London mints, with Calais especially prolific in 1422–9 but falling

134 England; gold noble, 1363–9, Edward III, Calais. The noble was, the coin which was eventually established as the standard English gold coin. The activity of the Calais mint was an index of the prosperity of English wool exports [actual size]

away sharply thereafter, provides an interesting commentary on the comparative importance of wool and other exports in English trade, on English sea power and on diplomatic relations with the Burgundian Netherlands.

The kings of England made as few changes as possible in the coinage. They pursued a relentlessly sound money policy, preferring when times were hard, as they were during the reigns of Richard II and Henry IV, to issue virtually no coins at all rather than to debase them or to increase their nominal value like the French. From time to time they had to make minor adjustments of gold against silver, which usually took the form of a reduction in the weight of coins of one metal or the other. Only twice, in 1411 and 1464 [figure 135], did the harsh realities of having an overvalued currency force them to make a general reduction in the weight of the coinage. This was remarkably little for a century of continuous war, in which, because of the Hussite wars in Bohemia and the exhaustion of many central European mines, the supply of precious metals was drying up. Only a rich country could afford such a policy at such a time. Scotland, for example, which had formerly kept pace with England, began to fall away. In 1374 the Scottish groat was worth only threepence sterling, and in 1390 only twopence, the first stages of a process which was to leave the pound Scots at only one twelfth of a pound sterling by the time of the union of the crowns in 1603.

The English policy of sound money, though sometimes severe in its social effects and probably a root cause of the Peasants' Revolt and the lesser upheavals which followed, worked to the long term benefit of the economy. English coin was well received abroad, especially the noble which, after the weight change of 1411, became the exact equivalent of two florins. Another result of the policy was the difference which arose between the English and others in their attitude towards the coins in common use. To most Europeans the coin was one thing, the value another. To the English a groat was always fourpence and even the noble, in spite of the fluctuations inseparable from a bimetallic system, was usually 6s. 8d. until the devaluation of 1464; its successors, the *ryal* tariffed at 10s. and the *angel* at 6s. 8d. remained at those rates until the reign of Henry VIII and even the *sovereign*, first issued by Henry VII at 20s., held that value for long enough for the name to become identified with the pound sterling in the public mind. This stability was to make the experiment in debasement by Henry VIII all the more shocking when it came, but it followed that in England, much earlier than anywhere else, coinage and money of account were able to come together with the issue of such coins as the *shilling* and the *sixpence*. Money of account was not discredited as it was elsewhere and the £ s d system was able to survive until 1971.

Just as the development of the new feudalism in France left its mark upon the French coinage, there was a parallel development in Italy. In many of the communes, oligarchy gave place to the rule of

135 England; silver groat, 1480–3, Edward IV, London. Only two changes were made in the weight and specification of the English silver during the whole of the fifteenth century [actual size]

136 Modena; silver grosso, Marquis Azzo d'Este (1293–1306). Verona, silver grosso, Cangrande della Scala, imperial vicar (1311–29). Two early instances of the lords of Italian cities placing their own marks on the coinage, in Azzo's case his name and in Cangrande's the little ladder (scala) in the legend [enlarged 2 : 1]

137 (opposite) Flanders; franc à cheval, demi lion, heaume d'or and lion d'or (reverse), Count Louis de Maele (1346–84); Hainault; double royal, Count William III (1356–89). Exuberance, both in size and design, characterise these Flemish coins of the late fourteenth century [actual size]

single families or individuals. The earliest instance of this constitutional development revealing itself in the coinage occurred at Modena and Reggio during the lordship of Azzo d'Este (1293–1306). On grossi of those cities Azzo substituted his own name and title for that of the emperor Frederick II which had been customary hitherto [figure 136]. However, the juridical basis of this act is not quite clear, since Azzo's old feudal title of marquis figures very prominently on these coins, and it was perhaps by virtue of that and not his lordship of the cities that he assumed the right to issue them. The first coins which unquestionably refer to a new kind of constitutional authority are grossi of Verona with the name of the emperor Henry VII and the little ladder of the Scaligers in the legend [figure 136]. These were issued soon after Henry appointed Cangrande della Scala perpetual imperial vicar of Verona in 1311. Within the next few years the arms of imperial vicars obtruded upon the coins of a number of cities, in some cases appearing along with the imperial title just as the monograms of Ostrogothic kings had done on imperial solidi some eight centuries before. The aquilini of the Ghibelline cities were especially prominent during this transitional phase, with the arms of the Bonacolsi appearing on those of Mantua [figure 96] and the arms of successive non-hereditary captains of the people on those of Padua. At Milan the first sign of the Visconti was the appearance of the letters AZ for Azzo Visconti on an otherwise unremarkable soldo of the emperor Louis IV in 1329.

In 1329 the emperor Louis IV petulantly withdrew from Italian affairs. There was a curious interlude the following year when John of Bohemia, the son of Henry VII, descended upon Italy and assumed

139 Parma; silver grosso 1331, John the Blind, king of Bohemia (1305–46). This remarkable portrait coin is one of the few relics of John's abortive venture into Italy [enlarged 2:1]

140 Padua; gold ducat, Francesco I Carrara (1355–88). The only gold coin struck by the Carrara lords of Padua. The stylised chariot on the obverse is the badge of the dynasty [enlarged 2:1]

138 (opposite) Illuminated frontispiece c. 1490 of a manuscript of *De Moneta* by Nicolas Oresme, the fourteenth–century political economist. The opening words translated, run as follows: 'Some believe that any king or prince can by his own authority, by law or prerogative, freely alter the coin current in his realm' . . .

the government of several cities. This quasi-imperial intervention left its mark upon the coinage of Parma in particular [figure 139]. Thereafter the signori were left to themselves and it became the normal practice for them to put their full names on the coins of their cities without acknowledgement of any suzerain. Azzo Visconti did this at Milan in the later years of his lordship. Elsewhere Taddeo Pepoli (1337–47) at Bologna, Ludovico II Gonzaga (1369–82) at Mantua, Francesco I Carrara (1355–88) at Padua [figure 140] and Carlo Malatesta (1389–1429) at Rimini all issued coins in their own names. Only at Verona the Scaligers got no further than using their family device and their initials on their coinage, for they were dispossessed by Giangaleazzo Visconti before they could carry their early initiative in this matter to its logical conclusion. At Ferrara the Estensi issued grossi of the traditional Emilian type but in their own names from the time of Obizzo III (1344–52). Tuscany was more republican. At Florence, the Medici were wise enough not to tamper with the florin; their consitutional position was in any case far more precarious than that of the Lombard and Emilian lords. Siena fell into the hands of Giangaleazzo in 1399, but whether for economic or political reasons he did no more than add his viper badge to the traditional design of the Sienese florin. This was far removed from the later practice of the Visconti at Milan and Pavia, where after about 1360 there was a prominent display of the dynasty's name and arms on the coinage of

141 Milan; gold florin,
Galeazzo II Visconti (1345–78).
A coin type showing the
Visconti vying in chivalric display
with the feudal nobility of France
[enlarged 2:1]

Galeazzo II and Bernabò. Galeazzo went a stage further, replacing the figure of the patron saint on his gold coinage by a representation of himself armed and mounted after the manner of the French feudal nobility [figure 141].

While the florin of Florence itself remained unchanged, its many imitations in northern Europe began to develop on their own. An early example was the florin of Louis of Hungary, who replaced the Florentine lily with his own arms [figure 126]. Within a few years the Count Palatine Rupert (1390–96) took a similar step. Nor was it long before St John the Baptist went the way of the lily. Usually he was supplanted by a similar standing figure of a locally revered saint, St Wladislas in Hungary, St Lawrence at Nuremberg [figure 142] and so on, but the archbishop of Mainz, John of Luxemburg (1371–3) and William V, count of Holland (1350–89), went so far as to replace the saint by representations of themselves. Even where the Baptist remained, as on the florins of Gerhard von Schwarzburg, bishop of Würzburg (1372–1400) [figure 142] or those which the margraves of Brandenburg struck at their city of Schwabach near Nuremberg, he began to wear a different aspect from the Florentine original.

It is at the point, when the German florin parts company with the Florentine, that it becomes convenient to call it by the name which was commonest in Germany, that is the *gulden*. The two names are in fact interchangeable and to this day the abbreviation fl. is used for the Dutch gulden. The gulden varied not only in appearance but in content. In weight they did not often depart much from the Florentine norm, but some rulers were more prone than others to debase the metal. The Hungarian coins had a particularly good reputation in this respect, the lesser princes of the lower Rhine a bad one. This in due course gave rise to a further distinction in nomenclature. As the Venetian ducat was not much imitated in northern Europe, the name ducat, unlike florin or gulden, was always associated with a coin of good quality. The best coins in circulation, such as the Hungarian, came in the fifteenth century to be known as ducats, while the poorer ones were still called gulden, though both classes had a common origin in the florin of Florence. The final irony was when the Florentine coin, which unlike the imitations was never debased, came to be called in common parlance a ducat.

The differing values of the German gulden and of the various German silver coinages were a source of great confusion in a country which had far greater economic than political cohesion. The history of German coinage from the late fourteenth century to the late nineteenth consists quite largely of the successive attempts to remedy this. The form which these attempts took was usually an agreement between a group of issuing authorities to strike coins of the same weight, fineness and nominal value, and sometimes to incorporate common features in the design. Frequently this would form part of a wider economic union, for in nearly every case the commercial inter-

142 Würzburg; gold gulden, Bishop Gerhard von Schwarzburg (1372–1400). Nuremberg; gold gulden of the imperial city, struck after 1464. The gulden at two stages of its development, the first with the Florentine figure of St John modified but clearly identifiable, the second with a different saint, whose pose shows just a trace of his Florentine origin [enlarged 2:1]

143 Wismar; silver witten, c. 1380. The little star which figures on both sides is the mark of the Hanseatic monetary convention, the so-called Wendische Münzverein of which Wismar was a founder member [enlarged 2:1]

ests of the parties were closely identified. Such for example was the treaty made in 1379 between Lübeck, Hamburg and Wismar, three of the foremost cities of the most famous of German economic leagues, the Hanse. These three agreed to issue *witten*, small silver pieces of about the same value as the English sterling and perhaps based on that coin, all according to the weight and standard of Lübeck. Each city kept its own emblem as the main design, but all put a star [figure 143] somewhere on the coin as the badge of the monetary union. Two years later three more Hanseatic cities joined, namely Rostock, Lüneburg and Stralsund. In its original form the Wendische Münzverein, as this union was called, lasted for only a few years, but it was renewed from time to time as new coinages incorporating larger pieces were required. It formed the basis of the issue of the *schilling* by the same six cities in 1432 and of the double schilling in 1468. Its last formal act was in 1569.

The example of the Wendish cities was soon followed by others; in 1382 the Barrenmünzverein was formed by a group of lower Saxon cities including Brunswick, Hanover and Goslar. In 1386 the three electoral archbishops of the Rhineland combined with the elector palatine in a treaty which covered both gold and silver. The gold coin of this league was the *gulden*, the silver the *weisspfennig* [figure 144], a groschen of medium size with a representation of St Peter on the obverse which had first been struck by Kuno von Falkenstein as

144 Cologne; gold gulden *c.* 1407, and silver weisspfennig, *c.* 1380, Archbishop Frederick von Saarwerden, Bonn. The gulden, struck after the formation of the Rhenish monetary convention, shows the arms of the other members beside that of the archbishop. These were the typical gold and silver coins of the Rhineland [actual size]

archbishop of Trier in 1368. On the coins of this convention, the distinguishing mark was the shield of the issuing elector surrounded by smaller escutcheons of the other three [figure 144]. Since the Rhenish league included gold coins and since also the Hundred Years War had driven much of the trade between Italy and the Netherlands from the Rhône-Saône route to the Rhine, this was commercially the most important of the German conventions. The Rhenish gulden was the nearest thing in the Empire to a generally acceptable German coin in the fifteenth century, and it had a profound influence on the currency of the Netherlands.

In 1407, a monetary treaty, covering gold and silver coins, was made between a group of Franconian rulers, the bishops of Bamberg and Würzburg, the burgrave of Nuremberg and, once more, the count palatine acting on this occasion in respect of the upper Palatinate. In 1403 a number of cities of the upper Rhine, including Basel, Colmar and Freiburg, made a monetary treaty with the Austrian landvogt who governed the imperial lands in Alsace and Breisgau. This convention lasted in various forms until 1553. It was known as the Rappenmünzbund after the *rappen* or double pfennig on which it was based, and its chief importance lay in its influence on the later development of Swiss coinage. Another south-western convention was made in 1423 in connection with the loose economic federation known as the Swabian League. The chief participants were Württemberg, Constance and Ulm with other cities of the upper Danube. Already it is possible to see foreshadowed in these agreements the geographical 'circles' of the Empire, Franconian, Swabian, Westphalian, upper and lower Saxon etc., through which German coinage and much else was to be ordered in the sixteenth century.

The two main areas of economic activity in the middle ages were northern Italy and the Netherlands. The Italian cities were active in all sorts of ways, manufacturing, exporting, importing, banking and carrying. Consequently Italian coins, the florin and the ducat especially, had a wide circulation and influence. The cities of the Netherlands on the other hand were principally industrial centres. It is probable that only the English, who supplied the wool for the looms, and perhaps the Venetians were net sellers in the Flemish market. It followed that there was a steady flow of foreign coin into the Netherlands. Nowhere was the trade of the money-changer more complicated or more necessary; it was so much a part of everyday life that it became one of the most popular genre subjects of Flemish painters [figures 110 & 151]. As for the local coinage, it was cosmopolitan in character and rich in content. The early influence of the florin, the gros tournois and the sterling has already been noticed. In the fourteenth century French influence became paramount for a time.

In gold, the coins most frequently encountered were the *chaise*, known in Dutch as the *klinkaart*, and the *mouton* or *lam*. Philip VI of France poured great quantities of chaises into the Netherlands to

145 Holland; gold chaise or klinkaart, Count William V (1346–89). Guelders; gold gros mouton, Duke Edward (1361–71). Two gold coins of French inspiration (see figure 122) which became popular with the Dutch princes [enlarged 2:1]

subsidise his allies there and, as a counter-measure, Edward III of England prevailed upon the emperor Louis IV to set up a mint at Antwerp, where, with English gold, an imperial version of the same coin was issued. The two factions, by their subsidies, made the klinkaart the commonest gold piece in the area, and it was much copied by the various princes, among them William V, count of Holland, the emperor's nephew [figure 145].

The mouton, so called because of the Agnus Dei to which the obverse design and legend were devoted, was first issued in France by John the Good in 1355, but its antecedents went back to a coin of Philip IV named, more reverently, the *agnel*. The French king no doubt selected the type out of piety, but it was probably the mundane association of the sheep with the textile industry which made the coin a popular subject for imitation by the princes of the Netherlands.

In silver, the typical coin of the Netherlands was the *leeuwengroot* or *gros au lion* [figure 146]. This was instituted in Flanders when Philip VI of France abandoned the issue of the gros tournois at the beginning of the Hundred Years War, but it was effectively a Flemish version of the French coin with the lion of Flanders substituted for the châtel. It was soon adopted by the neighbouring princes, most of whom could

146 Flanders; silver leeuwengroot, Count Louis of Nevers (1322–46). The Flemish version of the gros tournois which became the standard silver currency through much of the Netherlands [actual size]

147 Hainault; gold ange à la haie, Count William IV, (1404–17). One of the prettiest and rarest of the large gold coins struck in the Netherlands in the early fifteenth century [actual size]

point to a lion in their own coats of arms, and before long it became the normal unit of account in the whole region. A Flemish and Brabantine version of it was the subject of a monetary convention between those two provinces in 1339.

As the Hundred Years War dragged on, dimming French prestige and driving the trade with Italy further to the east, German influence became more marked in the coinage of the Netherlands. Floris van Wewelinkhoven, bishop of Utrecht (1379–93), who began by striking klinkaarts, ended by minting gulden of Rhenish type and his successor issued no gold except gulden; similarly, in the southern provinces, Arnold of Hornes, bishop of Liège (1378–89), took up the issue of gulden like those of his neighbour the archbishop of Trier.

Eventually, with the growth of the Burgundian state under Philip the Good (1419–67), the coinage of the Netherlands took on that independent and national quality which it had previously lacked. As early as 1427 the former position was reversed and a king of France, Charles VII, found it to his advantage to issue a coin of purely Flemish antecedents at his mint of Tournai. This was the *plaque*, worth two Flemish gros.

The most typically Flemish characteristic of the plaque was its size. There was plenty of money about in the industrial cities of the Netherlands, a condition which was otherwise rare in the Middle Ages. Prices were correspondingly high and there was a call for big coins, perhaps exaggerated by a native delight in extravagant display. In gold, the *gros mouton* was issued in at least four provinces, Brabant, Liège, Holland and Guelders [figure 145], though this enlarged version of John the Good's coin was never struck in France. William III of Hainault (1356–89) struck a *double royal*. Louis de Maele, count of Flanders (1346–84), issued a whole series of less imitative large gold pieces; his Burgundian successors, Philip the Bold, John the Fearless and Philip the Good, chose to copy the big English noble. In silver the usual coin was a double gros, variously named *botdrager*, *plack* or *stuiver*. The botdrager, first issued by Louis de Maele, took its name from the helmeted lion which figured prominently on the obverse; it was struck in great quantities by Louis himself and by Philip the Bold, and was directly copied by Count William V of Holland and more than a dozen lesser lords. The placks and stuivers of the other provinces mostly displayed appropriate heraldic designs, those of Utrecht an eagle, those of Liège a griffin and those of Hainault a lion within a palisade. These large coins in both metals gave ample scope for the profuse ornamentation which characterised all forms of late gothic art. They are less refined than the best French work of the period of Philip IV but they rank among the most spectacular of medieval coins [figure 137].

Enough has perhaps already been said to show how, in an age when imitative coinage was common everywhere, it was in the Netherlands the normal monetary way of life. Some of the lesser lords whose coins

148 Flanders; silver plack or botdrager, Count Louis de Maele (1346–84). Utrecht; silver plack, Bishop Frederick van Blankenheim (1393–1423), Deventer. The plack, or stuiver, worth two groots, became common in the latter part of the fourteenth century [actual size]

could not be expected to gain wide acceptance on the credit of the issuer, carried copying to extraordinary lengths. There is an element almost of fantasy in the way in which Arnold of Orey, a fourteenth-century lord of Rummen, a territory of no economic or political consequence, copied everything in sight, from the mouton d'or of the king of France to the remote double sterling of David II of Scotland. However the practice, when followed more moderately, had the advantage of giving some cohesion to an otherwise hopelessly fragmented monetary system, and among the leading princes it was perhaps a matter of deliberate policy. As between Flanders and Brabant it was formalised by a monetary treaty as early as 1339 and again in 1384, by the terms of which the rulers of the two provinces agreed to strike the same silver coins in their joint names. Such treaties might have proliferated in the following century, as they did in Germany, but the whole situation was changed by the political union of the territories under Philip the Good.

Philip became duke of Burgundy and count of Flanders in 1419. Until 1433 he maintained separate coinages in each of the provinces of the Netherlands as he acquired them, Namur in 1421, Brabant in 1430, and so on; but in 1434 after he finally succeeded Jacqueline of Bavaria as sovereign of Hainault, Holland and Zeeland, he scrapped all the provincial coinages except that of Burgundy and issued a new one for the whole of his Netherlands dominions. This coinage was based on the groot of Flanders, still the most important province economically; the commonest coin in use was the double groot or stuiver, which was also sometimes known in this period as the *vierlander* because it was the coin of the four important provinces of Flanders, Brabant, Hainault and Holland. The gold coin in this reformed and unified system was the *cavalier d'or* or *gouden ridder* [figure 149], a coin

149 Burgundian Netherlands; gold ridder 1434–40, Dordrecht, gold leeuw 1454–60 and silver plack of Flanders, Philip the Good, duke of Burgundy (1419–67); gold andreasgulden, Bruges, Duke Charles the Bold (1467–77). Some typical coins of the Burgundian Netherlands after Philip's monetary reform of 1434 [actual size]

whose antecedents went back to the French franc but which in the new context was effectively an original native coin. Twenty years later there was a further change, a minor revaluation of the gold which involved the substitution of the *gouden leeuw* [figure 149] for the ridder. Finally in 1467, just before Philip's death and the accession of Charles the Bold, the silver coinage was slightly debased and gouden leeuw gave place to yet another new coin, the *andreasgulden*. This coin was essentially a gulden of Rhenish type with St Andrew, a patron saint of the house of Burgundy, substituted for St John the Baptist. Its introduction represented a major change of policy, since it brought the Burgundian states back into line with the independent provinces such as Utrecht and Guelders and with the whole of the Rhineland. It was at this point that the permanent place of the gulden in the monetary system of the Netherlands was confirmed.

During the first half of the fifteenth century coinage was deteriorating all over Europe. This was most serious in the two main theatres of war, France and Bohemia, and most spectacular in remote Prussia, where the Teutonic knights were ruined in 1410 by the military disaster at Tannenberg, but even in the peaceful and industrial areas of Europe, such as the dominions of Philip the Good, the impression left by the coinage is of a little precious metal being spun out to go further and further. Historians have been puzzled by the contradiction between the evident will to economic advance which existed at the time and the failure to achieve it. One reason for this failure may have been the shortage of liquidity caused by the lack of specie. That was not destined to be a problem for long.

150 Burying coins was a common practice in the middle ages, especially in time of war. Most surviving medieval coins come from the hoards that their owners never came back to collect. (from a fifteenth-century French manuscript of Boethius. Harleian MS 4399, British Museum)

7 New World Gold, Old World Silver

151 The *Gold Weigher* by Adriaen Isenbrant (active 1510–51). The coin in the foreground is a Bolognese double ducat of Giovanni II Bentivoglio. The little pile is typically international rather than Flemish.

152 *(opposite)* The miners of Kuttenberg. This Bohemian mine, the richest in Europe during its fourteenth-century heyday, was the scene of renewed activity late in the fifteenth century. The frontispiece of the Kuttenberger Kanzional by Matthaus of Kuttenberg, *c.* 1490

In 1445 the caravels of Prince Henry the Navigator first rounded Cape Verde. The discoveries in this area were the first in the age of exploration to bring the economic reward which all were seeking, for they gave the Portuguese direct access by river to the gold-bearing regions of upper Senegal. Europe had been using west African gold for centuries, but the Saharan route was expensive and liable to be cut from time to time. The Portuguese discovery put the supply line into Christian hands. It is impossible to judge how far this merely diverted an existing supply and how far it actually increased it, but some increase there certainly was, and it changed the whole economic situation of Europe. In a few years one of the poorest countries became one of the richest and the scanty gold coinage of Portugal became plentiful. In 1457 Alfonso V introduced a new gold coin, the *cruzado*, weighing 3.60 grams and worth about two per cent more than the ducat. Entirely medieval both in appearance [figure 153] and in purpose (since it was originally struck in order to finance a crusade), it was nevertheless the first important trading currency of modern Europe. It ushered in the great age of coinage in which new geographical and scientific discoveries, leading to the opening of new mines and a vast increase in the money supply, were to change the economy of the world. During the middle ages the money economy was still developing. By the late seventeenth century it had reached the stage when other forms of money such as bank deposits, credit and paper were beginning to play a more important part than coinage. In the intervening period however a money economy was in full swing in Europe and most of that money was coined. This justifies our calling those years the great age of coinage. Even so, too much importance must not be claimed for the subject. Money, not coinage, is the mainspring of economic activity and, if the gold of Senegal and Guinea had not been coined as the cruzado, it would still, in some other form, have given a boost to the European economy at that critical point. Nevertheless the cruzado was the form which that gold actually took, and it is therefore as important historically as a coin ever can be.

The heyday of the cruzado began after two more important geographical discoveries, that of the rich mining area of Guinea in 1481 and Vasco da Gama's rounding of the Cape of Good Hope in 1498.

153 Portugal; gold cruzado, Alfonso V (1438–81). The first coin struck with gold brought to Europe as a result of the explorations of the fifteenth century [actual size]

Thenceforward the Portuguese monopolised the East India trade, but though, like the Venetians before them, they were not exporters in their oriental commerce, the cruzado did not, like the ducat, tend to find its way eastwards. Gold was plentiful in the Indies, whereas silver was in demand there. It paid the Portuguese to ship African gold to Lisbon for coining, to buy silver with it on the European market and to use silver for buying merchandise in the east. The most convenient meeting for the seaborne traders of Portugal and the central European silver producers was the port of Antwerp, where an active bullion and foreign exchange market grew up. The financial expertise for this was already developed as a legacy of the complex monetary history and active economy of the Burgundian lands, described in the last chapter.

The increased trade at Antwerp greatly stimulated European mining. In 1451 there was a new invention for separating silver from argentiferous copper ores, and at about the same time new developments in drainage techniques were developed. This enabled a number of old mines to reopen, among them Kuttenberg which had been a centre of fighting during the Hussite wars, and Rammelsberg, near Goslar in the upper Harz. New seams were discovered at Schwaz in the Tirol, where output was tripled during the years 1470–90. By about 1500, new mines were operating at Mansfeld, where Luther's father was a miner, Schneeberg, Annaberg and Marienberg, all in Saxony, at Joachimsthal in Bohemia and also in Silesia. It has been estimated that there was a fivefold increase in central European output between 1450 and 1530.

Now the Portuguese only became active buyers of silver after the turn of the century. Schwaz was the first of the new mines to come into intensive production and the natural outlet for the Tirol was Italy. Consequently a large part of the early output went to the old financial centres there, whose appetite for it increased as the Portuguese diverted the source of their gold supply. Meanwhile the increasing production of silver naturally had some effect upon local coinage. There was a remarkable improvement, for example, in the quality of Saxon coinage under the brothers Ernest, landgrave of Thuringia (1464–86), and Albert, margrave of Meissen (1464–1500). In Tirol there was a more startling development. In 1450 Archduke Sigismund moved his mint from Merano to Hall [figure 156], a little up the Inn valley from Schwaz, and there in 1486 he instituted a new denomination, the *guldengroschen*, a coin of the same value as the gulden but in silver. This was the first really large silver coin [figure 176], the forerunner of many in central Europe and elsewhere in the sixteenth century.

In Italy the supply of silver was not so profuse as it was in the Tirol and, although Italian coins became larger, none was so substantial as Sigismund's guldengroschen. The first experiment was to issue a coin of one lira. This of course was what the florin had been

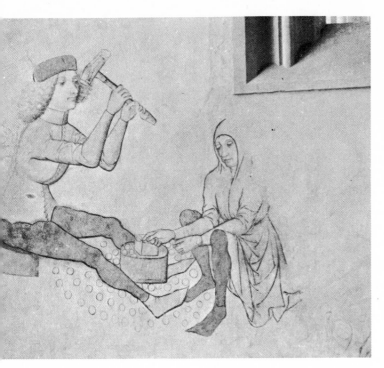

154 The moneyers of Kuttenberg.
A fifteenth-century wall painting
in the moneyers' chapel in
the cathedral of Kutná Hora

155 Venice; silver lira, 1472,
Doge Nicolò Tron. Venice's first
experiment with a high value silver
coin and her first and last
experiment with portrait coinage
[actual size]

worth in 1252, but the fall in the value of money since then had reduced 240 denari to quite a modest weight of fine silver. The earliest
of these coins was issued at Venice in 1472. It weighed 6.5 grams and
was remarkable for its portrait of the doge Nicolò Tron [figure 155]. It
was probably the portrait which made the coin unacceptable to the
Venetians, whose republican traditions were opposed to the cult of
personality. They did not give up large silver coins, but the lira Tron
was never reissued. In Milan a similar experiment by Galeazzo Maria
Sforza was more successful. His lira of 240 denari imperiali was rather
heavier than the Venetian, weighing 9.8 grams. This coin too carried
a portrait, and this in a few years gave it its name, *testone*, the coin
with a head.

The larger silver coins were ideal for those Italian princes who, in
the spirit of the Renaissance, wanted to issue portrait coinage after
the manner of the ancients. The first modern portrait medal was cast
by Pisanello in 1439. It was a portrait of the last but one of the Byzantine emperors, John VIII Palaeologus, who was in Italy for the council
of Florence. Pisanello's choice of subject thus makes a curious link
between modern coinage and the ancient world, but though portrait
medals quickly became fashionable, it was some years before portraiture was transferred to coinage. The conservatism always latent in
matters of coinage no doubt partly accounts for the delay, but there
were technical problems as well. Pisanello's medals were cast, not
struck; the thin fabric of coins as they were struck in 1450 did not
allow for the relief necessary for a satisfactory portrait. This failing

156 A sixteenth-century pen
and wash drawing of the mint
town of Hall in the Tirol, where the
first large silver coins of the
modern era were struck. The mint
tower, which still stands, is the
prominent building in the left
foreground

was apparent in the first portrait coin of the Renaissance, a ducat of
Francesco Sforza struck soon after 1450. This was simply not big
enough for an impressive portrait. Not until the next reign was the
artistic need for a bigger coin met by the issue of the double ducat and
the testone, both made possible by the increase in the supply of the
precious metals.

It was appropriate that Francesco was the first modern ruler to
issue portrait coins, for the essence of these was that they showed the
duke in his humanity, and Francesco was the very type of Renaissance
prince who governed by virtue of his personal qualities and not by
hereditary or constitutional right. That element in portrait coinage
which was so repugnant to the Venetians suited the Sforza well. They
made the most of it. As is so often the case with anything new in
coinage, new techniques or new designs, the earliest portrait coins
were the best. The Sforza dynasty came to an end before coin portraiture even began to deteriorate. The double ducats and testoni of
Galeazzo Maria (1466–76), his widow Bona of Savoy, his son Giangaleazzo Maria and his brother Ludovico il Moro (1494–1500) are some
of the most beautiful coins ever made [figure 157]. Giangaleazzo was
portrayed by the medallist Caradosso as a youth of ravishing beauty

157 Milan; silver testoni, Bona of Savoy, regent for Giangaleazzo Maria Sforza (1476–81), and Duke Ludovico Maria Sforza (1494–1500). Two fine portrait coins struck by the Sforza dynasty in Milan, one of the first states to adopt the new style of coinage [actual size]

and Ludovico, by the same artist, as the archetypal wicked uncle. The conjunction of the two on either side of the same piece in the years 1481–94 is dramatic.

Within a few years, Francesco Sforza's initiative in the matter of portrait coinage was followed at Mantua by Ludovico III Gonzaga (1444–78) and at Ferrara by Borso d'Este (1450–71). Compared with Milan, these were places of little commercial importance but the Estense and Gonzaga courts were among the most refined in Europe and acknowledged leaders of artistic fashion [figures 158 & 160]. For a time, however, coin portraiture remained a matter of building up personal prestige. It was taken up by princes such as Giovanni II Bentivoglio (1494–1506), balanced in a precarious diplomatic position between Pope and emperor as ruler of Bologna, by Charles I of Savoy (1482–90) [figure 158] and by his neighbour Ludovico II of Saluzzo (1475–1504). But the two Italian cities which were pre-eminent in the arts and commerce were behindhand with the new development. Venice, as we have seen, dropped the idea after a single experiment. At Florence the Medici, tactfully deferring to the forms of republicanism, set their face against it; as international bankers they no doubt also took into account the financial unwisdom of tampering with a

well-established trading currency. Both Venice and Florence did however start issuing larger silver coins and something of the Renaissance spirit showed in their designs [figure 159].

After Milan, the most important states to adopt portrait coinage were the Papacy and Naples. Avignon had been prosperous but Rome was not until 1462, when alum was discovered at Tolfa, the only deposit in western Europe of a commodity essential to the textile industry. Thus Rome gained a source of revenue in addition to the contributions of the faithful. For the first time the coinage of the popes became plentiful and the *ducato di camera* with its charming design of St Peter in a fishing boat first used in the reign of Calixtus III (1455–8) became a coin of more than local importance [figure 162]. The papal portrait was reserved for the bigger coins. These were mostly commemorative, for the Renaissance popes in this way restored the tradition of ancient Roman coinage. Sixtus IV (1471–84) issued a grosso [figure 161] and double grosso with his portrait engraved by Emiliano Orfini to mark his rebuilding of the city; for the jubilee year 1500 Alexander VI issued a portrait three ducat piece and both Julius II and Leo X occasionally issued similar coins.

The earliest portrait coin of Naples was a silver piece issued by Ferdinand I in 1458. Portrait coinage became as common at Naples as at Milan, but the quality was not so good. This was partly because the Neapolitan court was old-fashioned and the style of portraiture such that the humanity of the ruler was still overlaid with the trappings of royalty [figure 163] and partly because portraiture was extended to much humbler coins, including even the little copper *cavalli* which Ferdinand introduced.

Copper coinage was another new development of those fertile years. The earliest experiment with it was made at Venice in 1463, but that was abortive. It was first successfully pioneered at Naples in an area where, curiously enough, it had been in early use in ancient Greek

158 Savoy; testone, Duke Charles I (1482–90). Ferrara; testone, *c.* 1503, Duke Ercole I d'Este. Bologna; testone, Giovanni II Bentivoglio (1494–1506). Three remarkable silver coins of the early Renaissance issued by princes of more taste than political importance [actual size]

159 Florence; silver barile, 1511, mint-master Giovanni Battista Altoviti. The traditional figure of St John the Baptist treated in the Renaissance manner on a coin of a new denomination; the established Florentine coins, like the florin, remained untouched by the new style [actual size]

160 (*opposite*) Ferrara; gold double ducat, Duke Alfonso d'Este (1505–34) from dies by Giovanni Antonio da Foligno. A notable coin from the cultivated court of the Estense, with the reverse type of Christ and the Pharisee [enlarged 4:1]

162 Rome; gold ducato di camera,
Pope Calixtus III (1455–8).
The growing prosperity of Rome
in the second half of the fifteenth
century made the papal ducat
a more important piece
economically than any previous
papal coin [actual size]

161 *(opposite)* Rome; silver
grosso, Pope Sixtus IV (1471–84).
Scotland; silver groat, 1485,
James III, Edinburgh. Contrasting
exercises in coin portraiture
at the two ends of Europe
[enlarged 2.5 : 1]

times and slow to go out in the middle ages. In the fifteenth century
the debasement of Italian coinage was taken to such lengths that the
intrinsic value of the smallest pieces became negligible. Their alloy
was so heavy that in practice people ceased to care about the actual
silver content and the authorities were able to get away with issuing
them at rates well above their true value. The old position was reversed so that each currency had come to be assessed, not on the basic
unit, but on the silver content and official valuation of multiple coins.
It was a logical step from there to leave out the silver from the *moneta
piccola* altogether. For such coins, intrinsic value was irrelevant,
provided that the number issued was limited and that they were
convertible into good money. But this, the principle of fiduciary
coinage, was a sophisticated monetary concept which in the fifteenth
century smacked of financial trickery. It was onerous to guarantee
convertibility for base money when in any given area much of the coin
in circulation was issued by extraneous governments and it was not
easy to limit the size of issues when mints were mostly in the hands of
private farmers. The theory behind fiduciary coinage was still being
debated in the eighteenth century when Jonathan Swift, for example,
was able to play upon public distrust of it in his *Drapier's Letters*
dealing with a proposal to provide a new copper token for Ireland.
Copper coinage was not adopted in France until 1575 nor in England
finally until 1672. However Ferdinand's *cavallo* [figure 164] as the
forerunner of the fiduciary issues which make up by far the greater
part of the world's coinage today, was as important in its way as
the Venetian grosso or the gold genovino.

Copper token coinage was slow to be taken up outside Italy. Portrait coinage on the other hand, pleasing both to the private vanity of
rulers and to the public eye, spread quite quickly. The first instance of
it in a northern kingdom was a groat of James III of Scotland struck
in 1485 [figure 161]. The portrait was not in the Italian style, but it is
unquestionably a likeness related to other known portraits of James.
It is surprising that such a remote kingdom should have been so far
ahead of others in this single respect. In James's reign Scottish coinage

163 Naples; silver carlino,
Ferdinand II (1495–6). Naples
was, with Milan, the most
important, politically and
economically, of the states which
early adopted portrait coinage
[actual size]

164 Naples, copper cavallo,
Ferdinand I (1458–94). The first
successful experiment with
copper coinage in modern
Europe [actual size]

165 Asti; silver testone, Louis, duke of Orleans (1465–98). A forerunner of the portrait coins which Louis struck when he became King Louis XII of France [actual size]

166 France; silver teston, 1514, Louis XII, Rouen. The first French portrait coin influenced by the portrait testoni which Louis issued as duke of Milan and lord of Asti [actual size]

moved away from English influence into the Burgundian orbit. His standard gold piece was the *rider*, copied from Philip the Good's coin, and in billon he first issued the *plack*, whose name and general appearance were also Burgundian. There was nothing, however, in Burgundian or English coinage to inspire the new portrait groat, which appears to have been an isolated northern manifestation of the spirit of humanism. It was without influence, even in Scotland, where there was no more portrait coinage until 1526.

In France, Spain, England and the Empire, where portraiture was adopted later than in Scotland but more permanently, Italian stylistic influence was stronger. As in Italy, the new development was associated with the issue of larger coins. France, self-sufficient as ever, was rather isolated from economic developments elsewhere, but the annexation of Provence greatly strengthened her position in Mediterranean trade. The political adventures of Charles VIII and Louis XII no doubt also resulted in some increase in commerce with Italy. In 1500 Louis seized the duchy of Milan and there continued to issue portrait double ducats and testoni after the manner of the Sforza. By 1514 enough silver was being brought up the Rhône to enable him to order the striking of testons in his own kingdom. They were tariffed initially at ten sous tournois. In appearance they were very like his Milanese testoni, but artistically they were inferior [figure 166]. The teston continued to be issued until 1576 and, with the écu au soleil, a variant of the écu à la couronne first issued by Louis XI in 1475, accounted for all but the small change of the French coinage for most of those years. Paris was usually the busiest mint, but in some years towards the end of the reign of Francis I the output of silver, especially, was higher at Lyons where there was a free market in precious metals to which Italian, German and French traders all resorted. The heavy issues of écus and testons from this mint were one aspect of Francis' policy of making the city a second Antwerp so that he might have a source of finance equal to that of the emperor [figure 177].

Portrait coinage was introduced to England by Henry VII in 1503. There also it was associated with the appearance of a larger coin, the *testoon*, tariffed at one shilling [figure 167]. This new piece met with no more initial success in the face of English monetary conservatism than the groat had done in 1279, but the portrait was at the same time adopted for the existing groat and half-groat, thus becoming an established feature of the English scene. Its nature seems to have been imperfectly understood by the English, since, when Henry VII died, his portrait continued to appear for eighteen years on the coins struck in the name of his successor. Henry himself seems to have been as well aware as any prince of his time of the potential political impact of coinage and apart from the introduction of portraiture and the testoon, he made a number of changes. The most important of his other innovations was the *sovereign* of twenty shillings, the first coin to have the value of a pound sterling. First struck in 1489, the sovereign was

167 England; gold sovereign, 1489, and silver testoon, *c.* 1508, Henry VII, London. A contrast in styles: Burgundian and Italian influence at King Henry's court. The sovereign was the first coin tariffed at one pound sterling and the testoon the first silver shilling [actual size]

copied from the réal d'or issued in the Netherlands two years before by the emperor Maximilian as regent for his son Philip the Handsome [figure 168]. Both coins were issued in economic response to the inflow of Guinea gold into northern Europe, but the sovereign also unquestionably carried political overtones in the design of the king enthroned wearing an arched imperial crown, in the prominent display of the royal arms and a Tudor rose on the reverse [figure 167] and in its very name. When Henry died there was not a single coin in issue which he had not either himself introduced or modified, a point which tends to confirm the old-fashioned historical view that in England the middle ages ended when he came to the throne.

In Spanish history there has never been much doubt that the great turning point was the reign of Ferdinand and Isabella. For coinage the decisive change can be precisely dated to 13 June 1497 when, by the Pragmatic of Medina del Campo, the Catholic Kings abolished all previous monetary systems and instituted a new coinage based upon the *maravedi* as the unit of account. The Pragmatic was essentially a Castilian ordinance. It made rules for the seven mints of Castile providing that every coin issued should bear the mark of the mint and of the assayer who was responsible for its weight and fineness. It

168 Burgundian Netherlands; gold grote reaal, 1487, the Emperor Maximilian I (regent for the Archduke Philip the Handsome), Dordrecht. The Dutch forerunner of the first English sovereign [actual size]

169 Burgundian Netherlands; gold nobel, 1487–8, Archduke Philip the Handsome under the regency of the Emperor Maximilian I, Dordrecht. England, gold ryal, c. 1489, Henry VII, London. Another example of the mutual influence of Burgundian and English coins in the late fifteenth century [actual size]

specified the designs for the most important Castilian coins, namely the silver real of 34 maravedis, its fractions and multiples, and the gold excelente of 375 maravedis. However, its provisions regarding the weight and value of these coins were applied all over Spain. Only Valencia kept its own system until 1707, but that was regarded as an anachronism and downgraded as a provincial coinage. In Barcelona and Aragon all the more valuable coins conformed to the standards laid down by the Pragmatic though their designs and legends were sometimes different from those of Castilian pieces. Thus from 1497 the coinage of Castile became virtually the national coinage of Spain. This in itself was a great advantage, but the new coinage had one more merit; it was not wholly Castilian in its nature. The specification

170 Gold excelente, Seville, and silver real, Burgos, Ferdinand and Isabella (1479–1504). The principal coins in gold and silver issued after Ferdinand and Isabella's far-reaching monetary reform in 1497 [actual size]

of the excelente made it the exact equivalent of two Venetian ducats. The hand of Ferdinand of Aragon with his Mediterranean interests may perhaps be discerned in this stroke of policy which, just before the discoveries in America thrust an important monetary rôle upon Spain, ended her isolation from the older financial centres of Europe.

The Pragmatic of Medina del Campo was one of the best timed monetary reforms ever made. Its authors could scarcely have foreseen the scale of shipments of bullion to Spain in the sixteenth century, yet they set up a mint organisation efficient enough to cope with them and, by providing from the start for the issue of indefinite multiples of the excelente and the real, they met the demand for larger coins which a big influx of precious metals was bound to create. The motley coinage of Spain before 1497 was scarcely adequate for the monetary needs of a group of second-rate medieval kingdoms. The system which replaced it proved good enough to meet the requirements of the whole Spanish Empire for three hundred years.

By tradition the first gold which Ferdinand and Isabella received from America they sent to Pope Alexander VI, who used it to gild the new ceiling of Santa Maria Maggiore. The later shipments found a more practical use. The bullion was received by the *Casa de la contración de las Indias* whence the royal share, consisting of one half of all booty and one eighth of mined metal, was sent directly to the mint. From 1503 the mint was required to coin gold brought by private holders without charging any fee except the bare expenses of minting, so that the metal should pass quickly into circulation. In the early days of the Spanish conquest and exploration, gold was practically the only commodity which was shipped home in commercial quantities. The amounts sent at first were not fabulous, for no major deposits were discovered. In 1516 for example the royal share amounted to only 35,000 ducats, most of that presumably taken from the Indian population. However, what was sent was a net addition to European supplies and that was enough to establish the excelente as an international trading counter of some importance. The decision taken when Isabella died in 1504 to go on striking both gold and silver in the joint names of Ferdinand and Isabella with no change in their designs no doubt helped the coin to achieve that position. The distinctive facing portraits of the Catholic Kings continued in use long after both were dead, their double portrait on what was effectively a double ducat eventually giving the excelente the new name *doubloon* in the international market [figure 170]. The doubloon's heyday was in those posthumous years. The conquest of Mexico in 1519–27 and of Peru in 1532–41 put into Spanish hands the whole stock of gold accumulated by two great civilizations. Still no important new deposits were found, but all that the Aztecs and the Incas had amassed in years of conquest and mining was there for the taking. The amount was enormous and the doubloon with the S mark of the Seville mint became the commonest gold coin in Europe.

171 A famous picture of a
sixteenth-century mint. The
moneyers' trade explained to the
Emperor Maximilian I; a
woodcut from the Weisskunig
by Hans Burgkmair

172 Hungary; silver half-guldiner,
1506, Wladislas II, Kremnitz.
One of the first heavy silver coins
from the Hungarian mining
city of Kremnitz [actual size]

It has been estimated that in the years 1521–30 the ratio of gold
to silver in shipments from America to Spain was 97:3 computed by
weight. This would have upset the monetary balance of Europe even
more than it did in fact if the same years had not seen the full development of central European silver production. The initiative of Sigismund of the Tirol in striking a great silver coin of the value of a
gulden in 1486 was followed by others even before the close of the
fifteenth century. In Hungary Wladislas II issued a similar coin in
1499. Several early guldengroschen were struck in Switzerland. One
of these, issued by the canton of Berne in 1494, seems to have had a
satirical significance, for the canton's ungainly bear was substituted
for the gallant figure of the Hapsburg archduke in a design otherwise
closely related to that of Sigismund's coin [figure 176]. In 1498 a
guldengroschen was issued by Nicholas Schinner, the bishop of Sitten
whose titles included that of count of Valais; Zurich first issued one
in 1512 and Lucerne in 1518. The Swiss coinage at that time showed
a curious combination of German and Italian influence, for the Swiss
were as quick to copy the testone, which in German they called
dicken, meaning the thick coin, as they were to copy the guldengroschen; only, because of their republicanism, they were obliged to

154

173 Saxony; silver klappmützen-thaler, *c.* 1500–10, the Elector Frederick III, with Dukes George and John. An early example of a heavy silver coin from the mining country of Saxony [enlarged 2:1]

substitute a patron saint or a heraldic device for the princely portrait which characterised the testone.

In Germany the first to copy Sigismund was the ruler of another mining area, the elector of Saxony, Frederick the Wise (1486–1525). His was one of the first German portrait coins; in fact it had three portraits for like so many other Saxon coins it was issued by the elector jointly with other members of his family, in this instance his uncle Albert and brother John. William II, landgrave of Hesse, issued a similar large coin in 1502 and Ulrich duke of Wurttemberg in 1509. At St Veit in Carinthia a few years later Maximilian I issued a series of handsome portrait pieces in his capacity as emperor and archduke. Another early guldengroschen was issued by John III, archbishop of Bremen, in 1511 and the first of a long series at Salzburg was issued in the name of Archbishop Leonard von Keutschach who died in 1519. However, none of these issues was plentiful except the Saxon one, which continued after Albert's death in 1500 in the names of Frederick, John and their cousin George [figure 173].

In 1519 Stephen count of Šlik, a Czech nobleman whose family had been granted coining rights in northern Bohemia but had never exercised them, decided to open a mint. The Šliks were lords of Joachimsthal (Jáchymov) on the Bohemian slope of the Erzgebirge and they wanted to exploit its rapidly growing output of silver. Their natural course was to strike big coins like the elector of Saxony; and like Saxony in one more respect Stephen of Šlik brought his brothers in on the issue. In political terms the Šliks were nobodies by comparison with the neighbouring electoral house, but their mine was richer than any in Saxony and by 1519 was probably the most productive in Europe. The Šlik coins [figure 174], of slightly baser alloy than anything which had gone before in that line, were seen in circulation as

174 Joachimsthal (Jáchymov);
silver joachimsthaler or thaler, *c.*
1520, Count Stephen of Šlik,
in the name also of King
Louis of Bohemia. This was issued
in such quantities that the name
thaler became a generic term
for heavy silver coins in central
Europe [actual size]

often as the elector's. They were known from their place of origin as
joachimsthaler. Shortened to *thaler,* the name stuck not only to the
coins of that mint but to all coins of that size emanating from central
Europe, even to those which had been struck before the Joachimsthal
mint came into operation. The thaler was to have a great future, but the
Šliks did not share in it for long, for Ferdinand I took over Joachimsthal in 1528, two years after his accession to the Bohemian throne.
Thenceforward it was a royal mint. The Hapsburg takeover was well
timed for the mine's most productive period was just beginning. In
the next decade its annual output averaged 54,000 marks. In 1533
production is believed to have been over 87,000 marks, which was
more than the combined average of all the mines of Salzburg and the
Tirol. It was no wonder therefore that the name joachimsthaler came
to be applied to a whole class of coinage.

The success of the thaler prompted a great number of the princes
and cities of the Empire to issue similar coins. Among the first were
the counts of Mansfeld in 1521. They, like the Šliks, had mines to
exploit, less spectacular than Joachimsthal but, as it turned out,
longer lived; their distinctive but rather monotonous series of thalers
with the George and dragon device come to an end only with the
extinction of the dynasty in 1780. We may mention also among those
who first issued thalers in the same decade, the elector of Brandenburg
(1521), the bishop of Würzburg (1523) and the imperial city of Lübeck
(1528). Beyond the boundaries of the Empire, Frederick I of Denmark
issued a thaler in 1532 and Gustavus Vasa of Sweden in 1534.

Although the emperors had long since lost control of the German
silver currency, they still in the sixteenth century had jurisdiction in
matters of gold coinage when acting constitutionally through the
imperial diet. The thaler, which had the value of a gold coin but was
made of silver, appeared to offer the German princes a way round the
imperial authority. The emperors for their part claimed that they
were entitled to regulate this new coinage as they did the gold. The
controversy was kept going for more than sixty years. At a series of

175 Holy Roman Empire;
silver thaler, 1522, Frederick the
Wise, younger brother of the
Elector Palatine. A quasi-medallic
thaler struck to commemorate
Frederick's appointment as
stadhalter of the Empire during
the absence of Charles V
[actual size]

176 *(opposite)* Bern; silver
guldengroschen, 1494. County of
Tirol; silver guldengroschen, 1486,
Archduke Sigismund, Hall.
Sigismund's guldengroschen, the
first of all the heavy silver coins
struck in Europe, was soon copied
(and parodied) by the republican
Swiss [actual size]

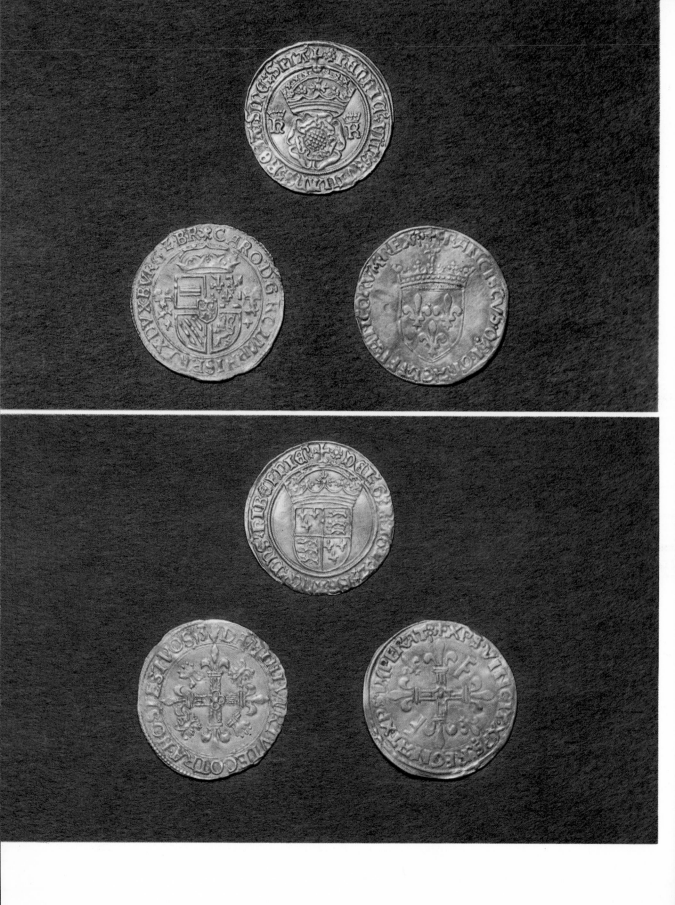

In meiner Müntz schlag ich aericht/
Gute Müntz an kern vnd gewicht/
Gülden/Cron/Taler vnd Batzen/
Mit gutem preg /künstlich zu schatzen/
Halb Batzen/Creutzer vnd Weißpfennig/
Vnd gut alt Thurnis / aller mennig
Zu gut/in recht guter Landewerung/
Dardurch niemand geschickt gferung.
J iij   Der

178 The mint-master; a wood engraving from Hans Sachs *Eygentliche Beschreibung Aller Stände auff Erden*, Frankfurt, 1568

177 *(opposite)* England; gold crown of the double rose, 1526–44, London. Burgundian Netherlands; gold zonnekroon, 1542–55, the Emperor Charles v, Antwerp. France; gold écu à la couronne, 1519–40, Francis I, Lyons. A concert of European coinage, crowns of similar type and value issued from mints at the three chief commercial centres of the age [enlarged 1.5:1]

diets held between 1500 and 1551 the emperors Maximilian and Charles v attempted to impose some order upon the coinage. They prescribed the weight and alloy of the thaler and its current value in terms of kreuzers, then the basic unit of account in some parts of the Empire. On one occasion Charles v prohibited its issue to all except those who were in actual possession of silver mines. However, these edicts were only partially effective. The comprehensive edict of Esslingen (1524), for example, was rejected by Charles's own brother, the future emperor Ferdinand I, who maintained that it could not bind princes of the house of Austria. The mining lobby, of which Saxony was the natural leader, proved too powerful to be browbeaten even in the years after Charles's defeat of the elector John Frederick at the battle of Mühlberg in 1547. The interests of that group lay in minting a rather heavier thaler but one of baser alloy than the imperial diets prescribed. In 1559 Ferdinand I promulgated yet another system based upon a *reichsgulden* valued at 60 kreuzers, but it was only after this was in turn modified by an edict of 1566, which included the Saxon type coin to be known as the *reichsthaler* and valued at 68 kreuzers, that a generally acceptable solution was found.

The truth was that in the political conditions of sixteenth-century Germany it was impossible to bring order out of the monetary chaos. At best the imperial edicts could only standardise the gold and larger silver coins. For in three hundred years the various parts of Germany had evolved not only different coins but different accounting systems, and even modern states find those difficult to change. At the level of small change therefore an enormous variety of coins was permitted to circulate. The trouble was that these smaller coins became virtually foreign currency as soon as they were taken away from their place of origin. To meet this difficulty the monetary authorities within the Empire were formed into geographical groups called circles. There were ten of these in theory, but one, the Burgundian circle which included the Netherlands, went its own way and was only counted for form's sake. The circles were supposed to hold their own meetings every six months to co-ordinate the issues of coinage within their areas and to specify the foreign coins, such as Danish and Swedish thalers, which were permitted to circulate. Essentially they fulfilled the function of the *münzvereinen* of the previous century, but they were more comprehensive and were strengthened by imperial sanction. The system at least ensured that the schilling of Lübeck, to take an example, was good money in say, Hamelin, even though it was still at a discount in Ulm or Regensburg.

In the middle of the sixteenth century the circle principle was extended by arranging the nine effective circles into groups: the Upper and Lower Rhine and Westphalia in one, Upper and Lower Saxony in another, and Franconia, Bavaria, Swabia and sometimes Austria in a third. Prussia and Bohemia took no part in these dispositions. Still less did Hungary, which was not constitutionally part

Der Stadt Regensburg Thaler.

Der Stadt Nürmberg Thaler.

Der Stadt Lübeck Thaler.

Der Stadt Constantz Thaler.

Der Stadt Franckfurt Thaler.

179 A sample of thalers issued by the free imperial cities of Germany in the mid-sixteenth century. A page of woodcuts from a traders' handbook showing all the types of thaler current in the Franconian, Swabian and Bavarian circles

of the Empire. However, that kingdom was claimed by the Hapsburgs after the battle of Mohacs in 1526 and Ferdinand I was at pains to bring the Hungarian coinage into line with his Austrian and Bohemian issues. The first Hungarian thaler was struck at Kremnitz in 1553, a coin of quite remarkable beauty, much more delicate in treatment than the great majority of contemporary German thalers [figure 180]. Unfortunately it was not struck for long, for within a few years the Hungarian mint was made to comply with the Austrian in the design as well as the denomination of the principal coin.

While silver production was in full swing everywhere in eastern Europe, that area made little contribution to the pool of gold which was being so rapidly filled from the west. In the disturbed years after Mohacs mining was much curtailed in Hungary; the Hapsburgs did not control the mining districts of Transylvania. However, for the traditional needs of eastern Europe there was enough Saxon and Silesian gold; enough even for Poland to make its first issue of gold coin. In 1528 Sigismund I, inspired by the monetary theories of the

180 Hungary, silver thaler, 1553, the Emperor Ferdinand I, Kremnitz. The first and most beautiful Hungarian thaler struck by the Hapsburgs [actual size]

181 Danzig; silver dreigroschen, 1539, Sigismund I of Poland. Notable portraiture distinguished Sigismund's reformed coinage for Danzig and for his kingdom of Poland [actual size]

182 Guelders; silver snaphaan, 1509–38, Duke Charles of Egmont. Still medieval in its general aspect, the snaphaan was in content and purpose the first modern coin struck in the Netherlands [actual size]

great Copernicus, swept away the debased coinage of his predecessors and of the Teutonic knights, his vassals in east Prussia, to replace it by a fine coinage in gold and silver. Nevertheless, throughout this period and until well into the following century, the thaler was the really important coin everywhere in central Europe, even for big transactions.

The flood of gold from America and of silver from central Europe greatly increased the prosperity of the Netherlands, especially that of Antwerp. Surprisingly however it was not the Hapsburgs who first introduced a large silver coin to the Netherlands, but Charles of Egmont who in 1492 was proclaimed duke of Guelders in defiance of the pervading dynasty. The *snaphaan*, which he first issued in 1509, was still medieval in appearance, as all Dutch coins were at that date, with its gothic lettering and chivalric design [figure 182], but in weight it was a modern piece comparable with the Italian testone or the Swiss dicken. In spite of its undesirable political background, the snaphaan was highly favoured in the Netherlands. Nor was it Charles's only innovation, for he was also the first Dutch prince to strike an equivalent to the German thaler. For one whose rule was so insecure, he was remarkably forward-looking in his monetary policy.

The silver coinage of Philip the Handsome who ruled the Burgundian Netherlands at the turn of the century differed little from that of his grandfather Charles the Bold. His gold coinage also was essentially conservative. The *réal d'or* struck in 1494 during his minority has already been noticed in connexion with the English sovereign [figure 168]. It was copied in Denmark as well as England, but it seems to have been regarded as something of a sport in its country of origin. The great real of Austria, *den grooten Reaal van Oostrijc*, the Dutch called it, as if it did not really belong to them at all but was just one more of the regent Maximilian's grand ideas. Philip's gold coinage as finally arranged consisted of the gulden and its double, the *gouden vlies*. The gulden of this reign was called *philippusgulden* after the duke's name saint, who took the place which Saint Andrew had occupied on Charles the Bold's similar coin. It was not by any means the only coin of that denomination to circulate in the Netherlands at that

183 A placard issued in 1499 by the Archduke Philip the Handsome to inform his subjects which foreign coins might circulate in the Netherlands and at what rate. This is the earliest surviving placard with illustrations. These are mostly of Rhenish gulden: of the many similar coins, only those illustrated were allowed currency

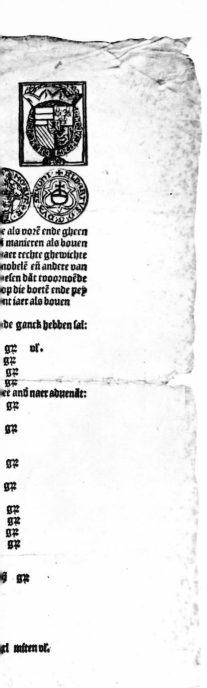

184 Burgundian Netherlands;
silver karolusgulden 1542–8,
the Emperor Charles v, Antwerp.
The first thaler-sized coin struck
at Antwerp, the financial
centre of Europe in the mid-
sixteenth century [actual size]

time. German, English, French, Italian and later Spanish and Portuguese pieces were allowed to circulate at an approved rate, and
German gulden were among the most plentiful. These were a great
problem, however, for, though homogeneous in appearance, they
varied in fineness. The moneychangers' handbills, of which the earliest
one surviving dates from Philip's reign, had to specify in great detail
the good Rhenish gulden which alone were permitted currency in the
Netherlands [figure 183].

It was during the reign of Charles v that the great influx of precious
metals from the New World and from central Europe began to tell on
the Netherlands. For the first time the coinage of the area took on a
modern aspect. Its evolution during Charles's long reign provides an
interesting commentary on his widespread political and economic
interests. To accommodate his coinage to the accounting systems of
Flanders and Brabant was merely the first of his problems, inherited
from the dukes of Burgundy, his predecessors. In a country where so
much foreign coin circulated, a great deal of it issued in his own name
or from his own mints, it was convenient also that his coins should
correspond to those of the Netherlands' chief trading partners.
Finally, he could not, as emperor, utterly ignore the fact that in some
quarters his Netherlands coinage was regarded as that of the Burgundian circle of the Holy Roman Empire. Following belatedly in the
steps of Charles of Egmont, Charles v introduced a thick silver coin,
the *vlieger* of four stuivers, in 1536 and a silver equivalent of the gulden, the so called *karolusgulden*, a handsome portrait coin, in 1540
[figure 184]. He was the first ruler to issue copper coinage in northern
Europe. He was of course already striking such coins for his kingdom
of Naples and in 1543 he transplanted the idea to the Netherlands to
issue the copper *korte*, worth three mites of Brabant or two of Flanders, thenceforward the lowest value coin in circulation. In gold
Charles issued four coins: the gulden, the real with the fractional half-
real and the kroon. Each had its separate function. The gulden was
the traditional Dutch coin corresponding to the similar Rhenish pieces
and suitable for trade with the Empire. The real, though much smaller than Maximilian's great real of 1487, was still quite a substantial
coin of the sort required now that American gold was reaching the
Netherlands in quantity; it was worth three gulden. The kroon was
especially designed both in weight and type to circulate beside the écu
in trade with France [figure 177].

France during the first half of the sixteenth century was rather
isolated from economic developments elsewhere. Its commercial links
with Spain were slight and the financial currents which met at Antwerp
flowed round France not through it. Little Spanish gold therefore
found its way there and the money supply increased relatively
slowly. Prices were comparatively steady throughout the reign of
Francis i and the current value of the coins in issue remained, by
French standards, remarkably stable. The écu au soleil, valued at

Lon doibt auoir Vng bon Architecteur/
Diuiseur et ouurier quant on baftist Vne
cite. Tiltre premier.

185 A woodcut showing moneyers
at work in Paris and, possibly,
the Cour des Monnaies in
session. This was the public
body which exercised general
jurisdiction in coinage matters in
France. From *De l'institution
et administration de la chose
publique*, by François Patricius,
1520

186 Tournai, besieged by the
Emperor Charles v in 1521,
silver six gros, Francis I. One of the
earliest known siege coins
such as were later commonly
issued in the wars of the
late sixteenth and seventeenth
centuries [actual size]

36¾ sous tournois in 1515, was still only tariffed at 45 sous tournois
when Francis died in 1547. During the same period the teston rose only
from 10 to 11 sous tournois. There was a reduction in the weight and
fineness of the écu in 1519 and in the fineness of the teston in 1521. If
allowance is made for that, the depreciation of the currency in terms
of gold was about 28 per cent and in terms of silver only about 11 per
cent during more than thirty years of intermittent warfare.

Though Francis's reign brought few alterations in the type or value
of the coins issued, there were important changes in mint organisation. It became a general rule for all coins to be marked not only with
the mint mark but also with the personal mark of the mint-master
who was responsible for their weight and fineness. A regulation to
similar effect was made in Spain in 1497, but the practice seems to
have developed independently in France, where such marks had been
used with increasing frequency since the reign of Louis XI. In 1540
Francis abandoned the old system of indicating mints by a code of
numbered letters. He replaced it by a simpler system of code letters:
A for Paris, B for Rouen, and so on. The mint letter system was one
of the few ordinances of the ancien régime to survive the revolution
of 1789; it lasted until 1870, for almost as long in fact as there was
more than one mint in France. In 1546 there were twenty-seven mints
in operation, not including Turin. That rather overstates the position,
for some were only active in striking small change. More than three
quarters of the gold and the silver testons issued in the years 1540–7
were struck by four mints only, Paris, Rouen, Lyons and Toulouse.
Nevertheless, in spite of this and although the whole mint administration was subject to the Cour des Monnaies at Paris, there was
still a certain quaint provincialism about much of Francis's coinage.
In two provinces only recently united to the kingdom, Brittany and
Dauphiné, the coins were of a quite distinctive type from those of the
rest of France [figure 187], as they had been since the days of Louis XI
and Charles VIII. Dies were locally made and sometimes of poor workmanship. Francis's features, curious at the best of times, were positive-
ly grotesque as portrayed at some mints. In 1547 his successor
Henry II remedied this by appointing a *tailleur général* to supervise
the making of the punches for the king's portrait at Paris for distribution to the provinces. He also strengthened the central administration
by promoting the Cour des Monnaies to the rank of a sovereign court.

England, like France, lay rather outside the mainstream of monetary development in Europe in the early years of the sixteenth
century. The reign of Henry VIII was not until its closing years a
particularly eventful one so far as coinage was concerned. Henry
inherited a well filled treasury and a healthy national economy from
his father and for seventeen years he left the coinage virtually unchanged, not even replacing his father's portrait, as we have seen. In
1526 there was a recoinage. The weight of the silver coinage was
slightly reduced and a new gold coin of 22 carats as compared with the

187 France; silver teston du Dauphiné, 1526–9, Francis I, Romans (mint-master Pierre Carme). An example of provincial separatism persisting in French coinage well into the sixteenth century [actual size]

188 England; silver groat, 1526–30, Henry VIII, York. One of the last English coins from an ecclesiastical mint: the cardinal's hat below the royal arms is the badge of the archbishop, Thomas Wolsey, whose initials are on either side of the shield [actual size]

old English standard of 23¾ carats was introduced. The opportunity was taken to put the king's own portrait on the silver, but this was soon out of date again, for Henry grew a beard the following year. The 1526 recoinage was not a serious debasement but an adjustment to the fact that, with the rise in prices in Europe, the English coinage, especially the gold, had become seriously undervalued. English angels and sovereigns were being exported and for current use the people were taking to using the French écu which was realistically valued at 4s. 4d. sterling. The new gold coin was intended to undercut the French piece in the home market. It looked like an écu with the main feature of its design the royal arms surmounted by a crown [figure 177], and its intrinsic value and fineness were approximate to that of the écu; but it was tariffed at 5s. sterling, which gave it the edge over the French coin in circulation. It was called the *crown*, the name given to the *écu à la couronne* in the countries of northern Europe. In its original form it did not, as it turned out, play a particularly important part in English monetary history, but the name crown became associated with the value of five shillings, and so was given to the large silver five shilling pieces which were issued in the next reign.

Henry's coinage of 1526 was the last in which the ecclesiastical mints played an active part. Since the tenth century all English coinage had been issued in the king's name, but certain prelates had retained the right to administer and take the profit from mints of their own. Successive kings, regarding these mints with a jealous eye, had gradually reduced their number. By the fifteenth century only the archbishops of Canterbury and York and the bishops of Durham were left with minting rights. They were restricted to the issue of the smaller and less profitable coins, typically half-groats and pennies, but of those, in the years after 1464 when Edward IV reduced the weight of the coinage, they produced the greater part of the national supply. These were marked with the initials and sometimes the personal badge of the prelate who issued them. Cardinal Wolsey with characteristic ostentation struck a groat at York bearing a cardinal's hat and his initials TW [figure 188]; this caused no trouble at the time, but for him to issue so large a coin was *ultra vires* and it was remembered against him when the indictment was drawn up after his fall. The last archbishop of Canterbury whose initials appeared on coins was, suitably enough, Thomas Cranmer, for with the English reformation and the passing of the Act of Supremacy these mints were suppressed.

By 1543 Henry's treasury was almost exhausted by foreign war and domestic extravagance. The great increase in the European money supply was pushing prices up everywhere, but not much of this money was coming the way of the English government. For a few years the king kept going by pillaging the Church. When that source was drained he turned to debasement of the coinage. His first step was to lay hands on all the silver that he could by paying slightly over the market rate for it. He then minted it at a profit by reducing the silver content of his pieces from the old English standard of 11 ozs. 2 dwt. in the pound troy to 9 oz. For this purpose he introduced an entirely new coinage with his bearded full face portrait; the issue consisted mostly of groats and testoons, the latter tariffed at a shilling like those in which Henry VII had issued tentatively in 1503. A debasement of this order, though unprecedented in England, was common form in Europe and even the kings of England, Henry VIII included, were accustomed to practise it on their Irish subjects. Its effects were therefore not sensational. The merchants of Antwerp were wise to it at once and adjusted the exchange rates accordingly, but England did not live on imports and in the home market prices were slow to rise. The chief practical disadvantage of the operation was that the gold coins were not debased in the same proportion as the silver and therefore, since it was forbidden to pay or ask a premium for them, they went out of circulation.

It took about three years for Henry's devaluation of 1542 to work through to prices. Eventually the sterling price of silver was up to a level at which it was no longer profitable to take it to the mint and Henry began to run short again. He therefore decided to repeat the operation, and in 1545 he reduced the fineness of the silver coins from 9 oz. to 6 oz. and raised his offer for the metal. Once again the trick worked, but economic processes of this kind gather their own momentum and get out of hand. This time it was only two years before the ensuing inflation caught up with the government. In 1547 Henry was impelled to raise his bid again and to reduce the standard of his coinage still further to 4 oz. Then he died.

For some two years the government under the regency of the duke of Somerset made no attempt to clear up the mess. Timidly it continued to issue coins of the 4 oz. standard, most of them in the name of the old king so that he should bear the odium of it. In 1549 an issue of shillings in the name of Edward VI was made, of improved standard but reduced weight; this was a futile gesture which simply muddled the public still further. In 1551, by which time the duke of Northumberland was regent, a reform was resolved upon. By yet one more debasement of the silver to 3 oz. fine the Council obtained enough of the metal to contemplate the issue of a coinage of almost the old English standard. A new coinage was struck of silver 11 oz. fine; it included silver crowns [figure 190] and half-crowns as earnest that the silver in this coinage was as good as gold. The lower denominations were marked with their value in order to inspire confidence and to avoid disputes. Debased testoons of whatever fineness were called down to 6d. at which price the mint undertook to exchange them for the new coins. However the new scheme did not quite work. Debased coins were brought to the mint surely enough, for there was more silver in a new sixpence than in an old testoon, but the price of silver was so high that it was tempting to hoard or to melt down the new money. Consequently base coin still predominated in circulation and

189 England; base silver testoon, 1549, Edward VI, Southwark. A much devalued coin, issued at one shilling and called down in 1551 to 6d. and in 1558 to 4½d., when, by Queen Elizabeth's order, it was countermarked with the portcullis [enlarged 2:1]

this state of affairs persisted right through the reign of Mary (1553–8) who was too honest to issue anything except coin of good quality, but too preoccupied with other matters to take any effective measures to remedy the evil which she had inherited.

It was not until Elizabeth I had been more than two years on the throne and William Cecil was secretary of state, who was one of the moving spirits behind the attempted reform of 1551, that the nettle was firmly grasped. In 1560 a careful assessment was made of the coins in circulation. Testoons of the better sort were then called down from 6 d. to $4\frac{1}{2}$ d. and the baser ones from 6 d. to $2\frac{1}{2}$ d. The two classes were distinguished by countermarks [figure 189]. The queen undertook to exchange all base coins at the proclaimed rate for coins of good silver during a period of about six months; after which the base coins were to be no longer current. The price of silver having fallen since 1551, there was no more temptation to melt the old testoons or to hoard the new pieces. From the administrative point of view the operation went through smoothly and the queen made a profit of about £50,000, which must have delighted her. The social effects of the recoinage are not so clear. Its deflationary impact was softened by the increase in the supply of silver which was taking place at the time, and there was no general fall in prices. The recoinage certainly made the transaction of the nation's business more straightforward. On the other hand the proclamation of 1560 calling down the value of the coins in circulation must have caused real hardship to some and it may have been a contributory cause of the poverty which became a national problem in Elizabeth's reign. By European standards Henry VIII's depreciation of the currency was not abnormal. In England however the debasement and its aftermath left a deep impression and a strong determination that it should not be repeated.

190 England; silver crown, 1551, Edward VI, London. The first English coin of thaler size, issued as a pledge of reform of the currency after the debasement started by Henry VIII [enlarged 2:1]

8 The Great Inflation

192 Spain; gold double escudo or pistole, Philip II (1555–98), Seville. The characteristic twenty-two carat gold coin of the second half of the sixteenth century [actual size]

For an understanding of the monetary developments of the mid-sixteenth century it is necessary to consider again the position in Spain and America. The first gush of gold from the New World lost much of its force in the 1530s. Valuable shipments of gold were still often made, but the quantities were no longer so large that the Spaniards could afford to ignore the silver. By 1536 the authorities were concerned that more gold coin was going out of Spain than was coming in. In the changed conditions the pure gold excelente was probably undervalued. Charles v stopped issuing it in that year and replaced it by a 22 carat coin after the new fashion. This was called the *escudo*. Its design was a shield of arms, and like Henry VIII's gold crown it was closely related in type and name to the French écu which it was intended to undercut. It was not a large coin and thirty years later Philip II started to issue multiples of it, the double, commonly called the *pistole*, and the quadruple escudo. Before the end of the century the pistole had supplanted the escudo as the gold coin in commonest use, especially in international transactions. The introduction of the escudo was not quite the end of the old doubloon. This remained a popular coin in the Netherlands and, like the English rose noble whose issue in its native land had been discontinued for much longer, it was commonly imitated there until the end of the century. The facing portraits, its characteristic feature, set the fashion for the coinages of the married heiresses of the 1550s, Mary Tudor, Mary Queen of Scots and Joan of Navarre.

When Charles v altered his Spanish gold coinage in 1536 he was under no pressure to make substantial changes in the silver. Of that metal he had plenty, for by that time it was being mined in Mexico, whence fabulous quantities were shipped to Seville. It passed, as gold did, through the *Casa de la Contratación* to the mint. All that Charles did then with the silver coinage was to bring it up to date by putting his own name on it, with that of his mother, Joanna the Mad, who was still queen of Castile. He continued to issue the real and the pieces of two and four reals. For some reason he suspended the piece of eight reals, a coin the size of a thaler which had been issued at some stage during the currency of Ferdinand and Isabella's coinage. It is not clear why he did so just when silver was beginning to come in so

191 *(opposite)* Florence; silver scudo, Duke Cosimo I de' Medici (1536–74). Too beautiful and scarcely intended for use, a quasi-medallic piece from dies by Domenico Poggini [enlarged 3:1]

193 New Spain; silver four reals, *c.* 1570, Philip II in the name of the Emperor Charles V and Queen Joanna, Mexico. An early coin from the first mint established in America [actual size]

freely. Philip II was to take up the issue of this coin again to some consequence.

At about the same time as Charles V was modifying the Spanish coinage there was an important development in the Spanish empire overseas. Quite a big Spanish population was settled in New Spain (Mexico) within a few years of the conquest. These people required a means of exchange. It was absurd to ship metal to Seville for minting and then back to the colony, and it was dangerous for them to use bullion, which was contraband until tax had been paid on it. The obvious solution to this problem was to set up a mint locally and representations to that effect were made as early as 1528. However, transatlantic consultation over matters of that sort took many years and it was not until 1535 that royal authorisation was forthcoming. The mint, housed in the palace of Hernando Cortes in Mexico City, came into operation in the following year. This was the first mint in America; it was authorised to strike silver and copper coins, but not gold. The copper coinage did not get very far because the native population would have nothing to do with it, so effectively the mint issued silver coins only. These were of the same denomination as those of metropolitan Spain except that in the early days a piece of three reals was issued. The designs, which were prescribed by the royal letter of authorisation, were essentially the same as for the new Spanish silver coins in the names of Charles and Joanna. The rule of Ferdinand and Isabella, that every coin must bear the mark of both the mint and the assayer responsible for it, was applied to Mexico as if it were one more of the provincial mints of Spain. The assayer was strictly enjoined to accept no bullion for coining which was not marked by the king's officers as tax paid.

The coinage of Mexico in the names of Charles and Joanna continued until 1572, by which time Philip II had been king of Spain for seventeen years. Since the amount issued increased steadily, most of the pieces must actually have been struck in Philip's reign [figure 193]. Given the amount of silver available, it was not a heavy coinage, since unlike most later Spanish American issues, it was made primarily for local use and not for convenient accounting in making shipments of silver to Spain. That came later.

In 1545 silver was discovered at Potosí in the viceroyalty of Peru [figure 194]. It was the biggest silver deposit ever found up to that time, and in spite of its inaccessibility it was quickly developed. This inaccessibility is the clue to the sort of coinage that was struck there when Philip II made Potosí a mint in 1575. For, though in its heyday it was a fine baroque city of more than 100,000 inhabitants, it was always economically a shanty town. The surrounding country was almost uninhabited. The whole viceroyalty of Peru had a much smaller European population than New Spain, and the output of the mint at Lima, established in 1565, was more than enough for local needs. The only reason for having a mint at Potosí therefore was that it had

194 The Cerro Rico, the silver mountain of Potosí, seen from the city with the roofs of the Casa de Moneda, the mint building in the foreground

195 A patio of King Philip's Casa de Moneda at Potosí

been found administratively more convenient to get the silver away as coin than as bullion. Its establishment signals a change in Spanish policy. From about that time the much increased output of the American mints, including Mexico, seems to have been devoted primarily to filling the Spanish plate fleets. The issues were made up chiefly of pieces of eight reals, a big denomination suitable for bulk transport. They were villainously struck, evidently by unskilled Indian labour working under great pressure [figure 196]. It is open to doubt how far they were intended for ordinary circulation. In theory they were good currency in Spain where the coinage was of exactly the same type, though of better manufacture. In practice, however, so much was pre-empted by the bankers of Antwerp, Augsburg and Milan, the paymasters of Philip's armies, who would have it all recoined, that not much of any shipment found its way into circulation. An increasing amount, however, stayed in America as the European population multiplied. In due course also the rough piece of eight followed the trade route westwards from Acapulco to Manila and so became the regular currency of merchants in the Pacific.

The influx of American silver, following hard upon that of gold, had a profound effect upon the European economy. Spain came near to suffering the fate of Midas. Prices began to rise in Andalusia right at the beginning of the century, and, as the inflation spread through the other provinces, Spanish industry priced itself out of the European market. The certainty of vast annual shipments of revenue had a most pernicious effect upon the Spanish crown. Both Charles v and Philip ii were encouraged to overspend wildly on war and grandiose diplomatic projects, for neither found any shortage of lenders on the security of the next Spanish plate fleet. A perceptive Venetian called Vendramin, who visited Spain in 1556, described the gold and silver as flowing out of the country like water off a roof. The government became obsessed about the export of bullion. In 1536 Charles v reduced the fineness of the gold coinage expressly to prevent it, but he never reduced his own foreign expenditure, which was the most unproductive of all. Contemporaries were at a loss to explain how a country could be at once so rich and so poor. In 1558 Francisco Lopez de Gomara demonstrated the causal connexion between the increase in the supply of gold and silver and the rise in prices. His was the first practical formulation of the quantity theory of money, but he propounded no remedy for Spain's economic problems. The sixteenth century produced no Adam Smith and it was not in keeping with their national temperament that the Spaniards should come upon the true source of national wealth in the light of practical experience, like the Dutch.

The Low Countries were the area which chiefly benefited from Spain's adverse balance of payments. They lent the king money and supplied his army. The war with France which ended with the treaty of Cateau Cambrésis in 1559 was fought from bases there. The army was not withdrawn after the treaty and within a few years it was reinforced to deal with the local unrest which developed into the full scale Dutch war of independence. It is not surprising therefore that during the early years of Philip II's reign the coinage of the Netherlands in gold and silver was very plentiful. For gold Antwerp was, after Seville, the most prolific mint in Europe, but with this difference, that the escudos of Seville were common in Antwerp, whereas the gold reals of Brabant rarely turned up in Andalusia. For silver Antwerp was without a rival, for it still had access to supplies from central Europe as well as America. It so dominated the Netherlands economy in those years that it is easy to overlook the other mints: there were in fact six, one more in Brabant and one in each major province. Dordrecht in Holland and Nijmegen in Guelders were especially active.

Philip's gold coinage in the Netherlands, like that of his father, consisted of reals, crowns and florins, but the florin faded out as its functions were taken over by silver coins, and the crown was always a specialised piece. The bulk of the coinage was therefore made up of reals and half-reals. The important developments took place in the silver, which assumed more monetary duties as it became more plentiful. Philip replaced the karolusgulden by an even larger coin, tariffed at 35 stuivers, the *philippusdaalder* [figure 196]. This, as its name implied, was the counterpart of the German thaler. The new silver coinage was based upon it, the other pieces being quoted as fractions of it, namely one half, one fifth and one tenth. Like the thaler, it took over the functions of the smaller gold coins; it was of the same value as the gold half-real. However the florin-sized coin was missed, and in

196 Spanish viceroyalty of Peru; silver eight reals, Philip II (1555–98) Potosí. Spanish Netherlands; silver philippusdaalder, 1557, Philip II Antwerp. The two ancestors of the dollar; the piece of eight, the characteristic coin of the Spanish plate fleets and trade in the Americas and the Pacific, and its European counterpart from which the piece of eight took a new name [actual size]

1567 it was found convenient to supplement the philippusdaalder by a slightly lighter piece, which became known as the *Burgundian rijks-daalder*. This was intended to do duty for the gold florin and to be the Dutch counterpart of the emperor Ferdinand's reichsgulden of 60 kreuzers. It was distinguished from the philippusdaalder by having no portrait. It was never such a popular coin as the other.

The philippusdaalder was the ideal coin for a wealthy trading community in which gold had become relatively dear but silver was plentiful. It also turned out to be an important piece in the history of the world's currencies, for in the philippusdaalder the silver of the old world and the new was mixed and the German thaler and the Spanish piece of eight found parity. The word daalder, transliterated into Spanish *dollaro*, was transferred to the piece of eight, and thus became the name of the currency of the Americas and the Pacific.

The traditional route for the transfer of funds from Spain to the Netherlands was by the Bay of Biscay and the English Channel. The safety of this route depended upon Spain staying on friendly terms with England, which it did until 1567, when English sympathy for the rebellious Dutch caused a diplomatic breach between the two countries. At the same time the situation in the Netherlands made it more necessary than ever for Philip II to send money there. He was therefore obliged to look about for another route. He could not rely upon receiving regular safe conduct from the king of France for convoys across the shortest overland route. His best alternative therefore was by way of Italy and Germany, which gave him the incidental benefit of the services of the Genoese and Milanese bankers.

This change greatly stimulated the Italian economy. Since the turn of the century Italy had drifted into a financial backwater. The signs of stagnation can be seen in the Italian coinage. The Italian states lacked the resources and the inducement to strike the larger coins which were being issued in Germany, Spain and the Netherlands. Venice still clung to her ducat. It was in this form that much of the gold which came into Europe by way of Seville finally departed again, for the ducat lost none of its old prestige in the Levant. However, the Levant trade, though undiminished in volume, was relatively less important to the European economy than it had been before the

197 Ferrara; silver testone, 1534, Duke Ercole II d'Este. A commemorative piece in the style of the High Renaissance [actual size]

198 Florence; silver testone, Duke Alessandro de' Medici (1533–5), from dies by Benvenuto Cellini. Not since ancient times had such famous artists been prepared to work for the mint as those who engraved dies for the cultivated Italian courts of the 1530s [actual size]

oceanic routes were opened and the ducat, though more plentiful than ever, also declined in relative importance. Significantly it changed its name at this juncture. During a period of stability late in the fifteenth century it had become a money of account at the fixed rate of 124 Venetian soldi. When the price of gold resumed its upwards course, the value of the ducat of account diverged from that of the coin, which to avoid confusion, came to be called the *zecchino* or *sequin*, meaning the little piece from the mint *(zecca)*.

The largest silver piece normally struck in Italy was still the testone, as it had been in the later years of the fifteenth century. In about 1536 Frederick II, duke of Mantua, struck a bigger piece, a *scudo d'argento*, the silver equivalent of the gold scudo, but only one of these exceptionally beautiful coins has survived and we may assume that it was quasi-medallic, an artistic rather than an economic initiative. The same was probably also true of the silver *ducatone* which Charles V issued at Milan in 1551.

In artistic quality Italian coinage retained its pre-eminence. The dukes of Ferrara and Mantua maintained the high standards set by Borso d'Este and Ludovico Gonzaga [figure 197]. The Italian princes could still call upon the best engravers in Europe. In 1529 Clement VII appointed Benvenuto Cellini *maestro delle stampe* at the papal mint. Six years later Benvenuto moved to Florence where, under the patronage of Alessandro de' Medici, he engraved the dies for the first Florentine portrait coinage [figure 198]. At Milan Charles V employed Benvenuto's rival, Leone Leoni, an artist who in this specialised field is thought by many to have excelled his more famous contemporary. It was Leone who engraved the dies for the ducatone of 1551. Never before, except perhaps in fifth century Syracuse, had such eminent artists been content to work in this field. 'Your Holiness may boast a coinage more perfect than that of the ancients', declared the pope's secretary when Benvenuto produced his dies for the approval of Clement VII. He was right: more perfect was just the word, but the freshness of vision which characterised the portrait coinage of the late fifteenth century had given way to a more conscious imitation of the antique. The resulting coinage was somewhat mannered, suitable only as long as it was not wanted in great quantity. A comparison of the testone which Leone Leoni struck at Milan for Charles V [figure 199] with a karolusgulden from the Netherlands [figure 184] contrasts not

199 *(opposite)* Milan; silver testone, the Emperor Charles V (1535–56), from dies by Leone Leoni. A fine coin by the great rival of Benvenuto Cellini; the reverse is adapted from a sestertius of the Emperor Caligula (37–41) [enlarged 3.5:1]

201 Milan; silver ducatone, 1608, Philip III of Spain. More and bigger coins, but poorer workmanship were an index of north Italy's renewed prosperity, when Milan and Genoa became the scene of the Spanish crown's financial operations [actual size]

200 *(opposite)* Scotland; gold twenty pounds, 1576, James VI, Edinburgh. James's reign saw a long succession of coinage experiments, and some remarkably beautiful coins [enlarged 2.5:1]

202 Savoy; silver ducatone, 1588, Duke Charles Emmanuel I, Turin. An early experiment in baroque coin design [actual size]

only beauty with plainness but also a coin made for enjoyment and prestige with one made for heavy commercial use. When therefore after 1567 Spanish silver was diverted through Italy, the increase in the volume of Italian coinage was accompanied by a deterioration in its artistic quality. The scudi and ducatoni which were then struck in abundance at Milan and Genoa were warriors for the working day [figure 201], fit to rank with pieces of eight and philippusdaalders.

That was not quite the end of the tradition of beautiful coinage. It survived in cities of lesser commercial importance and even in quite big ones, as long as they were remote from Spanish influence. At Florence, for example, the first scudo d'argento of Duke Cosimo was most elegantly engraved by Domenico Poggini [figure 191]. At Piacenza and Turin the large flan of the new pieces was regarded as a priceless opportunity for experiment in the new baroque style [figure 202]. Nevertheless it was not these but the rough pieces of Milan and Genoa which brought in the Indian summer of Italian prosperity.

The increase in the supply of precious metals was everywhere followed by a deterioration in the quality of the work turned out by the mints. The busiest mints were the worst. Potosí and Mexico, employing Indian labour and shipping most of their production to Europe as if it were bullion, were special cases, but in fact Seville was not much better, and Antwerp, Genoa and London were all poor. The best made coins of the late sixteenth century were struck either at the lesser Italian cities which have just been mentioned, or at outlying mints such as Edinburgh and Danzig [figures 200 & 203]. If the deficiency of the busier mints had been merely artistic, it might long have gone uncorrected, but it was more than that. Badly struck coins were easily clipped or forged, and clipping and counterfeiting led to the depreciation of whole currencies, since by the operation of Gresham's law the bad pieces drove the good out of circulation. It therefore became a matter of prime public importance to find a remedy. This was to be found in the invention and use of coin-making machinery.

In the fields of metallurgy and engineering the Germans, with their long experience of mining, were technologically far in advance of the rest of Europe. It seems probable that for some years before 1550 German engineers had been experimenting with machinery for rolling

203 Scotland; silver testoon, 1562, Mary, Edinburgh. Fine workmanship and strong French influence (cf. figure 205) characterise the Scots coinage during the queen's first widowhood [actual size]

bullion out to a required thickness, for cutting blanks out of the rolled metal and then for stamping the blanks, without recourse to the clumsy process of holding two dies in one hand and a hammer in the other. The principle of such machinery is simple enough. What is difficult is to make a rolling mill that will not leave lumps, a cutter that will not blunt and a press which is reasonably quick to operate and will not crack the dies. In 1550 Charles de Marillac, the French ambassador in Augsburg, heard that an engineer in the city had perfected such an invention.

Although the episode which followed Marillac's information is well documented, an air of mystery still surrounds it. Marillac was anxious that his government should have sole rights in the new machinery. He was therefore at pains to keep the negotiations secret and to complete them quickly before any other governments, particularly that of Charles v, got wind of the invention. In all the correspondence therefore the inventor's real name was never mentioned. His code name was 'le chevalier de St Sepulchre'. He would not leave Augsburg to supervise the erection of his machinery in France. If he had, we might have known who he was. As it is, he has never been identified, though the theory is widely held that he was an Augsburg engineer called Marx Schwab.

Marillac, having determined to obtain the new invention for France, managed to get support for his scheme from the constable, Anne de Montmorency, who was then the councillor who stood highest in the king's favour. The constable sent a delegation to Augsburg, consisting of two men, Guillaume de Marillac, the ambassador's brother, who held the financial offices of *contrôleur général* and *intendant*, and François Guilhem, master of the mint at Lyons. These two were commissioned to offer the 'chevalier' three or four thousand écus if the machinery appeared to be satisfactory. There followed a series of experiments in the ambassador's lodgings. The mint-master made difficulties, and called for modifications. He was opposed to the whole operation, as nearly all members of his profession were when they were faced with it, for it threatened their livelihood. However, Marillac's enthusiasm was not to be thwarted. The mint-master was sent home and the constable was asked to replace him by someone who understood engineering. A distinguished engineer called Aubin Olivier [figure 204] was sent at once, but meanwhile the ambassador felt obliged to complete the prelimary negotiations in a hurry, for he heard that Charles v was sending a mint-master from Spain to examine the new process. The engineer's journey was by no means wasted however, for, since the 'chevalier' would not travel to France, Olivier was to learn from him how to assemble and work the machine. He learned quickly, for within six months of the start of the whole negotiation the ambassador was able to report: 'Nos instrumens a faire monnoye advance fort et desja, Monseigneur, votre serrurier (Aubin Olivier) avecques l'aide de deux ouvriers qu'on lui a baillez a parachevé celluy

qui coupe en rond par lequel il appert occulairement qu'ung homme, voire un garçon de quinze ans, coupera plus de monnoye en ung jour et en la perfection que cinquante ne pourroit arrondir.'[1]

When Aubin Olivier had fully mastered the new invention, the travellers returned to France. They were well rewarded. By letters patent dated 27th March 1551 Henry II appointed Guillaume de Marillac superintendent and Aubin Olivier chief engineer of a mechanised mint to be set up in Paris. A man called Claude Rouget was appointed master of the mint. Water power to drive the rolling mills was the chief physical requirement of the new establishment, which was therefore situated near the river at the tip of the Ile du Palais. This was where the palace baths *(étuves)* stood. They had fallen out of use because of the changing manners of the age, but gave their name to the mint, which came to be known as the Moulin des Etuves. For the first year it struck only trial pieces, but in 1552 it came into regular production. Its years of heaviest activity were 1553 and 1554. By then Claude Rouget had been succeeded by a mint-master from Troyes called Etienne Bergeron, who was responsible also for setting up coining machinery in the mint of his home town.

The Moulin des Etuves was authorised to strike coins in both gold and silver. Although it was looked upon with hostility by the moneyers' guild, artists such as Marc Béchot, the *tailleur général*, were anxious to do their best for it. The new pieces fully justified the enthusiasm of Charles de Marillac and the pioneers of the new process. They were always well struck and perfectly round [figure 210]. Their style, like that of contemporary Italian coins, was rather self-consciously derived from antique models, but the lettering was the best ever done on coins and they were certainly among the most elegant pieces struck during the sixteenth century.

However, the excellence of the coins was not in itself enough to save the new mint in the face of the entrenched opposition of the moneyers' profession. It would appear that Guillaume de Marillac had a difficult personality and laid himself open to charges of maladministration. There were also genuine difficulties: the costs of the enterprise turned out to be heavier than expected. After 1554 the output of the Moulin des Etuves fell off sharply and for the rest of the reign it remained low. In 1559 Etienne Bergeron left to take up service with the queen of Navarre. In 1563 the Cour des Monnaies was induced by the opposition to restrict the Moulin des Etuves to the striking of medals and presentation pieces. For some years it struck no more coins of the realm, though as late as 1573 it was employed

204 Aubin Olivier, the engineer who brought the mechanical minting process to Paris and there supervised its first practical operations. An engraving dated 1581 in the Bibliothèque Nationale, Paris

---

[1] Our coin-making machinery is coming on well and already, my lord, your engineer, with the aid of two workmen who have been seconded to him, has completed the cutting machine; by which, one can see for oneself, that one man, even a boy of fifteen, will cut out more coins in a day, and more perfectly, than fifty men otherwise could

205 France; silver teston, 1562, Charles IX, Orléans (mint-master Etienne Bergeron). A coin of regular appearance but irregular in fact. The Orléans mint was set up by the Huguenots during the first war of religion and was never authorised by the king [actual size]

by Henry of Navarre to strike coins in his name for the lordship of Béarn. It got no support from Charles IX as he grew up. He had a forge of his own and fancied himself sometimes as a moneyer of the old school. Brântome describes how the king 'voulut tout scavoir et faire jusques a faire l'éscu, le double ducat, le teston, et autre monnoye, ores bonne et de double alloy … et prenoit plaisir à la monstrer.'[1] With so powerful an ally the conservative moneyers had nothing to fear and the establishment of milled coinage in France was postponed for nearly a century. The machinery of the Moulin des Etuves did not lie completely idle, however, since it was used to make copper coinage when that was introduced in 1577.

In the long controversy over the introduction of coin-making machinery, historians have generally been on the side of the progressive party. The beauty of the first milled coins and the saving of labour are powerful arguments in favour of the machines. It may however be unjust to assume that the conservative moneyers were simply obscurantists. No doubt their chief motive was to save their own jobs, but there was some force in their contention that, in the early days of the mill and press, the old-fashioned coining process was cheaper and more reliable. The techniques of cost accounting had not been developed in those days, but the ability to make a true estimate of profit can be learned by experience. The mint-masters of the sixteenth century were business men. The mill and screw press was an expensive machine which repeatedly broke down and they assessed as it unprofitable. That may have been short-sighted of them, but, given their limited outlook, they probably made the right decision. It may be significant that the Dutch, whose business methods in the seventeenth century were the most advanced in Europe, did not employ the new machinery until 1670. Of course, the Dutch had no water power and guilds such as that of the moneyers' enjoyed more power under the constitution of the United Provinces than under the French or English crowns. Even so the delay in the changeover to machinery is most easily explained by the provincial estates' realistic assessment of profit or loss.

The prevalence of Huguenot influence among the staff of the Moulin des Etuves may have been an auxiliary cause of the opposition which the enterprise aroused. The departure of Etienne Bergeron to join the queen of Navarre has already been mentioned. In 1562, during the first war of religion, he was master of the mint which was set up by the Huguenots in Orléans without royal authority and was reported to have coined a quantity of church plate there [figure 205]. In 1561 a humbler employee of the Moulin des Etuves, Eloi Mestrel, whose name suggests that he also was a Huguenot, presented

[1] The king wished to know and to do everything, even to make écus, double ducats, testons and other coins, both good ones and doubly alloyed ones . . . and he took pleasure in showing them off

206 Trial plates from the Tower mint in London for testing the two standards of gold in use at the time of Elizabeth's great recoinage. Fine gold was the old English standard, 23 carats 3½ grains fine, which the conservative English were reluctant to abandon. Crown gold of 22 carats was the new standard for which Charles v set the pattern in 1536. Most of the commonly traded English pieces were of crown gold.

207 England; silver shilling, 1561–2, Elizabeth I, London. An early English milled coin issued at the time of the queen's great recoinage [actual size]

himself to the Privy Council in London and offered to set up machinery at the Tower to help with the great recoinage. His offer was accepted and the first English milled coins, mostly sixpences, were struck before the end of that year [figure 207]. They were admirable, well struck and round; their lettering, like that of the French milled coins, was exceptional. This matter of the lettering was no coincidence, for the special excellence of the milled coin lay not in the middle but round the edge, which was where hammered pieces were usually defective. Engravers therefore found that it was worth taking trouble with the lettering for milled coins. However, in spite of the excellence of Eloi Mestrel's coins, his undertaking met a similar fate to that of the Moulin des Etuves. Throughout 1562 he was very active, but with the completion of the recoinage he had less to do and the mint authorities had time to give to the business of getting rid of him. The warden of the mint, Sir Richard Martin, reported to the Privy Council that the machinery was less efficient than the moneyers of the old school and that 'neither the said engine nor any workmanship to be wrought thereby will be to the Queen's Majesty's profit'. The Privy Council was convinced and in 1572 Mestrel was dismissed. Unfortunately that was not the end of his coining activites, for six years later he was hanged at Norwich for counterfeiting.

The next experiment in milled coinage was in Spain. Machinery was set up at the mint of Segovia in 1586. This time all went well and the establishment was permanent, but the use of machinery was not extended to the other mints. For a few decades therefore the well made Segovia pieces [figure 208] stood out in the general shabbiness of the Spanish coinage.

208 Spain; silver eight reals,
1590, Philip II, Segovia.
This piece of eight, made by the
mechanical process, contrasts
strangely with the same coin made
by Indian labour at Potosí
(figure 196) [actual size]

It is at first surprising that France should have been the first
nation to experiment with milled coinage, for in 1552 it was still isolated monetarily and economically from the rest of Europe. The
coinage, consisting of the 23 carat gold *henri*, a slightly heavier portrait version of the écu, and the silver teston, was old fashioned by
the standards of Spain and the Netherlands, or even of England and
Germany. Scotland, tied to France economically as well as politically
by the Auld Alliance, was the only kingdom in Europe at that time
whose coinage was closely related to the French [figure 203]. However,
it was during the reign of Henry II that American bullion really made
itself felt in France. As prices and wages rose in Spain, French labour
was attracted across the Pyrenees. The Spanish source of the increase
in the supply of money in France is clearly indicated by the replace-
ment of Lyons by Toulouse as the most important mint for silver
coinage. Not enough of this new wealth came the way of the government, which was therefore reduced to its usual expedient of increasing
the value of the coinage in terms of money of account. The gold écu,
valued at 45 s.t. in 1549, rose by stages to 60 s.t. in 1576 and the teston
over the same period rose from 11 s.t. to 14s. 6d. tournois. This of
course added to the inflation which was already being caused by the
increase in the supply of coinage. Many of the lesser nobility who lived
on fixed rents were ruined by it, and with dire consequences, since
their discontent was one of the root causes of the wars of religion.

Mutation of the currency was well known to be a cause of rising
prices. In 1568 the political economist Jean Bodin, in his *Reply to the
Paradoxes of M. de Malestroit*, published a deeper analysis of the
financial situation. Formulating for the first time in detail the quantity theory of money, he drew attention to the shipments of American
bullion as the primary cause of 'la vie chère'. For that of course there
was no remedy but, in the public controversy which followed, opinion
hardened against the aggravation of the problem by continued currency mutation. Finally the government gave way. By a series of
measures dated between 1575 and 1577, some of which were undoubtedly owing to the pressure of the States General which met at Blois
in 1577, the traditional system of accounting in £ s d tournois was
abolished and a number of new coins were introduced. The écu was to
be stabilised at the equivalent of three livres tournois and the new
monetary system was to be based upon it, with all prices quoted in
écus. The currency was to be identified with the coinage. As earnest
of this intention, two new silver coins were introduced to replace the
teston, both firmly anchored to specific monetary values. One of these
was the *franc*, whose name was always associated with coins stabilised
at a value of one livre. The other was the quarter-écu, the first French
coin to bear a mark of value [figure 209]. For the lowest values, the
double and the denier, a fiduciary copper coinage was issued. This was
an integral part of the stabilisation process. Formerly the double and
the denier were the theoretical foundation of the whole monetary

209 France; silver quarter-écu, 1595, Charles x (Pretender), Dinan. A coin issued by the Leaguers during the Wars of the Catholic League. Charles actually died in 1590, but in default of another prince of the blood acceptable to them, the Leaguers still struck coins in his name [actual size]

system: any alteration in their weight or alloy implied a whole sequence of changes in value further up the scale. As fiduciary pieces they could no longer play that rôle. They became simply the lowest fractional coins in a monetary system based upon the écu.

If Henry III had really wanted to abolish money of account, he could have done so more effectively. The survival of the livre in the form of the franc and of the denier as a copper coin, even though these were now theoretically only fractions of the écu, left the way open for his successors to revert to the old system. The reform probably made no difference whatever to the way in which the people of France conducted their everyday transactions. Nor was it wholly effective as an essay in stabilisation. Prices continued to rise, for production was disrupted by the recurrence of civil war and the money supply was further increased by Philip II's subsidies to the Catholic League. During this disturbed time there was a tendency for the value of the écu to diverge unofficially from the écu of account. In the troubled years which followed the assassination of Henry III in 1589 each of the opposing parties issued the same sort of coinage at the mints under their control, but neither could always resist the temptation to debasement, and the Leaguers at Dijon and Troyes were prone to make excessive issues of copper. The royalists struck in the name of Henry IV and the Leaguers in the name of their claimant, the Cardinal de Bourbon, as Charles X. Those who were unwilling to commit themselves to either, such as the Catholics in Toulouse, continued to use the name of Henry III. Some irregular mints were opened. Most of the big cities held out for the League and the royalists were obliged to compensate for them by opening their own mints nearby; thus Compiègne stood in for Paris, Dieppe for Rouen and Sémur en Auxois for Dijon. The Leaguers likewise established a mint at Dinan [figure 209] when they lost Rennes and made up for Clermont in Auvergne by a mint at Riom. In all these instances, however, the status of the temporary mints was made as regular as possible by giving them code letters related to those of the mints they were supposed to replace. The apparent normality of the coinage of both sides during those years says much for the continuity and efficiency of French civil administration.

The uniformity of French coinage throughout the wars of the League contrasts strongly with the monetary disarray which the revolt against Philip II caused in the Netherlands. The single currency system, which successive Burgundian and Hapsburg sovereigns had eventually achieved, was dismantled. The first act of monetary defiance was committed by the estates of Holland and Zeeland, which in 1573 called in Philip's silver and any foreign pieces in circulation and reissued them with a provincial countermark [figure 213] at a premium of 15%. In 1575 the estates of Holland improved upon that profitable operation by issuing a coin of their own, the *leeuwendaalder*, so called because of the lion (*leeuw*) rampant of Holland which occupied the principal place on one side [figure 213]. Such was the financial

210 *(opposite)* France; silver
teston, 1552, Henry II,
Paris (mint-master Claude Rouget).
A coin of the first regular issue
made by machinery at the
Moulin des Etuves
[enlarged 3.5:1]

reputation of the province that the leeuwendaalder, which bore no reference to the king of Spain, was an immediate success even though, by the standards of the time, it was slightly overvalued at 32 stuivers.

In 1577, after the constitutional settlement known as the Pacification of Ghent, it appeared that unity might be restored to the Netherlands currency with the issue, by order of the States General, of a new coinage in the name of Philip II. For the next four years the States' coinage was in theory the principal currency of the whole area, but in practice its success was confined to the southern provinces, which alone were eager for the Pacification. The northern provinces found themselves drawn, economically as well as politically, into the orbit of the dynamic outsider Holland, which would have nothing to do with the States' coinage and continued to issue its own, more profitably. Utrecht, for example, stopped issuing the States' coinage in 1578 and launched its own version of the leeuwendaalder instead.

By 1581 the Pacification of Ghent was a dead letter. Most of the southern provinces returned to their allegiance to Philip II and reverted to the coinage in his name which they had issued before the revolt began. The others struck whatever their provincial estates ordained. In Brabant and Flanders coins were struck in the name of the French prince Francis of Anjou, whom William the Silent called in to rule those provinces. They are interesting relics of a curious political experiment; his portrait daalders and copper coins are related to the normal coinage of Brabant, but his gold écus give a hint of the intended French take-over of the region. After Francis's overthrow in 1583, coins were struck independently by the estates of both provinces and by the city of Ghent, but these issues also were short-lived, because by 1585 the whole district was reclaimed by Philip. Thereafter the coinage of Brabant and Flanders conformed to that of the loyalist provinces.

In the north, the provincial estates and cities, left to themselves and uncertain constitutionally in whose name they should issue coins, reverted to the old Dutch monetary tradition of imitation. The gold pieces which they most frequently copied were the Spanish doubloon, which thus took a new lease of life, and the English ryal, which they called the *rose noble* [figure 213]. The rose noble played a brief and unimportant part in English monetary history as the successor of the noble, but it was popular all over northern Europe. The choice of an English model by so many Dutch provinces at this juncture no doubt had a political motive. To have imitated the contemporary coinage of Elizabeth would have offended English sovereignty, but to copy the century old rose noble was flattery. Moreover it symbolised the old alliance between England and the Burgundian provinces, which Edward IV, who had first issued it, had done much to promote.

The doubloon and the rose noble were not the only coins revived during this period. Three provinces reverted to the old Burgundian type of the *rijder* [figure 213]. Holland and later Friesland opted for

212 The sixteenth-century gateway of the old mint of Holland at Dordrecht

211 *(opposite)* England; gold half-pound, 1592–5, Elizabeth I, London. A fine example of Elizabeth's later coinage in crown gold, that is of the normal international twenty-two carat standard [enlarged 4:1]

a version of the Hungarian ducat. In silver there was less room for variety or antiquarianism, since there was only one coin worth copying, namely the thaler, but there were many versions of that to choose from. In Germany the *reichsthaler* of Saxon origin was the favourite. It had been adopted by a number of the mints of the imperial cities, some of which, such as Nijmegen and Kampen, became involved in the Dutch struggle for independence. The reichsthaler, translated *rijksdaalder*, was therefore already in a sense naturalised as a Dutch coin when it was adopted by some of the independent provinces in 1584. Holland and Friesland both took it up, closely following Saxon prototypes in their designs. The Frisian rijksdaalder showed an anonymous figure wearing an electoral cap; the other portrayed the stadholder, William of Orange, also in the pose of an elector of Saxony, armed and with a great sword on his shoulder [figure 213]. These were not, however, the only daalders current in the Netherlands. Holland still continued to issue the leeuwendaalder and so did Utrecht. The old philippusdaalders still circulated. To add to the confusion, some provinces, instead of copying the reichsthaler, went for their prototype to Philip's so-called *kruisrijksdaalder* or Burgundian rijksdaalder, based originally upon the German *reichsgulden*. A foreigner might be forgiven for supposing that one Dutch daalder was as good as another, but there was in fact a bewildering variety of type, weight, fineness and value among coins issued in some instances from the same mint in the same year.

The Earl of Leicester, who was appointed governor general of the Netherlands after the assassination of William the Silent and who for twenty-five years had been used to the well-ordered currency of Elizabeth's England, was appalled by the monetary confusion which he found and attempted to remedy it. The principle of Leicester's reform was that the States General of the United Provinces should determine a uniform currency for the whole country, which the mints of each province would then issue as the provincial estates thought fit. Leicester did not usually see eye to eye with the states of Holland, but he rightly judged that it was that province which really mattered in currency matters, as in so much else. Accordingly, the two most important coins in the system which he proposed were the Hungarian type ducat and the rijksdaalder, both recently adopted by Holland. But although control of the issue was still reserved to the provincial estates, the scheme foundered on the rock of provinces' rights. As early as 1589 Gelderland began to issue independently a new coinage which included a doubloon and a leeuwendaalder, and within a short time most of the other provinces were also following their separate ways. As for the old imperial cities, they were never even included in Leicester's ordinances. However, as the war proceeded and the United Provinces emerged as the foremost economic power in Europe, it became clear even to the provincial estates that their multitude of coinages was a luxury which they could not afford. At last in 1606 a

213 Some Dutch coins of the years of rebellion against Spanish rule. Spanish Netherlands; one-fifth philippusdaalder, 1566, Philip II, Nijmegen, countermarked by the estates of Zeeland in 1573 to circulate at a premium of 15%. Haarlem, besieged by the Spaniards, silver daalder 1572. Middelburg, besieged by the Dutch, silver daalder, 1572. Holland; silver leeuwendaalder 1589, and rijksdaalder with portrait of the stadholder William of Orange, 1584, Dordrecht. Zeeland, gold doubloon, 1580–5, Middelburg, copied from the Spanish coin (see figure 170). Friesland; gold rijder, 1582, and ducat, 1591–4, copied from the Hungarian ducat. Utrecht; gold rose noble, 1602, copied from the English ryal, and silver rijksdaalder, 1612, of the type and standard agreed for all the United Provinces. A coinage of extraordinary complexity owing to the uncertain constitutional basis on which the Dutch estates issued coins and to the great commercial activity of the Netherlands throughout the war [actual size]

unified currency system was agreed upon. The doubloon and the noble were abandoned, but not on this occasion the leeuwendaalder, which had become a well-established trading counter overseas, especially in the Levant and further east, and was therefore still required in spite of the obvious inconvenience of putting it into circulation beside the rijksdaalder. The ducat, as introduced by Holland, remained one of the principal gold coins, but the English connexion was not abandoned with the rose noble, for the rijder, which was chosen as the other principal gold piece, was made to conform in both weight and alloy to the English unit or sovereign recently issued by James I.

The ordinance of 1606 remained in force without any important modification until 1659, that is to say for the greater part of the Dutch golden age. It was a simplifying measure, but only by Dutch standards, for the currency was still very complicated and was made more so by the great quantity of old and foreign coins still in circulation. In the great Serooskerke hoard, deposited in Zeeland on the eve of the Thirty Years War, the mints of Seville and Antwerp both account for more coins than any Dutch mint except Harderwijk, the mint of Gelderland. This is remarkable, even if allowance is made for the fact that many of the coins date from before the Dutch revolt and the emergence of the northern provinces as a separate and important economic unit.

As regards silver coinage, unrepresented in the Serooskerke hoard but nevertheless more important than gold in the condition of Europe at that time, the situation in the United Provinces was really unusual. The leeuwendaalder, as we have seen, became a popular coin in the Levant. The rijksdaalder, presumably because of its similarity to the Saxon thaler and its Danish and Swedish derivatives, achieved a similar success in the Baltic lands, which as the chief source of naval supplies and the only part of Europe to produce a regular grain surplus, kept a persistently favourable balance of trade with the Dutch. Both coins were therefore largely exported. At home the Dutch replaced them to a great extent by two comparatively overvalued coins from the Spanish Netherlands, namely the *patagon* [figure 214], introduced by the Archdukes Albert and Isabella in 1612 as a modified version of the Burgundian kruisrijksdaalder, worth 48 stuivers, and the *ducaton* [figure 214], a rather finer and heavier coin tariffed at 60 stuivers, which was first struck in 1618. Vast quantities of both were taken northwards to Amsterdam and the other Dutch cities. Much has been made of the decline of Antwerp and the Spanish Netherlands after their submission in the 1580s. But, though Antwerp's trade was ruined, it had great reserves of wealth which served to support an important financial and banking community for another sixty years. The prolific coinage of the Spanish Netherlands during the reigns of the Archdukes and their successor Philip IV is impressive evidence of this.

The province of Holland's choice of the Hungarian ducat as the

214 Spanish Netherlands; silver ducaton, 1619, Archdukes Albert and Isabella, Brussels and silver patagon, 1631, King Philip IV of Spain, Antwerp. Two coins of the Spanish provinces which also circulated widely in the United Provinces [actual size]

215 Hungary; gold ducat, 1571, the Emperor Maximilian II, Kremnitz. With the slackening of American gold supplies, the Hungarian ducat again became an important currency during the latter part of the sixteenth century [actual size]

model for its principal gold coin in 1583 is an interesting symptom of the re-emergence of central Europe as an important source of bullion during the closing years of the sixteenth century. The stream of gold from America was much less than it had been. Meanwhile, the gold-bearing districts of Hungary had become more settled politically since the establishment of the independent principality of Transylvania. In the days when most gold coins had been of pure metal, the Hungarian florin, exceptionally, had been alloyed. It was thus one of the few pieces to survive in its original form when alloyed gold pieces became the rule in the sixteenth century. Its change of name, when the term florin became *déclassé*, was a mark of its continued acceptance in international circulation. Under the Hapsburgs one more minor change brought it right up to date. The traditional figure of St Wladislas, who had himself supplanted John the Baptist in the fifteenth century, was replaced by that of the ruling sovereign, Rudolph II. Not that that amounted to much, for the saint had already lost his halo and a change of legend was virtually all that was necessary to transform him into the bearded emperor [figure 215]. This standing figure, directly derived from that of the Baptist on the florin of Florence, continued to be the chief feature of the Hungarian ducat through all the changes of style, baroque, neo-classical and modern, until the end of Francis Joseph's reign in 1916. It was this also which characterised the imitations which were struck in the Netherlands and the German states in the sixteenth and seventeenth centuries. The gold coinage of the Hungarian mints, Kremnitz, Hermannstadt, Nagybánya and Kolozsvár, was not heavy compared

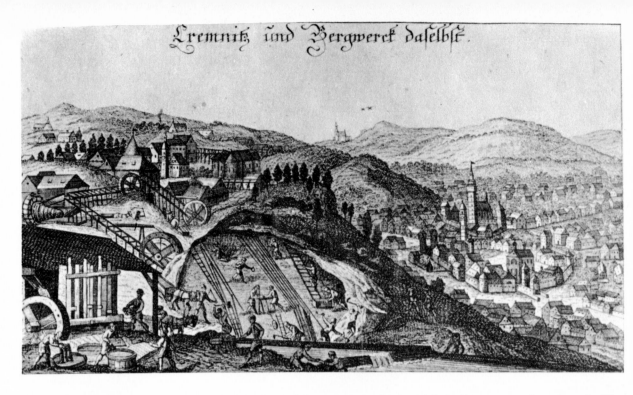

216 A view of Kremnitz in the
sixteenth century showing
a section of the workings of the
gold mine which supplied the
mint

217 Transylvania; silver thaler,
1592, Sigismund Bathory.
An example of the fine chasing
and quaint figure drawing
which distinguishes the
Transylvanian coinage
[actual size]

with that of the western cities which had access to American bullion,
but it was more than enough for local needs, since those places were of
little commercial importance except as mining towns. Consequently
much of it was put into international circulation, where it supplemented the more prolific output of Seville, Antwerp and London.

Since the production of American silver was so much better maintained than that of gold, the central European thaler played a less
important international role than the ducat. Nevertheless it accounted
for a great part of the coinage in circulation locally. At the turn of the
century the various Saxon dynasties and counts of Mansfeld still issued thalers in profusion. The emperor himself, whose mints extended
from Ensisheim in Alsace to Nagybánya in Transylvania, was
even more active, for Rudolph II, though an indifferent ruler, took a
serious interest in scientific and practical matters and gave real encouragement to the mining industry, especially in his favourite kingdom of Bohemia. He was also a notable patron of the arts. In 1579 he
appointed the distinguished Italian medallist Antonio Abondio to
engrave his portrait for the imperial coinage. Abondio's punches were
distributed to the various mints and, although in a few years his
refined and plastic style was coarsened in the hands of less talented
local craftsmen, his influence was decisive in bringing the baroque
style to coinage north of the Alps [figure 218].

The chief defects of German coin design, which Abondio's example
did much to correct, were overcrowding of detail and stiffness of
figure drawing. In one area, however, these characteristics were carried
to such mannered lengths that they became a kind of quaint virtue.
The independent princes of Transylvania, like the rulers of other

mining states, favoured large coins such as multiple thalers and ducats. But their country was remote and insecure. Skilled die-engravers were difficult to attract, and the mint authorities were therefore obliged to co-opt less specialised craftsmen, goldsmiths perhaps and chasers of plate or armour. These men produced some remarkable coins. Knowing that they lacked the skill to model a full-scale portrait bust, they commonly chose to represent the prince in half length. If they often made the figure clumsy and ill-proportioned, they overlaid these faults by their wealth of carefully rendered detail, either of armour or of the exotic half-oriental costume affected by the Hungarian nobility. Their portraiture was frank to the point of caricature, but this was treatment to which the wily and capable Transylvanian princes were eminently suited [figure 217]. The decorative heraldic designs for the reverse were especially well engraved. These coins were prized for their beauty even in their own day and were often made into jewellery or kept as curios. Consequently more of them have survived than their monetary importance has warranted.

218 A steel punch, engraved in relief, used to put the impression of the head on dies for thalers of the Emperor Rudolph II (1576–1612)

219 A pair of dies, pile and trussel, used for the Kremnitz thalers of 1579 in the name of the Emperor Rudolph II. For the method of use see figure 178

9 Towards Modern Coinage

221 Late seventeenth-century coining press from the Kremnitz mint

220 *(opposite)* Würzburg; silver thaler, Bishop Philip Adolf von Ehrenberg (1623–31). An example of unflagging artistic achievement in the coinage of Germany during the Thirty Years War [enlarged 2.5:1]

As the reign of Philip II drew to its close, Spanish imports of silver from the Indies reached their climax. During the last decade of the sixteenth century they are estimated to have averaged seven million pesos de minas (a weight of silver equivalent to one gold ducat) annually, touching twelve million in 1597. For the next thirty years the annual average was about five and a half million, in 1631–50 it was down to three million and in the 1650s it dropped to one million, which was about what it had been in the 1540s. It is against this background that the coinage of the first half of the seventeenth century must be seen.

The main reasons for the decline in bullion shipments were the falling yield of the Mexican and Peruvian mines, the increasing demands of the local population and, above all, the Pacific trade's growing appetite for silver. The normal annual export of silver from Acapulco to Manila in the early years of the seventeenth century has been estimated at four million pesos.

The effects of the contraction in the supply of precious metals were felt all over Europe, but first and most severely in Spain. The Spanish government had come to rely upon the annual shipment. This was nearly always pre-empted by foreign creditors and, when it fell short, there was nothing to spare for the current needs of the people. Consequently, soon after the death of Philip II it was found necessary to debase the coinage. During the reign of Philip IV (1621–65) this came to consist largely of copper. Private holders of gold and silver were persuaded to relinquish their stocks in return for copper money of artificially inflated value and then cheated when the value of the copper was called down in an attempt to stem the inflation. Gold and silver coins went to a high premium, which the government was powerless to control in spite of stringent legislation. The final point of irony was reached in 1643 when an armada arrived from the Indies laden with copper for the Spanish mints.

Spain's position at this time was exceptional. The domestic currency was weak but Spanish pistoles exported either by the government or, illegally, by private traders, were still important in the European monetary scene. Meanwhile dollars from both Spanish and colonial mints were becoming the chief currency in all the settlements on the

222 Savoy; silver ducatone, 1632, Duke Victor Amadeus I. In some Italian courts the fine medallic traditions of the previous century survived for a time [actual size]

American seaboard, of whatever nationality, and, through the Manila trade, were establishing in the far east a supremacy which has never been challenged.

The economic depression in Spain, of which the lack of a satisfactory coinage was part cause, part symptom, was one of the chief reasons for the revolt in Catalonia, Spain's most mercantile province, in 1640. It is worth noting that the French, during their brief occupation, pursued an active coinage policy there. They appealed to local sentiment by adopting for the reverse of their silver the old Barcelona type of the cross and pellets favoured by the Aragonese kings in Catalonia's medieval heyday.

Italy, whose commercial revival during the later years of Philip II was almost entirely owing to that king's financial policy, suffered almost as grievously as Spain from the change in conditions. At one or two centres such as Turin and Mantua the fine medallic traditions of the previous century were upheld for a time [figure 222] and at Rome notable commemorative pieces were still issued occasionally, but none of these was of commercial importance. The coinage of Milan and Naples fell into decay. Only the Venetian zecchino, which had never owed anything to Spanish patronage, still preserved a certain reputation in the dwindling Levantine trade. It was as pure as ever and unchanged in weight and design, but it had outlived its time. The Knights of St John at Malta still thought it worth imitating, but that was not from commercial principles. They had been doing so ever since they were at Rhodes; like Venice herself they were out of date but too tired to change.

The chief beneficiaries of Spain's continuing outflow of bullion were the Netherlands, as in the sixteenth century, and the rising mercantile and colonial powers, England and France. The Spanish Netherlands, as we have seen, remained an important source of finance for some years after their trade began to succumb to the rivalry of the independent Dutch. The Antwerp ducatons and patagons of Philip IV were a sort of northern manifestation of the Spanish dollar, and, like those of his predecessors, Albert and Isabella, they provided the greater part of the silver currency of the United Provinces. However, in 1648 the Peace of Westphalia, with its provisions for blocking the Scheldt, ruined the economy of the Spanish Netherlands. The coinage of the region was much reduced in quantity and became of no more than local significance, like that of Italy.

The Dutch, thrown upon their own resources, continued to strike rijksdaalders for the Baltic trade and leeuwendaalders for the Levant, but for their own use they preferred the larger and finer ducaton and the undervalued patagon. In 1659, as part of a general revaluation and reform they introduced their own versions of these, the silver rijder [figure 243] and the silver ducat, the latter worth one half of its golden counterpart. The rijder was of the same weight and standard as the ducaton, the other the equivalent of the patagon. This reform

223 An eighteenth–century
drawing of the mint of the estates
of Holland at Dordrecht, by
Aart Schouman

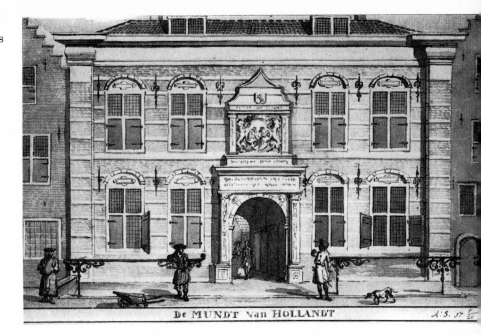

De MUNDT van HOLLANDT

224 England; silver crown,
1601, Elizabeth I, London.
The reappearance of this large
silver coin at the end of
Elizabeth's reign suggests that
an increasing share of the world's
silver supply was passing
through English hands
[actual size]

which did not touch the gold coinage, was apparently satisfactory.
In theory it redoubled the complications of the Dutch coinage, which
thenceforward comprised four big silver coins of different alloys and
weights, the rijder worth 63 stuivers, the rijksdaalder worth 52 stuivers, the ducat worth 50 stuivers, and the leeuwendaalder worth
42 stuivers. Moreover, since in the years before the revaluation the
value of 50 stuivers (two and a half gulden) had become associated
with the name rijksdaalder, this name tended to be transferred in
common speech to the new silver ducat. However, after 1659 the
domestic currency of the United Provinces was provided by Dutch
mints and that at least was a simplification.

England's increasing share of the European silver supply was
demonstrated in 1601 when silver crowns and half-crowns were issued
for the first time since 1553. This time they came to stay and within
a few years they made up the greater part of the money in circulation.
Elizabeth took the opportunity afforded by these larger coins for a
magnificent portrait of herself [figure 224] but James I reverted to the
equestrian design of 1551, which remained the unvarying type of the
crowns and plentiful half-crowns of his successor. For James the inflow of silver brought its problems. In 1611 he was obliged to revalue
his gold coinage, but he found that the English did not take so readily
as his other subjects the Scots to the odd values thrown up by revaluation. They preferred their gold unit to be worth one pound sterling.

225 England; gold laurel,
1623–4, James I, London.
James was the first English ruler
to adopt a system of marks
of value for his coins. This was
a consequence of his experience as
king of Scotland [actual size]

226 England; brass halfpenny
token, 1668, issued by James
Warwell, draper, of Groton,
Suffolk. This is typical of
the small change issued by small
traders in the middle of the
seventeenth century in default
of a satisfactory royal coinage
[actual size]

In 1619 James complied and issued a lighter gold coinage, whose clear system of marks of value [figure 225] showed the king's intention of abiding by this English tradition.

When James came to the English throne in 1603, the rate of exchange between the pound sterling and the pound Scots was one to twelve. This was a convenient rate at which to combine the two currencies, since the English shilling with its mark of value XII was worth twelve shillings Scots and the other English coins could be transposed into Scots currency with almost as little difficulty. The union of his two kingdoms was a project near to James's heart and he so ordered matters that his Scottish and English coins were the same in all respects except minor details of heraldry. However, the fusion of the two systems was only skin deep. The Scottish system retained its old substructure of base metal coins for small change and Charles II was able to revert to a policy of completely separate coinages for each kingdom without causing any disruption.

James I made a serious attempt to remedy the shortage of small change in England. In most countries there was only too much, but in England the smallest coin was the fine silver halfpenny, which was inconvenient to handle and yet still too valuable for some retail transactions. James's remedy was a token coinage of brass farthings. However, though a sound theoretical economist, he was politically inept. Instead of administering this coinage through the royal mint, he granted the patent for it to a private contractor, Lord Harington. Although the new farthings met the needs of the people, they were rejected because of their association with the private monopoly system. The patent did nobody any good: it changed hands several times at a loss and was finally abandoned. Consequently the need for small change arose again in the later years of the Commonwealth. This time, in default of government action, the people who were most affected, namely the retailers, took the law into their own hands and issued their own brass farthing and halfpenny tokens. From 1657 until about 1670 these illegal tokens [figure 226] were issued in profusion by grocers, apothecaries and coffee-house keepers and even by borough and city corporations. Few proved fraudulent but their extremely local character made them inconvenient. They only disappeared from circulation when a properly constituted royal coinage in copper was undertaken in 1672.

Charles I, unlike his father, was no innovator in the matter of coinage, but he was a man of taste and he improved its appearance by employing the best of contemporary French medallists, Nicolas Briot, as engraver at the royal mint. Briot was a practitioner of the mechanical process of coining, and like his predecessor Mestrel, he was opposed as a foreign innovator by the established officials of the Tower mint. The best that his patron the king was able to do was to appoint him as a sort of artistic supervisor, in which position he could exercise only a general influence. He proved more effective when he

227 Scotland; silver twelve shillings, c. 1642, Charles I, Edinburgh (mint-master John Falconer) [actual size]

228 England; silver half-pound, 1642, Charles I, Shrewsbury (mint-master Thomas Bushell). A very heavy silver coin issued by the king at the first of his war emergency mints [actual size]

was given a freer hand at York, whither the king sent him in 1642, and at Edinburgh where he was succeeded by his son-in-law, John Falconer [figure 227].

The opening of the York mint reversed the policy of centralisation which been followed by Charles's predecessors since Edward VI. Charles opened another mint at Aberystwyth in 1638 to take advantage of the renewed activity of the Welsh silver mines. This establishment proved of great value to the king when the civil war began in 1642.

Parliament's wartime control of London and the prosperous south-east of England put into its hands most of the precious metals which came into the kingdom by way of trade. Throughout the war the Tower mint was able to carry on quite normally, striking gold and silver in the king's name but by order of Parliament. So preoccupied were the parliamentary leaders with legitimacy and continuity that they did not even change the statement of divine right, CHRISTO AVSPICE REGNO, which Charles had chosen as the reverse legend for the silver.

The king's monetary situation was precarious. His control of the midlands and the west gave him access to silver from Wales, and his followers, especially the Oxford colleges, were generous with their private contributions; but not until Prince Rupert's capture of Bristol in 1643 did he hold an important commercial centre. Consequently Charles was rarely in a position to strike gold. His troops were paid almost exclusively in silver and most of his mints struck nothing else. Thomas Bushell, the mining entrepreneur and financier who had run the Aberystwyth mint, was responsible for the nucleus of Charles's war coinage, first at Shrewsbury and then at the king's Oxford head-quarters. At both cities an attempt was made to compensate for the dearth of gold by striking silver pound and half-pound pieces [figure 228]. Multiple thalers were commonplace in Germany and it is possible that it was German influence in the royalist camp which prompted this initiative. Late in 1643 some of Thomas Bushell's Aberystwyth personnel were sent to open a mint at Bristol, and this group, when Bristol was lost again in 1645, withdrew further to the west to set up yet another mint, tradition has it, in Bushell's own castle on Lundy Island. Coins from all these four mints were distinguished by Welsh plumes, the mark of their Aberystwyth pedigree, and on the reverse, by the words of the king's declaration that he was fighting for the Protestant Religion, the Laws of England and the Liberties of Parliament [figures 228 & 235].

A second important source of royalist coinage were the mints of Truro and Exeter set up to coin the silver extracted from the lead mines of Cornwall and Devon. Coins from this region were distinguished by a rose mint mark. Apart from the Welsh and west country groups of mints, the royalist output was light and spasmodic. A few half-crowns were struck at Chester and Worcester and others at mints which have never been identified. There were also emergency

229 England; gold half-unite, 1652, the Commonwealth, London. The Commonwealth coinage, though revolutionary in its outward aspect, was profoundly conservative in content and manufacture [actual size]

230 The gravestone in Kremnitz churchyard of Valentin Leiner (died 1624), sometime warden of the mint. A high proportion of the mint officials in all parts of the Hapsburg dominions was German

issues of crudely struck coins in Ireland; one of these, associated with the name of the marquis of Ormonde, the royalist commander, was substantial. Naturally circumstances left little scope for attention to matters of artistic detail at any of the royalist mints, but interesting designs were produced at some of them, and at Oxford Charles found time to patronise the medallic experiments of Briot's pupil Thomas Rawlings [figure 235].

After Charles's execution, the English coinage was issued in the name of the Commonwealth with a plain shield device on each side, bare of all decoration in the Puritan manner and with legends in English [figure 229]. In spite of its revolutionary appearance, this was fundamentally a conservative coinage, made by the old hammered process, unchanged in weight and consisting of the same denominations as in King Charles's day.

The Thirty Years War in Germany was on a far bigger scale than the English civil war, but its effect upon the coinage was less striking, since England was used to a single minting authority whereas the empire was accustomed to monetary disorder. In the first three years of the war the disorder became acute. All the mints in Germany, feeling themselves free from the restraint of the imperial diets, poured out unlimited quantities of small change. The market was flooded with copper and billon fractional pieces, while gold and silver went to a big premium. This period was known as the *kipper-und-wipperzeit*, the field day of the clippers of coins, when finally nothing passed for its face value and the moneychangers went through each payment to pick out the best pieces for hoarding or clipping. It did not last long, because after a time it ceased to be profitable to issue coin which no one would accept. In spite of the political anarchy and as if by common consent, the issue of worthless coin stopped and the mints returned to their pre-war practice. Gold was still exceptional. For the rest of the war armies and subsidies were mostly paid in thalers. The princes of the mining districts such as John George of Saxony and Count Leopold of Tirol had the heaviest output, but the war tended to increase the circulation of specie and to reduce the imbalance between the mining and the non-mining regions.

Some coins made direct allusion to the war. During the first religious phase, Christian of Brunswick struck thalers at Paderborn, supposedly from the abbey's melted plate, with the legend GOTTES FREUNDT DER PFAFFEN FEINDT (God's friend, the priest's foe) [figure 232]. Twenty years later, his kinsman Augustus the Young of Brunswick-Wolfenbüttel expressed the growing war weariness of the people with the legend TANDEM PATIENTIA VICTRIX on the bell thalers which he struck to celebrate the departure of the imperial army in 1643. Magdeburg struck a special thaler to commemorate its restoration after Tilly's terrible sack of the city in 1631. There were several issues which, though from regular mints, would never have been made but for the political changes wrought by the war. Such were the Bohemian

CIVITAS CREMNICIENSIS

231 Kremnitz, well outside the theatre of operations, was
nevertheless an important source of money for the
imperialists throughout the Thirty Years War. A pen and
wash drawing of the city (dated 1742) showing the old
mint building in the left foreground, near the stream

232 Paderborn; silver thaler, 1622,
Christian of Brunswick.
Christian, the first Protestant
champion in the Thirty Years War,
was uncompromisingly aggressive
in the design and legend of
these coins, supposedly struck
from abbey plate [actual size]

233 Bohemia, silver twenty-four
kreuzers, 1620, Frederick
of the Palatinate, Joachimsthal,
(mint-master Centurio Lengefelder)
[actual size]

234 Sagan (Silesia); silver thaler,
1629, Albert of Wallenstein,
duke of Friedland, (mint-master
Hans Ziesler). The right
to issue money was one of the
many rewards heaped upon
the imperialist general by his
master, Ferdinand II [actual size]

235 *(opposite)* England;
silver crown, 1644, Charles I,
Oxford, from dies engraved
by Thomas Rawlings. An
ambitious pattern coin with
a view of the city in the
background, rather after the
contemporary German manner

237 Regensburg; silver thaler, 1633, Bernhard of Saxe-Weimar, struck to commemorate the Protestant commander's entry into the city [actual size]

238 Bavaria; gold five ducats, 1640, the elector Maximilian, Munich. The long war did not prevent some mints from continuing to strike coins of great magnificence [actual size]

236 (opposite) Maryland; silver shilling, in the name of Lord Baltimore, proprietor of the colony, c. 1659.
Massachusetts; silver shilling, 1662–82 but dated 1652.
Two of the earliest north American coins; the pine tree shilling was made in Massachusetts, but the Baltimore coin was made in England and shipped to the colony

coins of the Winter King, Frederick of the Palatinate [figure 233], and the thalers struck by Gustavus Adolphus at Augsburg and by Bernhard of Saxe-Weimar at Regensburg [figure 237]. Wallenstein struck coins with his own name and portrait as duke of Friedland and Sagan [figure 234]. This duchy with its minting rights was specially created for him as a reward for his services to the emperor during the war, but his coins take their place quite normally beside those of other sovereign princes of the empire. On the whole, once the *kipperzeit* was over, German coinage during the war was remarkably normal. Monetary contention was postponed as long as more deadly issues were at stake. At some mints even the artistic quality was unimpaired [figure 220]. Machinery was much used. There was some experimentation at the imperial mints with the invention of engraving the die upon the surface of a roller. This was quicker to operate than the screw press, but it produced slightly cambered coins.

An important part of warfare during the sixteenth and seventeenth centuries was the formal siege. As long as money was only a marginal requirement of society, beleaguered cities simply did without it, but once Europe had become a wholly monetary economy, coinage was considered so necessary, even in the artificial conditions of a siege,

239 Scarborough, besieged
by the Parliamentary forces,
1644–5, silver five shillings.
The marks of the original
plate are clearly seen on this
crude siege piece struck during the
English civil war [actual size]

240 Sommer Islands; brass
sixpence, c. 1615. A piece of the
rare 'hog money' struck
for the English colony which
was later called Bermuda
[actual size]

that cities in that situation took to issuing emergency money. Early instances of this occurred at Tournai [figure 186], where the French were besieged by the imperialists in 1521 and at Pavia in 1524 where the situation was reversed. The Pavia pieces were stamped with the initials of the commander, Antonio de Leiva, and were presumably made for the benefit of the garrison rather than for the citizens. At Vienna, besieged by the Turks in 1529, gold and silver coins were struck bearing the head or coat of arms of the Archduke Ferdinand and the legend TVRCK BELEGERT WIEN. The Dutch war of independence was especially fertile in such expedients. There was no distinction in the rebellious cities between garrison and citizens and the Dutch carried on trading in the most trying conditions. The famous sieges of Haarlem (1572) [figure 213] and Leyden (1574) were both occasions of obsidional coinage, but there were some twenty more. At Middelburg (1572–3) and Amsterdam (1578) coins were struck by besieged Spanish garrisons. Elsewhere in Europe the phenomenon recurred at the celebrated sieges of Jametz (1588), Jülich (1610), Magdeburg (1629) and Lille (1708) and during the English civil war at Newark (1645–6), Scarborough (1644–5) [figure 239], Carlisle (1644–5) and Pontefract (1648–9). It was repeated quite often in the eighteenth century and even in the French revolutionary wars.

Obsidional coins have more in common with each other than with their own national coinages. They are often curiously shaped, having been roughly sheared from pieces of domestic plate, and are sometimes struck on one side only. The design is usually simple: at Haarlem, for example, it consisted of a punch like a goldsmith's hall mark [figure 213]; at Newark it was a crown, at Pavia a cypher and so on. Their legends on the other hand were sometimes elaborate, expressing the hope, defiance or despair of the garrison. At Middelburg the old Spanish general Mondragon stressed his garrison's loyalty with DEO REGI PATRIAE FIDEL, at Pontefract captain Morris evoked the spirit of the forlorn hope with DVM SPIRO SPERO. The Magdeburg garrison suggested a harsher view of their predicament with DVRAE NECESSITATIS OPVS. Others were purely factual. This one is quaint but explicit: POVR 30 SOLZ DE LA VAISSELLE DV MAR^{AL} DE TVRENNE ASSIEGEANT ST VENANT 1657. Obsidional coins were often deficient in weight or alloy; some were even made of card or leather. Consequently they did not usually get into general circulation. They were more in the nature of promissory notes, redeemable when the siege was over. Nevertheless they have always been valued as relics and therefore, though rare by definition, have had a higher survival rate than ordinary coins.

Besieged cities and newly settled colonies, both characteristic of seventeenth-century life, had this also in common; that they were isolated for long periods from the rest of the world. The coins of both were therefore often under weight and badly struck. Such, for example, were the brass shillings and other coins, the so-called hog money

241 Compagnie des Indes
Orientales; silver quarter–écu,
1670, Louis XIV, Paris.
Money minted in France and
transported to French possessions
in America [actual size]

[figure 240], struck for the Sommer Islands (Bermuda) in the seventeenth century. So far colonial coinage has only been mentioned in connexion with the early pieces of Mexico, but these were exceptional since Mexico, as an important source of silver, was in a state of constant monetary intercourse with Spain. From 1572 until 1650 the coinage of Mexico and Peru was in form and content an extension of that of Spain. After 1650 the old pillar design was reintroduced for the Peruvian coinage, which thereafter remained distinctive in appearance, but then it was too important and its circulation area too wide for it to be in any way typically colonial. For that we may look to North America. The earliest coinage there was struck in Massachusetts in about 1650. It consisted of light silver shillings and lesser coins stamped with a mark of value and the letters NE for New England. These were found too easy to forge, and in 1652 they were replaced by coins with the representation of a tree and the legend IN MASATHUSETS. These coins, the well known oak, pine and willow tree shillings, were struck during a period of about thirty years, but the date 1652 was never changed [figure 236].

The crude nature of the New England coinage suggests how difficult it was to sustain a locally operated colonial mint. One alternative was for those who planted the colony to supply it with coinage made at home. This solution was adopted by Lord Baltimore, who commissioned a quasi-royal coinage of silver with his name and portrait for his plantation in Maryland [figure 236]. This became a common practice, whether the coinage was royal or private. It was followed by the lords proprietors of Carolina for their coinage of halfpennies for that province in 1694. The French, with their strong tradition of centralisation, took to it wholeheartedly. The Compagnie des Indes Orientales, which held the monopoly of French trade with Africa and America and was given the right in 1670 to issue coins for those regions, struck all its quarter-écus and smaller silver at the Paris mint [figure 241]. Except for a distinctive reverse legend, these were just the same as the coins of metropolitan France. During the eighteenth century the bulk of French colonial coinage struck for general use with the comprehensive inscription COLONIES FRANÇOISES, was also made at Paris.

The danger of sending coins to the colonies instead of making them locally was that they would be shipwrecked or stolen at sea. Consequently governments usually restricted their minting operations for their colonies to base metal coinage, which was almost pure profit, and left to private traders the risk of transporting specie. The coins struck in the name of any colony were therefore only the small change, and we should draw a very false picture of colonial monetary circulation if we were only to look at those. Trade was conducted in any coinage used by the merchants who called at the colonial ports. In theory, because of the monopolies which nations tried to establish in the commerce of their own colonies, that was the coinage of the mother country, but in practice one trading currency, the Spanish dollar, came to predominate in all of them.

242 East India Company; silver dollar 1600, Elizabeth I, London. Compagnie van Verre, Amsterdam; silver daalder, 1601, Dordrecht. The chartered trading companies early recognised the dollar of eight Spanish reals as the best currency for their far eastern trade and had their own versions of it struck at their national mints for use overseas [actual size]

The Spanish dollar, shipped to the far east by way of Manila, is one point of contact between the colonial coinages of the East Indies and the New World. The very first attempts at coinage by the English and the Dutch for the East Indies were both versions of it [figure 242]. The English coin was the portcullis dollar struck in London in 1600 for the East India Company. The Dutch piece was first issued a year later at Dordrecht for the Compagnie van Verre of Amsterdam, one of the constituents of the United East India Company (VOC) formed the following year. However, neither of these issues was long lived and, apart from the dollar, there was not much in common between the colonial coinages of the east and the west.

So far from being isolated, the European settlements in the east were planted cheek by jowl with populous and economically active communities. The very first coins which can certainly be ascribed to a modern colonial mint are half-cruzados struck at Goa in the name of Manuel of Portugal (1500–21). These, though different from the normal Portuguese coins, are wholly European in style and the Portuguese, exceptionally, remained uncompromisingly European in their colonial coinage at all times. Other colonial powers in the orient tended to copy local coinage, just as the crusading Franks had copied Arabic dinars some five centuries before. Thus the English, when they set up a mint in Bombay in 1677, struck coins which, though they looked European [figure 244] with their heraldic design and English legends, were in fact silver *rupees* and copper *pice*, the standard values of the Mogul Empire. Before long the East India Company was striking coins

243 A sample not only of Dutch but of Dutch colonial currency. Silver coins from the wreck of *De Liefde*, a Dutch East Indiaman sunk off the Scottish coast on her outward voyage in 1711. They are: a half-ducaton, 1652, of Flanders and a ducaton of Antwerp, Philip IV of Spain; a ducaton of Brussels 1682, Charles II of Spain, and another of Antwerp, Philip V (1700–12); and Dutch rijders of the city of Campen and the estates of Utrecht and Westfrisia. The high proportion of coins from the Spanish Netherlands is interesting [actual size]

244 East India Company; silver rupee, 1678, in the name of Charles II, Bombay. A coin of Indian weight and value, but European in appearance. Soon the company adopted Indian types as well [actual size]

of Mogul type as well as weight for its trade in northern India, while at Madras it struck gold *pagodas* and silver *fanams* of Hindu type and standard for trade along the Coromandel coast. The French likewise at Pondicherry conformed to Indian practice, though their fanams were national in type, stamped with fleurs de lys and a crown.

The Dutch were faced with a different situation. In their sphere of influence there was no single widely recognised local currency. It was already a monetary hotch-potch with Chinese and Japanese coins circulating with the local pieces and the ubiquitous Spanish dollars. The United East India Company, after some experiment with a special coinage of its own, finally adopted the policy of circulating the coins which it shipped out from the Netherlands in the ordinary way of trade, rijksdaalders, ducats and rijders together with ducatons and patagons from the Spanish Netherlands [figure 243]. Thus the Dutch imposed one complicated coinage upon another and they so dominated the area that even Chinese and Japanese coins were countermarked with the lion of Holland or the company's VOC monogram and were made to fit into the accounting system of gulden and stuivers.

The early years of the seventeenth century saw the French coinage fall into increasing disorder. One cause of this was the inordinate quantity of old debased coin in circulation, the fruit of years of unrestraint on the part of successive finance ministers. Its measure was shown in 1640 when it was ordained that all billon coins should be officially countermarked and thereafter current at a flat rate of 15 deniers: fifteenth-century coins so countermarked are by no means rare.

245 France; silver écu, 1641, Louis XIII, Paris, from dies by Jean Varin. The first French coin of thaler size and the justification of the reinstallation of machinery at the Paris mint [actual size]

Having regulated the petty coinage, the government proceeded to reform the gold and silver. This was old-fashioned. The écu d'or was 23 carats fine whereas the international standard set by the emperor Charles v a century earlier was 22 carats; the écu tended to be undervalued at the official rate and was constantly exported. The silver coinage, for its part, was without a larger piece of the calibre of the thaler. It was resolved to bring the coinage up to date in these respects. Moreover it was accepted that clipping was the root cause of the deficiencies of the currency and that the remedy lay in the striking of perfectly round coins by mechanical process. A distinguished medallist from Liège, Jean Varin [figure 263], was appointed to superintend a new coinage and the conversion of the Paris mint to machinery.

By 1640, the value of the écu d'or had risen to over five livres. It was found convenient to issue a new coin of the same weight but of 22 carats to be current for five livres exactly. It was distinguished by a portrait of King Louis XIII, and was called for that reason the *louis d'or* on the analogy of the portrait *henri d'or* of the 1550s. Since all the subsequent kings of France were called Louis it was never found necessary to change this name, though as it happened it was soon transferred to another coin. Just as the pistole supplanted the escudo as the standard unit in Spain, so the ten livres coin which was provided in the new French system supplanted the piece worth five livres. The larger coin took the name *louis d'or* and the other was demoted to become the fractional *demi-louis*. Internationally, the name *pistole* was applied indiscriminately to both the new louis d'or and the Spanish double escudo.

The feature of the new silver coinage was the big *louis d'argent*, another portrait coin and one of Jean Varin's masterpieces as an engraver [figure 245]. This did not keep its original name for long. It was tariffed at three livres, which was the traditional value of the écu d'or as fixed in 1577. Although the écu d'or was worth more than five livres in 1641, the association of ideas was still strong enough for the term *écu* to become attached to the new silver coin. The reverse design, a large plain shield of arms, contributed to the appropriateness of the new name. From the reign of Louis XIV until the Revolution, the French dollar-sized coin was officially called the écu d'argent, whatever its design, and unofficially the name stuck to the five franc piece until late in the nineteenth century.

The *écu d'argent* of 1641 was accompanied by a series of scarcely less elegant fractional coins, but the old hammered coinage was still struck until 1646. This caused some confusion, for the centrepiece of the latter was the so-called quarter-écu, which was theoretically linked not to the new écu d'argent but to the écu d'or of 1577. Thus for some years the mint issued simultaneously écus tariffed at three livres and quarter-écus tariffed at one livre. It was not until 1656 that the French coinage was finally re-established on a homogeneous system.

There followed under the direction of Colbert one of those periods

246 Joseph Roettiers, who became engraver general to Louis XIV in 1682 and held the post trough the early phase of the *réformations*. An engraving by C. Vermeulen from a painting by Largillière

247 France; demi-écu aux palmes, *c.* 1694, overstruck on a demi-écu aux 8 LL, Louis XIV; an example of Louis's *réformations*, with the design and legend of the earlier piece showing through plainly [actual size]

of exceptional monetary stability which in France have punctuated the progress of inflation. Apart from one issue of petty coinage, there was no mutation of the currency during his ministry (1661–83) and in 1679 he even abolished the tax levied on bullion brought to the mint. However, a wretched episode then ensued. In the war conditions of the 1680s, prices rose so much that Frenchmen exported bullion rather than bring it to the mint at the official rate. In 1689, Louis XIV found it necessary to order that all plate in private hands be brought to the mint. In the same year he entered upon the first of his *réformations*. The technique of these was as follows. The government announced that on a certain date all major coins in circulation would be demonetised. Ecus brought to the mint in good time would be credited at, say, 62 sous, a small premium on the official current rate of 60, and other coins commensurately. They would then be struck with a new design and reissued at 66 sous, thus showing a profit to the king of four sous, less minting expenses. To save these expenses the coins were not melted down, but simply restruck over the old design, a technique facilitated by the recently installed machinery [figure 247]. After reissue the coins would be called down in value by a series of edicts to the original value of 60 sous. The process would then be started again. With variations in the actual figures involved, réformations were repeated five times between 1689 and 1715 and once again in the early years of Louis XV, when a réformation associated with the Noailles ministry taxed the

248 Thomas Simon, from the engraving by George Vertue in his work *Medals, Coins, Great Seals and Other Works of Thomas Simon*, 1753

public no less than twenty per cent. Nearly all the coins of those years bear the marks of restriking. It was sad work for the chief engraver, Joseph Roettiers [figure 246], whose sometimes distinguished designs were ruined by the overstriking to which they were subject.

Not only in France were members of the Roettiers family actively employed as die-engravers during the later years of the seventeenth century. In 1661 it was resolved to convert the London mint to the mill and screw press and Charles II appointed Jan Roettiers to engrave the dies for a new coinage. Jan was competent enough, but the appointment was unfortunate, since it displaced Thomas Simon, the Jean Varin of English medallists. Thomas Simon had held the post of chief engraver under the Commonwealth. There was no scope for his talents in the Commonwealth coinage, and the best of his work is therefore rare. It consists of a pattern coinage which he made for Oliver Cromwell as Lord Protector, work of a truly Roman severity [figure 249] and some more delicate but not more noble patterns of coins for Charles II. The most famous of these was the Petition Crown [figure 264] which he presented to the king in the hope of getting his job back. This masterpiece was perhaps too finely engraved to stand up to mass reproduction and everyday wear and tear, but Simon's Cromwell coinage shows that he could have made dies for a big coinage as satisfactorily as Jean Varin did in France, where even the smallest piece was a coin of dignity and distinction.

The English milled coinage of 1662 was issued in the same denominations as the old hammered coinage, but at slightly reduced weights. This deficiency in the new coins was more than compensated for by their immunity from clipping. A remarkable fact about the silver was that the crown, hitherto never a common piece, was more plentiful than the lesser coins. The reason for this was the surplus of silver at the mint caused by the payment of one and a half million écus d'argent by Louis XIV for the purchase of Dunkirk in 1662 and the subsidies which Louis paid Charles later under the terms of the treaty of Dover. Coins made from this French metal were not distinguished in any way, presumably because their origin was felt to be slightly discreditable. Otherwise the mint did at that time adopt the policy of marking coins made from certain classes of bullion. The plume and the rose, which had been the badges of the two main regional groups of royalist coinage during the civil war, were reintroduced at the Tower mint under Charles II to denote coins made from Welsh or west country silver. In later reigns coins made from bullion captured in the raid on Vigo Bay (1702) [figure 252] and by Anson in his Pacific expedition (1744) were appropriately marked. The initials of the South Sea Company were placed on silver coins of George I and those of the East India Company on gold of George II, when the metal was brought to the mint by those corporations. Over a long period coins made from bullion imported by the African Company were marked with a little elephant [figure 250].

249 England; silver crown, 1658, Oliver Cromwell, Lord Protector, London, from dies by Thomas Simon [actual size]

250 England; gold guinea, 1663, Charles II, London. This took its name from the Guinea gold from which it was made. The little elephant was the badge of the African Company which delivered the bullion to the mint [actual size]

251 England; silver shilling, 1696, William III, Norwich. A coin from one of the provincial mints set up to deal with the recoinage of the old hammered money in 1696–7 [actual size]

252 England; silver sixpence, 1703, Anne, London. The word VIGO under the queen's bust signifies that this was made from bullion captured in the raid on Vigo Bay the previous year [actual size]

It so happened that the African Company's gold from Guinea made up a high proportion of the total supply in the early years of the new milled coinage. It was thus that the name *guinea* arose to distinguish the new gold pieces worth one pound sterling from the theoretically heavier hammered gold broad pieces. The guinea kept this name long after most of the gold was coming from other sources, but its value soon changed. During a series of bimetallic crises towards the end of the century it rose from £1 to 30s. It then subsided to 21s. at which it held steady for the last eighty years of the eighteenth century. This stable period was long enough for the value of 21s. to become identified with the name. The guinea went out of circulation in 1816, but as money of account the term is in use to this day.

For some years the new milled money in England did not circulate freely because of the large quantity of clipped and worn hammered money which was still current. In 1695 it was resolved to demonetise the old silver, but a year was allowed in which everyone who brought it to the mint should receive full face value in new milled coin. There were many who, by giving the old coins a final clipping before handing them over, made a useful profit out of the operation. Nevertheless the English government, by its honest dealing on this occasion, laid the foundations of that reputation for financial probity which contributed so much to its prosperity in the next two centuries. The deficit, amounting to £2,700,000, was met by a house duty assessment, the so-called window tax. Five provincial mints were set up for the recoinage, the coins from which were all marked with the appropriate initial [figure 251]. They were closed again in 1697 when the recoinage was completed. The total amount struck in the operation was nearly £6.9 million; it was thus nineteen times bigger than Elizabeth's similar recoinage of 1561–2.

In 1707, by the union of England and Scotland, the Scots currency was merged with sterling. That was the end of the Scottish coinage as such, but the Edinburgh mint was very active during the next year or two recoining the old Scottish silver into coins of English denomination and type. These were distinguished by the initial E appearing under the ample bust of Queen Anne.

The Irish coinage, always a scandal because of the way in which the English government debased it, treating it as a means simply of exploiting the country, was reduced to a more lamentable state than ever as a consequence of James II's war of resistance against William of Orange. Having no gold or silver with which to pay his troops, James issued unlimited quantities of half-crowns, shillings and sixpences made of brass [figure 253]. These caused raging inflation, which James made worse still when he restruck the half-crowns with a new design and called them crowns. This coinage was called gun money because of the metal used for its manufacture. It was inscribed with the month as well as the year when it was minted, a feature which rather emphasised its ephemeral character. After the war William's

253 Ireland; brass half-crown 1689, James II. A half-crown of the so-called gun money which James, who had no bullion, issued to finance his war against William of Orange [actual size]

254 Ireland; brass halfpenny, 1722, George I. Issued by Mr. Wood under royal patent, these were rejected by the Irish and many were eventually sent to the American colonies to provide the small change there [actual size]

255 Russia; silver rouble, 1705, Peter the Great, Moscow. The coinage was one of the Russian institutions which Peter reformed on advanced western European principles [actual size]

government very properly called down the value of the crowns and half-crowns to a penny, the shillings to a halfpenny and the sixpences to a farthing. This episode left the Irish with a justifiable distaste for brass money which made the reintroduction of a proper token coinage extremely difficult. In 1722 William Wood, an English hardware dealer, was granted a monopoly for the supply of brass halfpence [figure 254] to Ireland. The patent system under which this coinage was imposed was open to objection, but otherwise the proposal was sound. It was opposed nevertheless and Dean Swift, who contributed his *Drapier's Letters* to the Irish cause, was able to appeal to all the prejudice against base metal coinage which a people once inflicted with gun money might have been expected to feel. He aroused such antagonism to the scheme that the government had to withdraw. Wood was permitted to export his halfpence to the American colonies instead, for which the next year he struck coins of a new type, the so-called Rosa Americana halfpence.

An experience akin to that of the Irish with gun money was imposed upon the Russians in the middle of the seventeenth century by Czar Alexis Mikailovitch. The native Russian coinage then consisted of little silver *kopeks*, but foreign coins circulated freely, especially ducats and thalers from Poland, Saxony and Silesia. The ducat was equivalent to a unit of account called the *rouble* and thalers were current at half a rouble. These coins were countermarked with the Russian eagle on one side and the mounted figure of the czar on the other which made them part of the official currency of Russia. In 1655 Alexis, financially straitened by war, conceived the idea of issuing copper coins of the same size and nominal value as the silver coins in circulation. Inevitably this drove the real silver coins to a premium, which rose to three hundred per cent before the copper coins were withdrawn to the loss of those who held them.

In 1698, Peter the Great set about the reorganisation of the Russian coinage to bring it up to western European standards. He began with a devaluation. He cut the value of the rouble from the equivalent of two thalers to one and in 1704 issued it for the first time as a coin [figure 255]. The accounting system was based upon the rouble of one hundred kopeks. The kopek was struck in copper. The gold coin, the *chervonets*, equivalent to the ducat was strictly outside the system since it was allowed to fluctuate in value, but later in the century, when more stable conditions prevailed, gold multiples of the rouble were issued. Peter introduced machinery to the Moscow mint, and in 1725 he opened a new mint at his new capital of St Petersburg.

As a result of Peter the Great's reforms, the Russian coinage, from being the most old-fashioned in Europe, became the most up to date. It was the first to be ordered on the decimal system. Those coins which did not fit into the decimal scheme, namely the *altynnik* worth three kopeks and the twelve kopek piece, were eventually withdrawn. Merchants from western Europe who traded with Russia were full of

256 Sweden; silver rixdaler 1642, Christina, Stockholm [actual size]

admiration for this system, which they urged their own government to copy. However, there was one other feature of Russian coinage during the eighteenth century which was not so convenient for the mercantile community. The czarina Catherine I (1725–7) commissioned a coinage of copper at the mint of Ekaterinburg in Siberia, in denominations ranging from one rouble to one kopek. This was not a fiduciary issue, like that of Alexis Mikailovitch. These pieces were in theory worth their weight in copper, which was the metal most plentiful in the area. The more valuable pieces however were extremely heavy, weighing several pounds each; they were therefore quite unsuitable for common use.

The idea of copper coins of vast proportions originated with Russia's neighbour, Sweden. Queen Christina (1633–54) issued similarly enormous pieces, known as *plåtmynt*, along with her normal coinage of *rixdalers*. The plåtmynt [figure 256], like the great copper coins of Russia, were issued at special mints set up at the mines. The intention behind both was to unload on to the market an important national product at a guaranteed price. Their effect was not very inflationary, partly we may assume because their velocity of circulation was low [figure 257]. It is true that the Swedish currency fell into disorder, but that was not because of the plåtmynt. There was serious tampering with the silver coinage by Charles XI (1660–97) and then there were the disastrous monetary experiments of Baron Görtz, the minister of Charles XII. The baron planned to repair the state's broken finances by the issue of an enormous token coinage of small copper rixdalers. Of course, far from repairing them, he only made them worse. The worthlessness of his coinage was all the more apparent in the country of the plåtmynt where everyone knew very well how big a copper rixdaler ought to be. The minister was unwise enough to put his own head on some of these *myntteken* as they were called [figure 258]. It was with his head that he paid when he fell from power after Charles XII was killed.

Ingenious financial experiments were generally fashionable in the early years of the eighteenth century. The most famous of these was the 'system' which John Law persuaded the French government to adopt in 1719. Law became *fermier général des monnaies*, but his influence on the coinage was negative since his idea was to substitute paper money for specie and to invalidate contracts which stipulated payment in the latter. Ideally he would have abolished all coinage except small change, and he came near to doing so in practice, since no gold was struck under his direction and two minor coins only in silver. These, the so called *livre de la Compagnie des Indes* and the *petit louis d'argent* tariffed at three livres, were both very much under weight. Law's system collapsed and this disaster, coming after twenty years of successive *réformations*, caused complete financial chaos. It was six years more before a new administration, that of Cardinal Fleury, determined to return to sound money. The louis d'or and the écu were

257 Sweden; copper daler, 1758,
Adolphus Frederick II, Gustafsberg.
An example of plåtmynt,
enormous copper pieces,
containing their full value in
metal, which were issued by the
Swedish and Russian authorities at
mints near their copper mines.
Pieces weighing up to 160 kg.
are recorded [actual size]

258 Sweden; copper daler, 1719,
Charles XII. A disastrous
financial experiment by Baron
Görtz, the prime minister,
who unwisely identified himself
with it by putting his own head
on the coins [actual size]

guaranteed against further *réformations* and established at the lowes[t]
values which it was thought that they could hold, twenty livres an[d]
five livres respectively. This was one of the first of those effective so[-]
cial reforms of the *ancien régime* which led to, or failed to avert, th[e]
French revolution. A twenty per cent devaluation of the livre too[k]
place in 1740, but that was the last. For the last half-century befor[e]
the revolution the louis d'or held at twenty-four livres and the écu a[t]
six. Mutation of the currency, which had caused so much social dis[-]
tress in France in previous centuries, was not one of the grievance[s]
which caused the revolution of 1789.

The eighteenth century was a period of exceptional monetary stabil[-]
ity in all countries. The economy of the world was expanding fast, bu[t]
so was the money supply. It is at this point, however, that the histor[-]
ian of coinage begins to have relatively less contribution to make t[o]
general economic history. For although the eighteenth century saw [a]
bigger increase in the supply of gold and silver than any previou[s]
century, this was not so important among the leading commercial na[-]
tions as the growing use of paper money and other forms of credit[.]
Coins began to lose their international role to these new forms o[f]
money. More were minted during the eighteenth century than eve[r]
before, but they were mostly only of local significance. However, ther[e]
was one important exception, one class of coins which achieved in th[e]
eighteenth century the international status of the doubloon in the six[-]
teenth or the ducat in the fifteenth.

259 Brazil; gold moidore, 1703,
Peter II of Portugal and dobra de
quadro escudos, 1739, John V,
both Rio de Janeiro. The
great gold deposits of Brazil
made the moidore one of the
foremost international coins
of the eighteenth century
[actual size]

260 Holland; silver gulden, 1749,
Dordrecht. The standard silver
coin of the United Provinces
as established in 1694 [actual size]

261 Olmütz; silver thaler, 1695,
Bishop Charles II von
Liechtenstein, Kremsier. The
sovereign prince-bishops of
Olmütz in Moravia kept up a
magnificent but old-fashioned
coinage of thalers until the
nineteenth century [actual size]

In the last decade of the seventeenth century, big gold deposits were found in south-eastern Brazil. Since the 1660s the standard gold coin of Brazil was the so-called *moeda da ouro* [figure 259]. This was of the same basic type as the old cruzado, but bigger and marked with the figures 4000 beside the shield signifying the value in *milreis*, the Portuguese unit of account. With the development of the Brazilian goldfields after 1700, there was a great increase in the minting of the moeda da ouro. Under the universal name of *moidore* it became the gold coin most commonly traded in the New World and it vied with the guinea and the louis d'or in the transactions of the bullion dealers of Amsterdam and the London bankers. Actually in Europe the figure 4,000 was misleading. The gold : silver ratio was abnormally low in Brazil, where gold was plentiful. In Portugal the value of the moidore in terms of silver was some twenty per cent higher and the moidore was usually worth about 4,800 milreis.

In 1720 John v of Portugal authorised a new mint at Villa Rica de Ouro Preto in the mining province of Minas Geraes. There and at Rio de Janeiro a series of larger gold portrait coins was struck, including some very heavy multiples. These coins did not have the universal success of the moidores, but they circulated extensively in North America where they were known as *joes* after the kings John v, John vi and Joseph i whose portraits and names (*Jo*annes and *Jo*sephus) figured on them so largely [figure 259].

Britain was the great commercial and industrial power of the eighteenth century and the guinea was, after the moidore, the most important coin in international trade. Its wider circulation was promoted by the government's policy of paying continental powers to fight Britain's European wars for her rather than fight them herself. Nevertheless, for all their worldwide acceptance, neither the moidore nor the guinea gave rise to imitations. Their era was one of growing nationalism, in coinage as in other affairs. The nations were settling down to their own currencies to the exclusion of each other's, in the Netherlands to the ducat and the gulden [figure 260] as established in 1694, in France to the louis and the écu as fixed in 1726, in Russia to the rouble of Peter the Great and so on.

Even Germany strove through a series of acrimonious conventions towards a national coinage. These were only partly successful since there always were some states which opted out, this time the Hanseatic cities, another time the house of Austria and almost always the kingdom of Prussia. These conventions between the adherents of three main accounting systems, thalers, gulden and marks, were the reason why so many German coins were struck in what appear to be complicated fractional denominations. The common two thirds denomination, for example [figure 262], is simply the silver gulden expressed in terms of the thaler. After the convention of 1753 it was normal for all major German silver coins to show in the inscription how many of them went to make up the fine mark of Cologne, which was the

262 Brunswick-Lüneburg; silver gulden, 1679, Duke John Frederick, Clausthal (mint-master Heinrich Bonhorst). Saxony; silver gulden 1690, Elector John George III, Dresden (mint-master Johann Kühnlein). German gulden of the late seventeenth century with marks of value signifying two thirds of a thaler. John Frederick was the uncle of George I of England [actual size]

263 *(opposite)* Jean Varin showing an antique medal to the young Louis XIV

commonly accepted bullion measure for the whole country. The history of German coinage in those years is extremely complicated and superficially it is made no easier by the cryptic legends which are found, especially on the smaller coins. From the time of the emperor Charles VI there was a great proliferation of titles and imperial offices all over Germany and the minor princes would abate none of them on their own coins. It was therefore necessary to shorten the titles to initials. The Elector Palatine Charles Theodore (1743–99) achieved a string of no less than fifty initials, and runs of up to twenty or so were quite common. When such legends are coupled with a much quartered shield of arms or an indecipherable monogram, quite difficult

problems of identification can occur. This practice was imported to Great Britain by George I on whose gold and silver the arms of England and Scotland were squeezed up into one small quarter to make room for those of Hanover and Brunswick-Lüneburg while the royal titles were quite outweighed by the important one of arch-treasurer of the Holy Roman Empire.

The exclusive nationalism which characterised so much of eighteenth-century coinage was in fact confined to the older and more settled European economies. The undeveloped parts of the world were still the sort of monetary free-for-all that Europe had been in 1400. Thus it was in the New World that the moidore originated and found a circulation area free enough and large enough for it to become a coin of universal repute within a few years. And in the New World also the Spanish dollar sustained and even extended its international role during the period. The productivity of the Mexican and to some extent also the Peruvian mines was reintensified by new industrial processes and in the reigns of Ferdinand VI (1746–59) and Charles III (1759–88) the output was higher than ever before. Moreover the American mints were now mechanised and the dollars of this epoch therefore were well made coins, fit for heavy use in an active and practical age. Few of them took the old route to Seville. Some were carried by the Dutch three-quarters of the way round the world to be traded in the East Indies. A great number were drained away from Mexico to China in exchange for silks and porcelain which the Creoles, with their rising standard of living, demanded. Chinese traders used to make a little chopmark on those which came into their hands in order to test their quality for themselves [figure 265]. Many dollars of Charles III and Charles IV have been treated in this way. They thus span three disparate civilizations with the head of a Bourbon king stamped on American metal and defaced by Asiatic money-changers.

Mexican and Peruvian dollars circulated widely in Europe. When Great Britain was cut off from this source during the wars with France and Spain the country suffered from a severe silver famine, though there was plenty elsewhere as abundant issues of French écus testify. With the rise in the price of the metal, English silver coins fresh from the mint were worth more than their face value and in the second half of the century virtually none were struck. When in the years of peace silver came flooding back into the country, it was in the form of Spanish dollars. However, their price was too high for them to be recoined at the old standard so they simply circulated as they were. A few were countermarked by industrial companies for circulation at a small premium and in 1797 the government itself adopted this idea and countermarked dollars with the king of England's head for currency at 4s. 9d. Finally in 1804 the Bank of England was authorised to restrike Spanish dollars to be current for five shillings [figure 266].

For the future of the dollar, the area of circulation which was most important was the American continent. More and more dollars were

264 *(opposite)* England; silver crown, 1663, Charles II. The Petition Crown, a pattern by Thomas Simon which he presented to the king in the hope of reinstatement after he was replaced at the mint by Jan Roettiers

265 Mexico; silver eight reals, 1782, Charles III.
Brazil, silver 960 milreis, 1819,
John VI of Portugal, Rio de Janiero.
Two Spanish dollars which met different fates,
the first one of many which was traded
in the area of the China Sea and was chopmarked by
Chinese traders and the second, a dollar of
Charles IV (1788–1808) which went to Brazil and was
overstruck in the name of John VI [enlarged 2:1]

required at home for the expanding economies of Mexico and Peru. Dollars circulated widely in the non-silver-producing provinces and countries of South America, where they were countermarked, overstruck and chopped up in endless variety [figure 265]. The dollar was the progenitor of the *peso*, which formed the basis of most South American coinages when the Spanish provinces gained their independence. In North America there was more competition from other currencies. The French alliance during the War of Independence was supported by big subsidies in louis d'or, which Congress distributed to its army and fleet and which circulated thereafter along with Brazilian joes and English guineas. Nevertheless contemporaries estimated that at the end of the war Spanish dollars outnumbered other coins current in North America by three or four to one.

266 Great Britain; silver dollar
1804, George III. A Spanish
dollar overstruck by the Bank
of England during the Napoleonic
war, when silver was short
and it was uneconomic for the
Royal Mint to strike silver
coins of full weight [enlarged 2:1]

10 The Retreat from Silver
–and from Gold

267 *(opposite)* United States of America; silver dollar, 1795, Philadelphia. An early striking of the US dollar as finally specified by the Mint Act, 1792 [enlarged 3:1]

The accounting system used in the American colonies was the same as in England, but the exchange rate between the colonies and sterling was not at par and parity was lost even between the several colonies. After independence it was agreed that the United States should have their own uniform currency system, but no state would accord primacy to any other. One theorist proposed to resolve the issue by basing a new system upon the lowest common denominator of the states' exchange rates, but Thomas Jefferson pointed out that the object of the reform was to get rid of the colonial currencies whereas that proposal merely perpetuated them all. Jefferson pointed to the Spanish dollar as the coin 'most familiar of all to the mind of the people' and suggested that that should be the unit and be divided by the most simple reckoning on the decimal system, 'The course of our commerce,' he wrote of the dollar, 'will bring us more of this than of any other foreign coin . . . I know of no Unit which can be proposed in competition with the dollar but the pound: but what is the pound? 1547 grains of fine silver in Georgia, 1289 grains in Virginia, Connecticut, Rhode Island, Massachusetts and New Hampshire, $1031\frac{1}{4}$ grains in Maryland, Delaware, Pennsylvania and New Jersey, $966\frac{3}{4}$ grains in North Carolina and New York. Which of these shall we adopt? . . . Or shall we hang the pound sterling as a common badge about all their necks?' A grand committee of Congress considered the proposals and decided, with some modification, in favour of Jefferson's; it recommended the dollar as likely in time to 'produce the happy effect of Uniformity in counting money throughout the Union', and only departed from the strictest decimal principles in suggesting a quarter-dollar and a half-cent piece among the lesser coins. In July 1785 Congress enacted that the money unit of the United States be the dollar; that the smallest coin be of copper, of which 200 shall pass for one dollar; and that the several pieces shall increase in a decimal ratio.

The 1785 Act was expressed in vague terms. It left open the exact value of the dollar and whether it was to be on the gold or the silver standard or both. The mint and the design of the coins still had to be decided. In 1786 Congress fixed the dollar at 375.64 grains of fine silver, but it had no real control of the matter as long as the actual coins in circulation were minted by the Spanish authorities, whose

268 United States of America;
copper cent, 1791, George
Washington, Philadelphia.
An early pattern for the United
States copper. The idea that this
should bear a portrait of the
President in office was opposed by
Washington personally and was
not adopted [actual size]

269 Matthew Boulton, the English
engineer who applied the
methods of the industrial
revolution to the English mint
and offered to make the first
coinage for the United States.
A portrait by a unknown artist
in the National Portrait Gallery

debasement of the coinage at any time would effectively devalue the United States dollar also. The solution was for the Americans to set up their own mint and issue their own coinage, but they were a long time in doing so. Money was short for anything except copper. Old colonial habits died hard and the government's first instinct was to place the contract for this copper coinage in Europe. It was only after failure in this direction that it became apparent that the United States must at once have a mint of their own. By the Mint Act (1792) a mint was established at Philadelphia. It was to strike coins in gold, silver and copper. The coinage was to be issued on a bimetallic standard and the unit was to be the dollar containing $371\frac{1}{4}$ grains of fine silver. This revised figure was arrived at by a sample test of Spanish dollars circulating in the United States. A mint Spanish dollar contained rather more silver, but naturally the coins in North American use were rather worn. The adjustment made sense from the domestic point of view, but it put the United States coin at a discount in the international market. The design of the gold and silver was to be on the obverse 'an impression emblematic of liberty' and on the reverse the representation of an eagle [figure 267]. It was originally intended that the copper should carry the portrait of the President. George Washington however deprecated the idea and the House of Representatives opposed it. 'However well pleased they might be with the head of the great man now their President,' warned Representative Page, 'they may have no great reason to be pleased with some of his successors'. After all it was decided to have Liberty on the copper also, but patterns of George Washington cents were made [figure 268]. The copper coins were not legal tender and were only to be accepted at will; nevertheless the cent, containing 264 grains of pure copper, was not overvalued.

The first mint of the United States of America was somewhat primitively equipped, since the government, in its anxiety to keep it independent, rejected offers of trained men and modern machinery from England. The man who made these offers was Matthew Boulton [figure 269] who had also made a bid for the contract when the Americans were considering importing their whole coinage from a European mint. Matthew Boulton was associated with James Watt in the development of the steam engine; his interests extended to many branches of industry, metallurgy and mines. He first began to consider the application of steam-power to the minting process in 1774 when the British government finally gave up what appeared to be the unequal struggle to provide an adequate domestic copper coinage in the face of wholesale counterfeiting by shady button-making and die-stamping concerns in Birmingham. Within a few years the government's abandonment of its responsibility was causing serious hardship among the industrial wage earners. These were the years of the silver famine in England. There was a shortage of all small change, which gave industrialists an excuse for paying their workmen in bad coin. In 1780 Boulton estimated that two thirds of the halfpence which he received

270 England; copper halfpenny tokens issued by Coalbrookdale Ironworks, Coalbrookdale, Shropshire, 1792, and by John Wilkinson, iron-master of Birmingham, 1793. Two tokens of the industrial revolution, manufactured by Matthew Boulton's new process. Their designs commemorate technical achievements of the age [actual size]

in change at tollgates and such places were counterfeit. They were sold by the forgers at one pound for thirty-six shillings face value.

What had happened in England was that the industrial revolution had generated demand for money on an unprecedented scale. The demand for big money, for industrial and commercial capital and for big payments between industrial concerns, was met essentially by the creation of paper money and credit, though here the mint did play a part with a heavy output of guineas. The demand for small money, on the other hand, for wage payments and the retail transactions of poorly paid workers could only be met by an increase in the supply of coin. The alternative of truck payments by the employers was recognised from the start as socially undesirable. However the mint, with its manually operated and horse-driven equipment, could not economically meet the increased demand. Coinage for an industrial nation had to be produced on an industrial scale. The Birmingham button manufacturers perhaps dimly recognised this. Boulton urged the argument upon the government and developed at his factory in Soho, Birmingham, machinery which could perform the task.

In spite of Matthew Boulton's urging, it was some years before the government took any action. In the meantime the public need was met by private enterprise. In 1787 Thomas Williams of the Anglesey Copper Mines Company issued full weight penny and halfpenny tokens payable in London, Liverpool or Anglesey. In the same year John Wilkinson, one of the great iron-masters of Birmingham, also began to issue copper tokens, later employing Matthew Boulton's machinery for the purpose [figure 270]. In the years 1790-5 halfpenny tokens became extremely common, especially in the industrial areas of the midlands and the north. Juridically they resembled those issued a hundred and thirty years earlier, but in other respects they forcefully illustrate the changes which had taken place in England in the meantime. Those were shabbily struck, these were made by the latest industrial process; those were issued by small retailers evenly spread all over the country, these by manufacturing concerns concentrated in a few industrial areas. The designs of the eighteenth century often proudly illustrate the pace of recent technological advance with representations of glass and iron furnaces, bridges and canals [figure 270]. They were favourably received at first and the issuers used them as prestige advertisements. Most were marked on the edge with the places where they were payable, usually an important centre such as London, Liverpool or Birmingham, and also the localities where the issuing company employed most labour.

The eighteenth-century tokens, like those of the seventeenth, were mostly honest. However, as they proliferated, more frauds were practised; moreover the war with France caused a rise in the price of copper and the average weight of the tokens was reduced. The public became uneasy about them. However, the point was proved, that it was physically possible to provide an adequate petty coinage for an industrial society. It only remained for the government to take up the challenge, which it did in 1797 by employing Matthew Boulton to manufacture a regal copper coinage at his Soho Mint. In the next two years more than one thousand tons of twopenny pieces, pence, half-pence and farthings were issued. In a systematic manner typical of his generation Boulton fixed the weights of the penny at one ounce exactly and the twopence at two ounces. The twopenny piece [figure 279] was the biggest coin yet minted on a substantial scale; it would have been an impossible project without the steam press. Even so it accounted for less that two per cent of the issue; it was always regarded as a curiosity and did not circulate much. It was the pence and halfpence of this and a subsequent issue by Boulton in 1806–7 which bore the burden of the common retail transactions of early nineteenth-century England, as the state of wear of most of the surviving coins proclaims.

The American, the Industrial and the French Revolutions all had an important effect upon the coinage of the countries most immediately concerned, and, after some interaction between those three, upon that of the rest of the world also. The French Revolution occurred at the end of a long period of monetary stability. In the first years the only change in the coinage was in its outward constitutional aspect. After a competition held in 1791 and judged by the painter J.-L. David, Augustin Dupré, an artist of the neo-classical school, was appointed to engrave a new coinage. He designed for the reverse, in place of the conventional heraldry, a representation of the spirit of the Constitution engraving a tablet. His portrait of Louis XVI was unflattering. The inscription was written in French instead of Latin and the king's titles were modified [figure 271]. However, for all its revolutionary appearance this coinage was conservative in spirit. The weights, alloys and values were the same as they were under the ancien régime. The most important monetary innovation of the period of constitutional monarchy was the reintroduction of paper money in the form of *assignats*, theoretically backed by the *biens nationaux* confiscated from the crown and the church. These, however, were nothing to do with the coinage.

One unforeseen result of the Constitution of 1791 was a spate of private coinage, issued mostly by industrial firms in Paris. The example for this was given by the English token coinage, then in full vigour, but its legal justification lay in article 5 of the Constitution which declared 'Tout ce qui n'est pas défendu par la loi ne peut être empêché'. No doubt these tokens fulfilled an economic need in the industrial quarters of Paris, though as a whole France was better provided than England with petty coinage and, being less industrialised, had less need of it. In 1792 the private tokens were specifically forbidden by law and no more were issued.

Louis XVI was deposed in August 1792 but the Convention Nationale was too much occupied with other matters to attend to the coinage, which continued in the king's name until after his execution in January 1793. Suitable republican emblems were then chosen to replace

271 France; écu constitutionel, 1792, Louis XVI, Paris, from dies by Augustin Dupré. The first coins of the French Revolution were from designs chosen by the painter J.-L. David [enlarged 2:1]

the king's head, but apart from copper coins only the silver écu and the gold twenty-four livres (the former louis) were struck in the early republican period, since the ever-multiplying assignats were beginning to drive gold and silver out of circulation. Thus, when in 1793 the Convention, inspired by the American example, set about a radical reform of the monetary system the reforms took place in a sort of coinage vacuum.

During the years 1793–1803 a number of tentative experiments were made. Their object was to replace the old system of account by a decimal one and to ensure monetary stability by identifying legally the unit of account with an actual coin of defined weight and alloy. The American solution to this problem was to take as the unit the coin most commonly in circulation. The French reverted to the policy foreshadowed by Henry III in 1577. They took the livre at its current value and gave it physical expression again as a coin, for which the name *franc* was at the same time traditional and in accord with the revolutionary spirit of French nationalism. They made it obligatory to express prices in terms of francs with decimal divisions into *décimes* and *centimes*, both of which were struck as copper coins. Old accounts were carried forward on the basis of the equivalence of franc and livre. In popular usage, because the French are a conservative people where money is concerned, the expression *sou* survived as the term for the five centime piece.

The monetary reforms of the First Republic were finally codified in the *loi du 17 Germinal an* XI (April 1803) which defined the franc in terms of both gold and silver. In silver the coin was to weigh five grams of a fineness of 0.900. The specification for the gold twenty franc made the franc equivalent to 290.3 mg. of pure gold, which gave the relationship between the two metals at 15.5 : 1. By 1803

272 France; silver franc, year XI (1803–4), Napoleon Bonaparte, First Consul, Paris. The franc of Germinal, 0.900 fine and weighing five grams, the currency unit of post-revolutionary France [actual size]

the assignats were demonetised and the inflation which they had caused was over. Gold and silver, which had been withheld during the years of instability, flowed again to the mint as soon as a sound money policy was adopted. The franc of Germinal therefore made its début in a heavy issue of both gold and silver. Unlike its tentative forerunners of the past ten years, it did not bear emblems of the republic and liberty, but a fine classical portrait of the First Consul Bonaparte [figure 272] executed by Pierre Joseph Tiolier [figure 273]. On the analogy of the louis, the twenty franc piece was commonly called the *napoléon*.

Napoleon was by no means solely responsible for the franc of Germinal, which was evolved over a ten year period. It was he however who, much as Charlemagne had done with the denier a thousand years earlier, first extended its use to other parts of Europe: to the Austrian Netherlands, when they were annexed to France, and then to Italy. Italy succumbed gradually, first Piedmont, then Genoa and Liguria. Tuscany adopted decimal coinage in 1803. Finally, after the establishment of the napoleonic kingdom of Italy, a decree of March 1806 ordained that the money of Italy should be uniform with that already current in France. It was deemed impolitic to change the name lira to franc, but the weight and fineness of the two coins were the same, and the same multiples and fractions were struck in gold and silver. To this system the kingdom of Naples, to which Napoleon's son-in-law Joachim Murat was appointed, also conformed eventually.

In France the franc of Germinal was regarded as one of the undoubted blessings of the revolutionary years. The restored Bourbons did not venture to tamper with it, though its outward aspect faithfully reflected the subsequent changes in the political scene with regal heraldry for the Bourbons, a civic wreath of oak and a utilitarian mark of value for the bourgeois monarchy of Louis Philippe, emblems of liberty and freemasonry for the second Republic and imperial laurels and eagle for Napoleon III. Throughout those years its content was unchanged. The Austrian Netherlands however reverted to Austrian currency after 1815, only returning to the franc when the Belgian monarchy was established in 1831. In Italy the restoration of the old regimes was followed by a reversion to monetary confusion. The Venetian and Lombard provinces were given over to the Austrian system. Tuscany, Rome and the Two Sicilies all returned to a revised version of their traditional currencies. Only the duchy of Parma and Savoy, where French influence remained strong, retained the lira of 1806 [figure 274]. However, the napoleonic experiment was not forgotten and it was under the house of Savoy that Italy was eventually reunited. In 1862 the lira of 1806 once again became the monetary unit of Italy.

Even in those countries where Napoleon did not reform the currency on the same lines as in France, a certain uniformity was imposed upon the coinage as a result of his conquests. This was a matter of style, not content, since in Spain, the Netherlands and Germany his brothers

273 Pierre Joseph Tiolier (1763–1819), engraver general of the French coinage during the reign of Napoleon

Joseph, Louis and Jerome struck reals, gulden and thalers as the rulers of those countries had done for years past. Nevertheless there was a strong similarity between their coins, with their austere portraiture and laconic inscriptions, which went far beyond the mere family resemblance between the brothers. This was the heyday of neo-classicism. These were also the first years in which minting by the steam press become common, and it often happens that a new process such as that is stimulating to the artists who work with it. This was therefore, as it transpired, the last period of really beautiful coinage, comparable with the first years of the mill and screw press. The coins of the Bonaparte brothers were all of fine quality, but the best work of the time was done in Italy where Napoleon's incursion caused an artistic revival. There the range of expression ran from the academic classicism of the jugate busts of Elisa and Felice Baciocchi, Napoleon's sister and brother-in-law, on the coinage of Lucca, to the Byronic bravura of Joachim Murat's portrait as king of Naples [figure 274].

One of the most influential patrons of contemporary Italian art was the Prince Regent, later George IV of England. It was through his taste and influence that an Italian medallist Benedetto Pistrucci was appointed to design and engrave new dies for a great recoinage in England in the last years of George III. For the several denominations of this coinage Pistrucci produced a series of busts of the old king no less monumental than the best portraits of the Napoleonic coinage, and more full of feeling. For the reverse of the sovereign and the crown he created one of the most successful coin designs ever; his George and dragon has such energy and yet fits so effortlessly into a small compass that even modern coinage materials and constant repetition have not spoiled it [figure 275]. It is one of the most popular works of art of its date and on more than one occasion has been restored to the British coinage because of public demand. It may nevertheless be wrong to ascribe its success as a coin type exclusively to its aesthetic appeal. It is in fact one of the last historical instances of a type which becomes so identified with a coin of great commercial importance that it survived many generations of changing fashion, like the figure of St John on the florin of Florence or the kneeling figure of the doge with St Mark on the Venetian ducat.

The recoinage of 1816–18 was a momentous undertaking. It completely changed the coinage policy of the world's foremost commercial power and set an economic example for all others to follow in the abandonment of bimetallism in favour of the gold standard. After long years of shortage, first of silver then of gold, the British government decided that stability could only be achieved by valuing the currency in one metal only and by reducing the other to the status of fiduciary coinage, struck underweight and legal tender in limited amounts. The standard was there for all to see: the guinea, current at 21s. for the better part of a century, was a measure of the value of sterling in terms of gold, and it was a simple operation to adjust the weight of the gold

274 Napoleonic influence on Italian coinage. Kingdom of Italy, five lire, 1812, Napoleon, Bologna. Principality of Lucca and Piombino; five francs, 1805, Felice and Elisa Baciocchi. Kingdom of the Two Sicilies; five lire 1813, Joachim Murat. Duchy of Parma and Piacenza; two lire, 1815, Archduchess Maria Louisa. Savoy; lira, 1830, Charles Felix, Turin. The first four are silver coins of Napoleon and members of the imperial family. However it was Savoy's adoption of the Napoleonic franc/lira which secured that currency for united Italy [actual size]

275 Great Britain; silver crown, 1818, George III, London from dies by Benedetto Pistrucci. Italian neo-classical influence on the coins of the great post-war recoinage in Great Britain [actual size]

unit to make it worth one pound sterling. It was for this coin, the sovereign, that Pistrucci's George and dragon was designed. In 1825 St George was replaced by a plain heraldic design, but he was restored in 1871 in time for the enormous increase in the output of sovereigns which followed the discovery of gold in Australia and then South Africa. Many sovereigns were actually struck at mints in those countries [figure 276]. It was during these prolific years that the close identification of Pistrucci's design with sterling came about. It is still used for the sovereign, and has been revived for a cupro-nickel crown piece as recently as 1951.

During the nineteenth century the tendency which has already been noticed in the eighteenth for coinage to become more prolific but at the same time relatively less important as a form of money, was carried several stages further. At times of crisis gold and silver gave way entirely to paper. This was so in England during the Napoleonic wars, where, apart from Boulton's copper, new coinage was on a trifling scale. The last guinea, struck in 1813, was made exclusively for export to supply Wellington's army in the Peninsula. In France the paper of the Banque de France was made legal tender and convertibility was suspended during the revolutionary period of 1848–50; coins were struck in the name of the Second Republic, but these were hoarded and bank notes accounted for nearly all the money in circulation. There was a similar course of events during the political crisis of 1870, aggravated by the German demand for war reparations; convertibility was only restored in 1874 and bank notes remained legal tender until 1878. In the United States gold and silver coinage was virtually suspended during the Civil War, and not fully restored until 1873.

Political crises were not the only causes of changes in coinage policy during the nineteenth century. There were also purely monetary upheavals caused by the working of the bimetallic system. This became increasingly difficult to manage, for two main reasons. Newly discovered deposits of precious metals were developed more quickly and exploited on a bigger scale than in previous centuries, which caused violent fluctuations in the supply position, and the improvement in transport and communications accelerated the process by which undervalued coins went out of circulation.

It was in the United States that the forces of bimetallism were given most free play. In 1834 a pressure group of congressmen, representing southern states with gold-producing interests, promoted an act to fix the relative values at which the mint coined gold and silver at sixteen to one. This overvaluation of gold was intended to encourage gold coinage at the expense of paper money and to be a slap in the eye for the financial community of New York; and of course it gave the southern gold producers a good price for their bullion. For their convenience branch mints for gold were set up at New Orleans and at Charlotte, North Carolina. In 1849, at the behest of the same interests, Congress authorised the minting of a gold dollar [figure 277], which extended

276 Australia; gold sovereign, 1858, Victoria, Sydney.
A coin from a new source of gold of the 1850s. [actual size]

the range of gold circulation to cover a whole class of lesser transactions. These measurements tended to drive silver coins out of circulation, but southern gold production was small beer, and in any case the tendency was counteracted by a local and temporary oversupply of silver from Mexico. The discovery of gold in California swept all that away. This goldfield was one of the richest yet discovered and with the mint ratio already biased in favour of gold the United States was soon flooded with gold coin while silver went right out of circulation.

One side effect of the California gold rush was the appearance of private gold coinage in the area [figure 277]. The eastern mints were unable to return coin quickly enough or in sufficient quantity to meet the exploding demand of the suddenly rich state, and the economy was still too primitive for paper money. Private mining and commercial concerns there issued their own gold coin as preferable to ingots or gold dust. In 1852 however Congress answered the need of the western states by establishing a mint at San Francisco.

By 1853 the shortage of silver coin in the United States was so acute that Congress was prevailed upon to issue a fiduciary silver coinage. The essential point was that these coins, valued at more than their intrinsic worth, should be legal tender in limited amounts and be issued at face value only against gold coin. In practice therefore the United States slipped on to the gold standard, but bimetallic theory was unimpaired since the fiduciary coinage did not embrace the silver dollar, the specification of which was unchanged. Nobody actually brought silver to the mint for free coinage into dollars since they could get a better price elsewhere, but in law they were entitled to do so.

For some years after the Civil War there was virtually no American coinage except for subsidiary silver, copper and nickel coins. Even in the history of these minor coins, something of the spirit of the free-for-all of nineteenth-century America is reflected in the lobbying and cajoling that was carried on by the various metal-producing interests. Eventually in 1873, in conditions almost of a coinage vacuum, a Mint Act was passed which abolished the free coinage of silver dollars and made an end of bimetallism.

The 1873 Mint Act was well conceived and well timed. Since 1867 world silver production had increased: new mines were developed in the western United States, and in 1871 Germany, in going on to the gold standard, had thrown large quantities of silver on to the market. The price went into such a steep decline as to make bimetallism virtually unworkable. However, those who framed the Act reckoned without the determination of those other Americans who had silver to sell. These made their first encroachment on the monetary situation with the so-called trade dollar [figure 280]. This especially heavy coin, weighing 420 grains, 0.900 fine, was originally intended to undercut the lighter Mexican dollar in the China trade, for which the standard US dollar (412½ grains) was inadequate. Since the trade dollar was so heavy it was not at first profitable for silver producers to have their

277 United States of America; gold dollar, 1849, Philadelphia. California; gold ten dollars, 1851 issued privately by Baldwin and Co. Two coins which throw light on the monetary upheavals caused by the gold rush [actual size]

bullion minted that way, unless it was for export, but by 1876 the market price of silver was so low that it paid to unload trade dollars in the home market also, where they were legal tender in amounts up to five. They flooded the western states and were a real nuisance since the government would not take them in payment of taxes. Meanwhile the silver states pressed for a further advantage, namely the reinstatement of the principle of free coinage of standard silver dollars. This they never achieved, but in 1878 the Bland-Allison Act obliged the Treasury to buy up to four million dollars worth of silver each month against standard silver dollars of unlimited legal tender. Since the silver dollar [figure 280] was worth intrinsically nine per cent less than its face value, this Act simply subsidised the silver mines at the expense of the currency. Silver dollars were only received in preference to paper in the southern and western states. In practice bullion was usually delivered to the mint against Treasury notes and when these were presented the holders asked for payment in gold. Many Bland-Allison dollars never left the government's hands until the silver boom of 1963, some eighty years after they were struck.

The silver purchase clause of the Bland-Allison Act was a persistent threat to the international stability of the dollar. For the mining states it was a valuable subsidy and for all of the United States it increased the money supply and, more than was realised at the time, helped to promote industrial expansion. However, it was anathema to the banking circles in New York, who were concerned to keep the dollar on a par with other currencies as more of these went on to the gold standard and to maintain the United States' own gold reserves. In 1893, under a Republican administration, the bankers managed to have the silver purchase clause repealed, but it remained a burning political issue for some ten years more. Democrat William Jennings Bryan, campaigning for president in 1898, took free silver as one of the main planks in his platform and was only narrowly defeated. It was on that occasion that he made his famous speech challenging the bankers of New York: 'We will answer their demand for a gold standard by saying to them "You shall not press down upon the brow of labour this crown of thorns, you shall not crucify mankind upon a cross of gold".' In another context some thirty years later these words were to find an echo in the writings of a man of very different stamp, the economist John Maynard Keynes, who insisted that gold as a monetary instrument was a barbarous relic.

The conflicts leading to the abandonment of bimetallism were nowhere so dramatically worked out as in the United States. Almost everywhere it came as a relief. The problems of German coinage and currency had mostly centred upon the valuation of silver. During the early part of the nineteenth century the number of states and free cities issuing coins was much reduced. There were about thirty left after 1815 and this number was down to about a dozen by 1871, Prussia having absorbed many of them in the interval. With those numbers and with

278 Free city of Frankfurt;
silver vereinsthaler, 1859.
On the silver coinage of Germany
before the union of 1871 it was
necessary to put the weight
as well as the value of the silver
coin [enlarged 1.5:1]

279 (opposite) Great Britain;
copper twopence, 1797, George III,
Birmingham. The modern
industrial process at last applied
to providing small change for
the industrial worker
[enlarged 2:1]

one state increasingly dominating the others, monetary conventions could be made to work, but they were still so complicated that all major coins had to state not only their value but their silver content [figure 278]. In 1871, when the German Empire was created, the whole system was jettisoned. Germany went on to the gold standard with a single unit of currency, the *reichsmark* divided into *pfennigs* on the decimal principle. Significantly it was the mark, traditional unit of the north-eastern states, rather than the more commonly used thaler or gulden to which the new unit was most closely related, though the other two did survive vestigially in the three mark and two mark pieces which were struck after 1871. Independent minting rights were retained by a few principalities and cities, such as Saxony and Bavaria, Württemberg and Baden, Hamburg and Lübeck, but their coins were all struck to the same standard and shared a common reverse design, the eagle emblem of the new empire [figure 281]. The petty coinage, of the value of one mark and less, was struck in silver, nickel and copper; this was of common appearance throughout the empire and carried the name of no ruler, not even the emperor. The standard gold coin was the twenty mark piece [figure 281], comparable in size to the sovereign, and the twenty franc piece.

Austria, which as late as 1857 participated in a German monetary convention, was excluded from taking further part in German monetary affairs by the political events of 1866–71. For some years after 1870 the Austro-Hungarian Empire maintained a bimetallic system with a silver florin and gold pieces of four and eight florins, but in 1892 the gold standard was adopted there also and the coinage reformed on what were by then the normal European principles. The chosen unit was the *korona* divided into one hundred *hellers*. The common gold pieces were of ten and twenty koronas. Hungary's privileged political position after 1848 was shown in the fact that, while both the bimetallic and the gold standard coinages were common to the whole empire, coins of the Kremnitz mint were inscribed in Hungarian and were often of special design [figure 282]. The last ducat with the standing figure of the emperor derived from the Florentine St John was in fact a ten korona piece of Francis Joseph got up to appeal to Hungarian national sentiment [figure 283].

The country which, after the United States, found it most difficult to abandon bimetallism was France. This was because the franc was enshrined in the law of Germinal as a unit of silver as well as gold. In the early years of the Second Empire the forces that in America had led to the minting of a gold dollar, similarly led to the issue of gold five franc pieces as a substitute for the silver ones, which the influx of gold had driven to a premium. As in America, silver went out of circulation. The Italians and the Swiss, faced with the same situation, reduced the fineness of their silver coins to prevent them from being hoarded, and soon Italian lire and Swiss francs were circulating in France, to the embarrassment of their governments. Tied by the Germinal definition,

the nearest the French could go to meet this challenge was to reduce the fineness of the coins of less than one franc, namely the fifty and twenty centime pieces. The position only became more confused until in 1865 France, Switzerland, Italy and Belgium made a monetary convention, known as the *Union Latine*, designed to preserve the parity of their currencies. The coinage of the Union Latine was in two categories. The subsidiary category consisted of silver [figure 284] up to the value of two francs (or lire). These pieces, 0.835 fine, were limited in issue and legal tender to a maximum of fifty francs in one payment. The second category was unlimited. It was made up of gold coins [figure 285] and silver five francs of the old Germinal standard. The silver franc of Germinal was thus preserved notionally in the five franc piece, though in 1865 it was not contemplated that that unwieldy coin would be struck in any quantity. Within two years, however, the market swung the other way, and as the price of silver came down bullion poured into the mint for coinage into five franc pieces. These were soon the commonest coins in circulation and the gold coins into which they were convertible began to go abroad. By 1873 Belgium had had enough and suspended the minting of silver altogether. The following year the Union Latine met again and agreed to limit the issue of five franc pieces, but this partial remedy, since it depressed the market in silver still more, created almost as many problems as it solved. The only solution was for the French to abandon the Germinal concept of the silver franc and to give up the free coinage of five franc pieces altogether. In 1878 this was agreed to by the Union.

280 *(opposite)* United States of America; silver dollar, 1884, the so-called Bland-Allison dollar, and silver trade dollar 1878. Two coins which owed their existence to the pressures of the silver lobby in the United States [enlarged 2:1]

281 German Empire; gold twenty marks, 1887, Kaiser William I, Berlin, and silver two marks, 1878, King Ludwig II of Bavaria, Munich. Under the German imperial system all coins were of common standard and value and shared a common reverse type [actual size]

282 Austro-Hungarian Empire;
silver forint 1868, Francis Joseph,
Kremnitz. A concession to
Hungarian national feeling in
the language [actual size]

283 Austro-Hungarian Empire;
gold twenty koronas, 1901,
Francis Joseph, Kremnitz. In
content a modern coin of
the gold standard, but in
appearance a descendant of the old
Hungarian ducat [actual size]

284 Switzerland; silver franc,
1875, Bern. A coin of the
Latin Monetary Union which
has continued in circulation until
the present time [actual size]

285 France; gold twenty francs,
1861, Napoleon III, Paris.
The napoleon, the gold coin
which became the centrepiece of
the Union Latine [actual size]

In forming the Union Latine Napoleon III had in mind the creation
of an international currency. The Union was joined at length by Spain
and Greece. It was copied by the Scandinavian countries who went on
to the gold standard and decimalised with a common currency of *krone*
and *öre* in 1875. But the more ambitious project never got any further.
The world's leading currency was sterling; that was not decimalised
and the sovereign was still twenty-two carats fine as compared with
the 0.900 standard which was the rule elsewhere. A Royal Commission
appointed in 1868 to look into the whole matter reported that the inconvenience of a change is 'greatest when a sound system has long been

in existence and is deeply rooted in the feelings and habits of a people'. But if the undesirability of disturbing a stable currency is one objection to the proposal, the whole idea is unworkable when currencies are in a state of flux. The 1914–18 war destroyed the gold standard, the Union Latine and any hope of achieving international currency for at least three generations. And if that hope revives, coinage will present no problems, for it will play no part in its realisation. For since the abandonment of the gold standard all coinage has been subsidiary.

More coins, probably, have been struck since 1918 than in all previous centuries put together. They have a story to tell. Sometimes it is political, as with the new emblems and inscriptions which reflect the changing politics of Africa. More rarely it is economic, as in the case of the Germans' use of iron and zinc in place of nickel and copper in the coinage of occupied Europe in the 1939–45 war, or Great Britain's abandonment of silver for coinage in 1947. Even in these instances, however, the coins have only reflected the changed situation; they have not helped to bring it about. Money and coinage have never been exactly the same thing, but it is the monetary function of coinage which holds most interest for the historian. It seems unlikely that historians of the future will glean much information about the economics of the mid-twentieth century from the coins of our own times.

286 Rome; silver five scudi, 1854, Pius IX [enlarged 2.25:1]

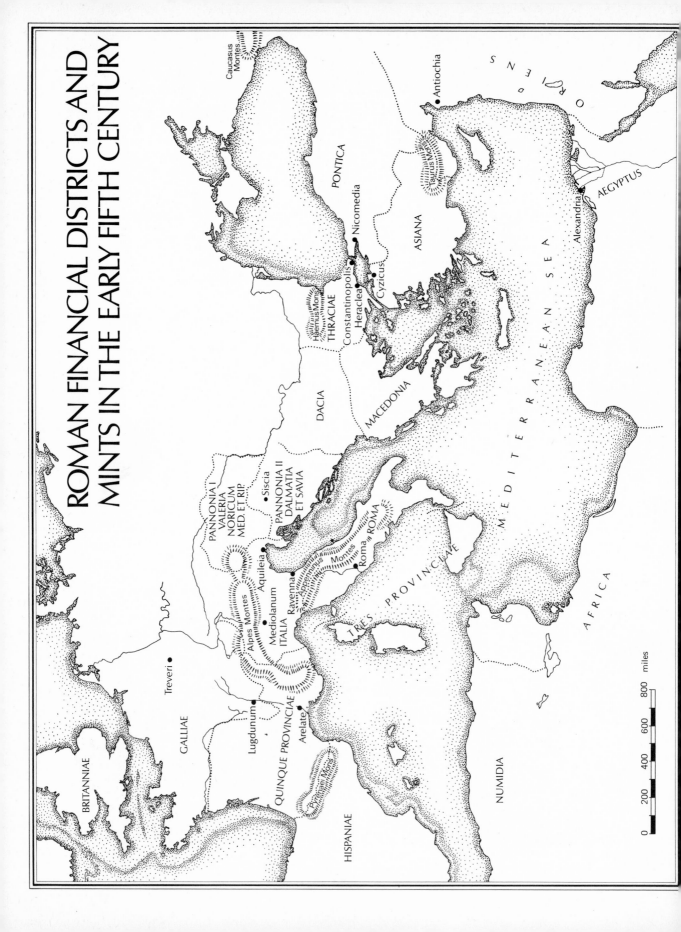

ROMAN FINANCIAL DISTRICTS AND MINTS IN THE EARLY FIFTH CENTURY

Caucasus Montes

PONTICA

Antiochia

Taurus Mons

ORIENS

Nicomedia

ASIANA

Cyzicus

Constantinopolis
Heraclea

Alexandria

AEGYPTUS

Haemus Mons

THRACIAE

MEDITERRANEAN SEA

DACIA

MACEDONIA

PANNONIA I
VALERIA
NORICUM
MED. ET RIP

Siscia

PANNONIA II
DALMATIA
ET SAVIA

Aquileia

Mediolanum

ITALIA

Alpes Montes

Apenninus Montes

Ravenna

Roma ROMA

TRES PROVINCIAE

AFRICA

Treveri

GALLIAE

Lugdunum

QUINQUE PROVINCIAE

Arelate

Pyrenaei Mons

HISPANIAE

NUMIDIA

BRITANNIAE

0   200   400   600   800   miles

WESTERN EUROPE IN THE EARLY NINTH CENTURY
showing the chief mints of the Carolingian Empire and the adjacent territories

Carolingian Empire

Byzantine lands

Other lands

● Mints of Charlemagne's reformed coinage and of Louis the Pious

✗ Mints outside the Carolingian Empire

Note: The list is not complete. Many coins of the period have no mint name and other mint names are unidentifiable. Aachen is included since some coins struck 'at the royal palace' may be presumed to have been minted there. The Byzantines almost certainly had more than one mint in Southern Italy

100   0   100   200   300   400   miles

NORTHUMBRIA

York ✗

MERCIA

SAXONY (772–803)

SLAVONIC TRIBES

London
Rochester ✗✗
Canterbury

Quentovic

Duurstede

Köln

Cambrai

Aachen

BOHEMIANS

AUSTRASIA

Rouen

Trier   Mainz

NEUSTRIA

Laon

Verdun

Regensburg

Meaux

Reims

Metz

Chartres

Paris

Strassburg

Rennes

Sens

BAVARIA (788)

Châteaudun

Orléans

Nantes   Tours

Bourges

Besançon

CARINTHIA

AVARS

Chalon

Melle

Lyon

Milan   Treviso

Bordeaux

Vienne

Pavia   Venice

AQUITAINE

BURGUNDY

LOMBARDY (774)

Dax

Arles

Lucca

Béziers

Toulouse

Marseille

Narbonne

SPANISH MARCH (778–806)

Ampurias

Gerona

Rome

DUCHY OF BENEVENTO

UMMAYAD CALIPHATE OF CORDOVA

Barcelona

Benevento ✗

Medina az Zahra ✗✗

Cordova (al-Andalus)

SICILY ✗ Catania

+ Bergen

NORWAY

SWED

NORTH SEA

SCOTLAND
+ Aberdeen
+ Perth
+ Edinburgh
+ Berwick
Newcastle ⊕
⊕ Durham

DENMARK

Stralsund
Lübeck
Rostock
Wismar
■ Hamburg
■ Lüneburg

For detail see map overleaf

IRELAND

Dublin ⊕

Waterford ⊕

York ⊕

ENGLAND Bury
⊕
Reading ⊕ ⊕ London
⚬ Canterbury
Calais

HOLY ROMAN EMPIRE

Meiss
BOHEM
Prag
+ Bamberg Kutter
Nuremberg

Danube

Rouen ⚬

Evreux △

BRITTANY

F R A N C E

Loire

△ Troyes

+ Sancerre

BURGUNDY

+ Auxonne
△

△ Mâcon

TIROL

Judenbu

+ Merano

Nantes △

BAY OF BISCAY

△ La Rochelle
△ Limoges

Bordeaux
+ △ + △ Bergerac

GUIENNE

△ Agen

Pamplona △ + Morlaas
△ Toulouse

NAVARRE

Perpignan +

For detail see inset

● Milan Venice
⊛

● Genoa
Savona +

Florence
⊕

ADRIATI

+ Gori

LEON

ARAGON

Barcelona + +
Tortosa +

PORTUGAL

CASTILE VALENCIA

Rome
* KINGD
OF NA
Na

SARDINIA

+ Lisbon

Valencia

+ Majorca

● Seville

GRANADA

M E D I T E R R

SICILY

miles 100   0   100   200   300

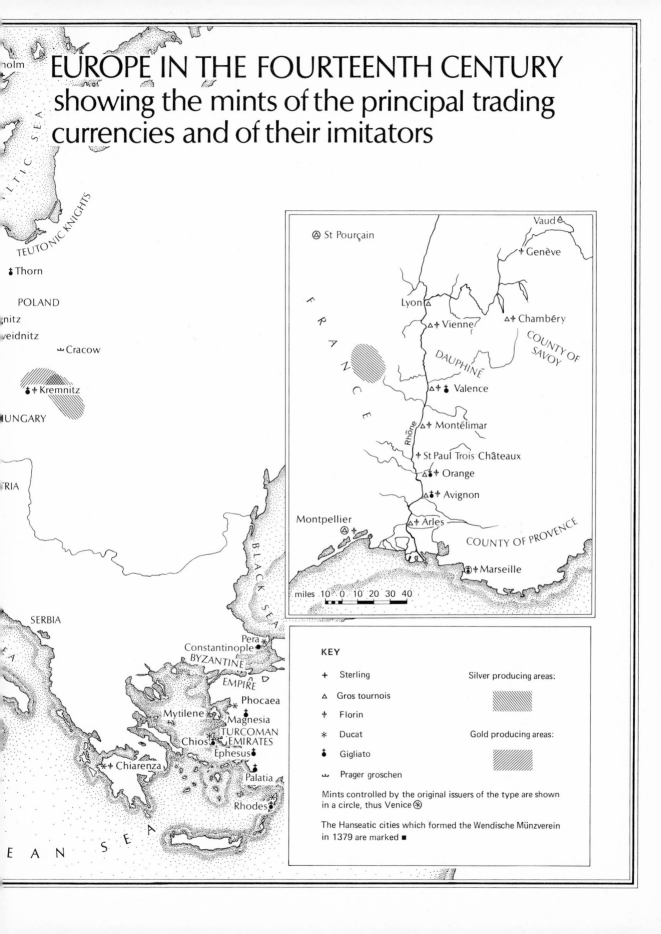

EUROPE IN THE FOURTEENTH CENTURY
showing the mints of the principal trading currencies and of their imitators

BALTIC SEA

TEUTONIC KNIGHTS

♣ Thorn

POLAND

nitz
veidnitz
⌣ Cracow

♣✦ Kremnitz

HUNGARY

RIA

SERBIA

BLACK SEA

Pera ✳
Constantinople ●
BYZANTINE
EMPIRE

Phocaea

Mytilene ✳✦ ✳
Magnesia ♣
Chios ✳ TURCOMAN
EMIRATES
Ephesus ♣
✳✦ Chiarenza
Palatia ♣

Rhodes ♣

E A N   S E A

⊕ St Pourçain

Vaud △

✦ Genève

F R A N C E

Lyon △

△✦ Vienne

△✦ Chambéry

COUNTY OF
SAVOY

DAUPHINÉ

△✦♣ Valence

Rhône

△✦ Montélimar

✦ St Paul Trois Châteaux

△♣✦ Orange

△♣✦ Avignon

Montpellier
⊕ ✦

△✦ Arles

COUNTY OF PROVENCE

♣✦ Marseille

miles 10 0 10 20 30 40

KEY

+	Sterling
△	Gros tournois
✦	Florin
✳	Ducat
♣	Gigliato
⌣	Prager groschen

Silver producing areas:

Gold producing areas:

Mints controlled by the original issuers of the type are shown in a circle, thus Venice ⊛

The Hanseatic cities which formed the Wendische Münzverein in 1379 are marked ■

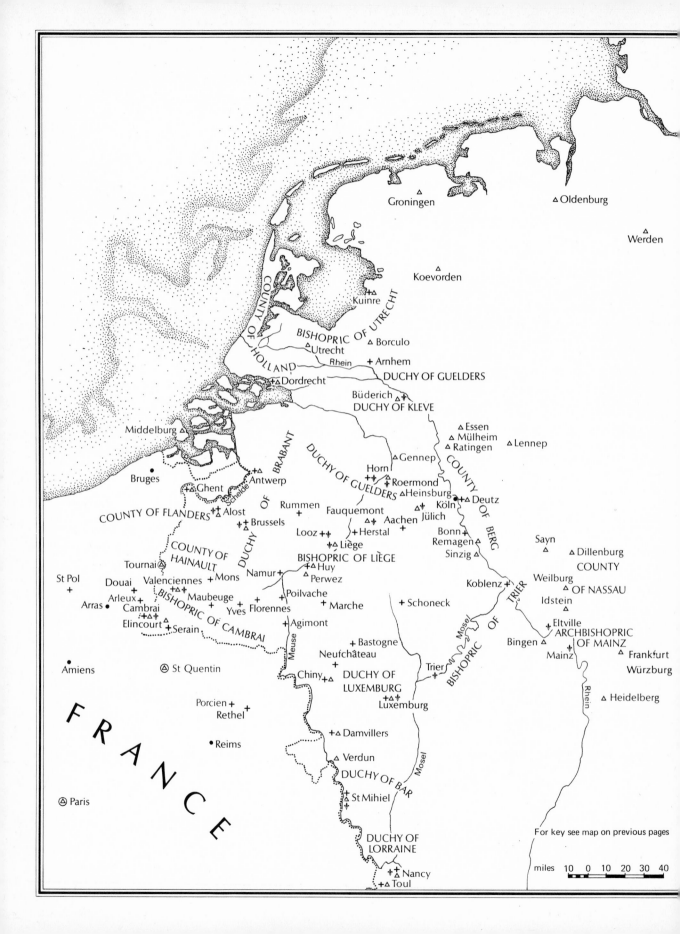

Groningen

△Oldenburg

△Werden

Koevorden△

COUNTY OF HOLLAND

Kuinre +△

BISHOPRIC OF UTRECHT

Utrecht△ △Borculo

Rhein + Arnhem

DUCHY OF GUELDERS

Büderich
DUCHY OF KLEVE

△Dordrecht

△Essen
△Mülheim
△Ratingen △Lennep

Middelburg △

△Gennep

BRABANT

DUCHY OF GUELDERS

Horn
+△

Bruges ●

△+Ghent Antwerp△

Scheldte

DUCHY OF

Roermond
△Heinsburg

Köln△
△Deutz

COUNTY OF BERG

COUNTY OF FLANDERS

++Alost
Rummen
++ Brussels

Jülich△

Fauquemont
△

Aachen

Bonn+

Sayn

△Dillenburg

COUNTY

COUNTY OF
HAINAULT

DUCHY OF

Looz ++
+Herstal

Remagen
Sinzig
△

OF NASSAU

Tournai△△

Namur +

++Liège

BISHOPRIC OF LIÈGE

Weilburg
△

Idstein
△

St Pol
+

Douai
+

Valenciennes +

+Huy

Koblenz+

TRIER

+Mons

Arleux
+

Maubeuge
+

Perwez
△

+ Eltville
ARCHBISHOPRIC

Arras ●
Cambrai
+△△

+
Yves

Poilvache
+

+Schoneck

+ Florennes
+ Marche

Bingen △

OF MAINZ

Elincourt
△ +Serain

BISHOPRIC OF CAMBRAI

Agimont
+△

Meuse

BISHOPRIC OF

Mainz△

Frankfurt
+△

Würzburg

●Amiens

⊚ St Quentin

+Bastogne

Neufchâteau
+

Mosel

Trier
++

DUCHY

Rhein

Porcien+
Rethel +

Chiny
+△

DUCHY OF
LUXEMBURG

△Heidelberg

●Reims

++
Luxemburg

+△Damvillers

Mosel

+△Verdun

DUCHY OF BAR

⊚Paris

++
St Mihiel

For key see map on previous pages

DUCHY OF
LORRAINE

miles 10 0 10 20 30 40

++
△ Nancy

+△Toul

F R A N C E

Appendix

This table shows the terms used in various languages to denote internationally recognised coins and money of account. In each instance the term is given in italics in the original vernacular of the country of origin. Similar words, e. g. real (Sp.), ryal (Eng.) used to denote coins of distinct origin and standard are not included in this table; nor, except in the important instances of the ducat and the sterling, are those terms which are simply transliterated, e. g. ducatone (It.), dukaton (Dutch) etc. For coins struck in the Netherlands for which French, Dutch and Spanish terms were normally interchangeable, the reader is referred to the concordance in Van Gelder H. E. and Hoc M. *Les monnaies des Pays-Bas bourguignons et espagnols 1434 to 1713*, Amsterdam, 1960 pp. 207–8.

LATIN	ITALIAN	FRENCH	ENGLISH	DUTCH	GERMAN	SPANISH
libra	lira	livre	pound	pond	pfund	libra
solidus	soldo	sou	shilling	schelling	schilling	sueldo
denarius	denaro	denier	penny	penning	pfennig	dinero (Portuguese: dinheiro)
sterilensis/ sterlingus	esterlino	esterlin	*sterling*	sterling	sterling	esterlin
grossus	*grosso*	gros	groat	groot	groschen	croat
florinus	*fiorino*	florin	florin/guilder	gulden	gulden	florin
ducatus	*ducato*	ducat	ducat	dukaat	dukat	ducado
*	scudo	*écu*	crown	kroon	krone	escudo
*	tallero	daldre	dollar	daalder	*thaler*	dollaro

* the heyday of these coins was after Latin went out of use in most mint documents.

Select Bibliography

For this necessarily short bibliography, the general works and national histories which cover the whole period are listed first, followed by some specialist works of prime importance which are relevant to one or two chapters of this book only. The best comprehensive numismatic bibliography is Grierson, P., *Coins and Medals: a select bibliography*, published by the Historical Association, London, 1954. A second edition was published in French by the Cercle d'Etudes Numismatiques, Brussels, 1966.

GENERAL WORKS: Engel A. & Serrure R., *Traité de numismatique du moyen âge*. 3 vol. Paris, 1891–5, reprinted Bologna, 1964, and *Traité de numismatique moderne et contemporaine*. 2 vol. Paris, 1897–9. Jesse W., *Quellenbuch zur Münz- und Geldgeschichte des Mittelalters*. Halle, 1924. Bloch M., *Esquisse d'une histoire monétaire de l'Europe*. Paris, 1954. Cipolla C. M., *Money, prices and civilization in the Mediterranean world from the 5th to the 17th century*. Princeton, 1956. Spufford P., 'Coinage and currency' in the *Cambridge Economic History of Europe*. vol III. Cambridge, 1963. Macdonald G., *The evolution of coinage*. Cambridge, 1916. Porteous J., *Coins*. London, 1964. Carson R. A. G., *Coins: ancient, medieval and modern*. London, 1962. Sutherland C. H. V., *Art in coinage*. London, 1955.

NATIONAL HISTORIES AND WORKS OF REFERENCE: Brooke G. C., *English coins*. 3rd edition, London, 1950. Oman C., *The coinage of England*. Oxford, 1931. Ruding R., *Annals of the coinage*. 3 vol. 3rd edition, London, 1840. Feaveryear A. E., *The pound sterling. A history of English money*. 2nd edition, Oxford, 1963. Stewart I. H., *The Scottish coinage*. 2nd edition, London, 1968. Blanchet A. & Dieudonné A., *Manuel de numismatique française*. 4 vol. Paris, 1912–36. Lafaurie J., *Les monnaies des rois de France*. vol I. Paris-Basel, 1951. Lafaurie J. & Prieur P., *Les monnaies des rois de France*. vol II. Paris, 1956. Poey d'Avant F., *Les monnaies féodales de la France*. 3 vol. Paris, 1858–62. Gaillard V., *Recherches sur les monnaies des comtes de Flandre*. 2nd edition, Ghent, 1857. Chalon R., *Recherches sur les monnaies des comtes de Hainaut*. Brussels, 1848. Witte A. de., *Histoire monétaire des comtes de Louvain, ducs de Brabant*. 3 vol. Antwerp, 1894–9. Van Gelder H. E. & Hoc M., *Les monnaies des Pays-Bas bourguignons et espagnols, 1434–1713*. Amsterdam, 1960. Van der Chijs P. O., *De munten der Nederlanden van de vroegste tijden tot aan de Pacificatie van Gend (1576)*. 9 vol. Haarlem, 1851–66. Van Gelder H. E., *De Nederlandse munten*. Utrecht-Antwerp, 1965. Suhle A., *Deutsche Münz- und Geldgeschichte von den Anfängen bis zum 15. Jahrhundert*. Berlin, 1955. Cipolla C. M., *Le avventure della lira*. Milan, 1958. Sambon G., *Repertorio generale delle monete coniate in Italia*. Part I. Paris, 1912. *Corpus Nummorum Italicorum*. vols I–XIX. Rome, 1910–40. Gil Farres O., *Historia de la moneda española*. Madrid, 1959. Spassky I. G., *The Russian monetary system* (English translation). Amsterdam, 1967. Huszár L., *The art of coinage in Hungary*. Budapest, 1963. Schlumberger G., *Numismatique de l'Orient Latin*. Paris 1878–82 (reprinted Graz, 1954). Taxay D., *History of the US mint and coinage*. New York, 1966. Burzio H. F., *Diccionario de la moneda hispano-americana*. 2 vol. Santiago, Chile 1958. Teixeira de Aragão A. C., *Descripção geral e historica das moedas cunhadas em nome dos reis, regentes e governadores de Portugal*. 3 vol. Lisbon, 1874–80.

SPECIALISED WORKS (Chapter 1) Sutherland C.H.V., *The Roman Imperial Coinage vol. VI, from Diocletian's reform (AD 294) to the death of Maximinus (AD 313)* London, 1967. Carson R. A. G., Hill P. V., and Kent J. P. C., *Late Roman bronze coinage AD 324–498*. London, 1962.

(Chapter 2) Wroth W., *Catalogue of the Imperial Byzantine coins in the British Museum*. 2 vol. London, 1908. Bertelè T., 'Lineamenti principali della numismatica bizantina'. *Rivista Italiana di Numismatica* LXVI (1964) 33–118. Grierson P., 'Coinage and money in the Byzantine Empire' in *Moneta e scambi nell' alto medioevo*. Spoleto, 1961. Lopez R. S., 'The dollar of the Middle Ages.' *Journal of Economic History* XI (1951) 209–234. Adelson H. L., *Light weight solidi and*

Byzantine trade during the sixth and seventh centuries. (Numismatic Notes & Monographs no. 138) New York, 1957. Walker J., *A catalogue of the Arab-Sassanian coins.* London, 1941, and *A catalogue of the Arab-Byzantine and post-Reform Umaiyad coins.* London, 1956. Grierson P., 'The debasement of the besant in the 11th century.' *Byzantinische Zeitschrift XLVII* (1954), 379–394. Zakythinos D. A., *Crise monétaire et crise économique à Byzance du XIIIe au XVe siècle.* Athens, 1948. Bertelè T., 'L'iperpero byzantino dal 1261 al 1453'. *Rivista Italiana di Numismatica LIX* (1957) 70–89.

(Chapter 3) Wroth W., *Catalogue of the coins of the Vandals, Ostrogoths and Lombards in the British Museum.* London, 1911. Miles G. C., *The coinage of the Visigoths of Spain: Leovigild to Achila II.* New York, 1952. Prou M., *Les monnaies mérovingiennes (Catalogue des monnaies françaises de la Bibliothèque Nationale)* Paris, 1892. Le Gentilhomme P., 'Le monnayage et la circulation monétaire dans les royaumes barbares en occident (Ve–VIIIe siècles)'. *Revue Numismatique* (fifth series)*VII* (1943) 46–112 & *VIII* (1944) 13–59. Lafaurie J., 'Les routes commerciales indiquées par les tré sors et trouvailles monétaires mérovingiens' in *Moneta e scambi nell' alto medioevo.* Spoleto, 1961. Grierson P., 'Monete bizantine in Italia dal VII all' XI secolo' in *Moneta e scambi.* Grierson P., 'Carolingian Europe and the Arabs; the myth of the mancus.' *Revue belge de philologie et d'histoire XXXII* (1954) 1059–1074. Sutherland C. H. V., *Anglo-Saxon gold coinage in the light of the Crondall hoard.* London, 1948.

(Chapter 4) Grierson P., 'Money and coinage under Charlemagne' in *Karl der Große: Lebenswerk und Nachleben,* ed. W. Braunfels, Düsseldorf, 1965. *Anglo-Saxon coins,* ed. R. H. M. Dolley, London, 1961. Dolley R. H. M., *Anglo-Saxon pennies.* London, 1964. Lombard M. 'Les bases monétaires d'une suprematie économique: l'or musulman du VIIe au XIIe siecle.' *Annales: Economies, Sociétés, Civilisations, II* (1947) 143–160. Bloch M., 'Le problème de l'or au moyen âge.' *Annales d'histoire économique et sociale V* (1933) 1–34 (translated into English in *Land and work in mediaeval Europe,* selected papers by Marc Bloch, London, 1967). Suhle A., *Hohenstaufenzeit im Münzbild.* Munich, 1963. Cipolla C. M., 'Currency depreciation in medieval Europe' *Economic History Review XV* (1963) 413–422.

(Chapter 5) Chautard J., *Imitations des monnaies au type esterlin frappées en Europe pendant le XIIIe et le XIVe siècles.* 2 vol. Nancy, 1872. Rigold S. E., 'The trail of the easterlings', *British Numismatic Journal XXVI* (1949) 31–55. Lopez R. S., *Settecento anni fa: il ritorno all' oro nel occidente duecentesco.* Naples, 1955.

(Chapter 6) Blancard L., *Essai sur les monnaies de Charles Ier, comte de Provence.* Paris, 1868–79. Ives H. E., *The Venetian gold ducat and its imitations.* (Numismatic Notes & Monographs no. 125) New York, 1954. Landry A., *Essai économique sur les mutations des monnaies dans l'ancienne France de Philippe le Bel à Charles VII.* Paris, 1910. Perroy E., 'A l'origine d'une economie contractée: les crises du XIV siècle' *Annales: Economies, Sociétés, Civilisations IV* (1949) 167–182. *The De Moneta of Nicolas Oresme and English mint documents,* ed. C. Johnson, Edinburgh, 1956. Murari O., 'La monetazione dell' Italia settentrionale nel passaggio del Comune alla Signoria' *Nova Historia XIII* (Verona, 1961) 31–45. Jesse W., *Der Wendische Münzverein.* Lübeck, 1928 (reprinted Brunswick, 1967). Grierson P., 'Le gillat ou carlin de Naples-Provence: le rayonnement de son type monetaire' in *Centénaire de la Société française de Numismatique (1865–1965)* 43–56. Paris, 1965. Homan B. 'La circolazione delle monete d'oro in Ungheria dal X al XIV secolo e la crisi europea dell' oro nel secolo XIV.' *Rivista Italiana di Numismatica XXXV* (1922) 109–156.

(Chapter 7) Nef J. U., 'Silver production in central Europe 1450–1518' *Journal of Political Economy XLIX* (1941) 575–591. *Der Tiroler Taler. Die Prägungen der Münzstätte Hall in Tirol 1477–1809.* Innsbruck, 1963. Panvini Rosati F., *Le monete italiane del rinascimento.* Rome, 1961. Hamilton E. J., *American treasure and the price revolution in Spain, 1501–1650.* Cambridge Mass., 1934. Grierson P., 'The origins of the English sovereign and the symbolism of the closed crown.' *British Numismatic Journal XXXIII* (1964) 118–134.

(Chapter 8) Nesmith R. I., *The coinage of the first mint of the Americas at Mexico City 1536–1572* (Numismatic Notes & Monographs no. 131) New York, 1955. Braudel F., *Le Mediterranée et le monde mediterranéen a l'époque de Philippe II.* Paris, 1950. Vaissiere P. de, *La découverte à Augsbourg des instrumens mécaniques du monnayage moderne et leur importation en France en 1550, d'après les dépêches de Charles de Marillac.* Montpellier, 1892. *La response de Jean Bodin à M. de Malestroit, 1568.* ed. H. Hauser. Paris, 1932.

(Chapter 9) Mailliet P., *Catalogue descriptif des monnaies obsidionales et de nécessité.* 4 vol. Brussels, 1868–73. Crosby S. S., *The early coins of America.* Boston 1878 (reprinted 1945). Atkins J., *The coins and tokens of the possessions and colonies of the British Empire.* London, 1889. Craig H., *Newton at the mint.* Cambridge, 1946.

(Chapter 10) Mathias P., *English trade tokens. The Industrial Revolution illustrated.* London, 1962. Neurrisse A., *Histoire du franc.* Paris, 1963.

Index